The Rocket

A Cultural History of

MAURICE RICHARD

BENOÎT MELANÇON

Translated by FRED A. REED

THE ROCKET

Foreword by ROY MacGREGOR · Afterword by JEAN BÉLIVEAU

GREYSTONE BOOKS

D&M Publishers Inc.

Vancouver/Toronto/Berkeley

FOR MY SONS, *Charles and Théo*

Copyright © 2009 by Greystone Books
Translation copyright © 2009 by Fred A. Reed
Originally published in 2006 as *Les yeux de Maurice Richard:*
une histoire culturelle by Les Éditions Fides, Montreal

09 10 11 12 13   5 4 3 2 1

Greystone Books
A division of D&M Publishers Inc.
2323 Quebec Street, Suite 201
Vancouver BC Canada V5T 4S7
www.greystonebooks.com

Library and Archives Canada Cataloguing in Publication
Melançon, Benoît, 1958–
The Rocket : a cultural history of Maurice Richard / Benoît Melançon ;
translated by Fred A. Reed.

Translation of: Les yeux de Maurice Richard.
Includes index.

ISBN 978-1-55365-336-3

1. Richard, Maurice, 1921–2000. 2. Hockey—Social aspects—Québec (Province).
3. Social perception—Québec (Province)—History—20th century. 4. Myth—Social
aspects—Québec (Province). 5. Québec (Province)—Social conditions—1945–1960.
I. Reed, Fred A., 1939– II. Title.

GV848.5.R5M4413 2009   796.962092   C2008-906903-X

Editing by Barbara Czarnecki
Cover and text design by Naomi MacDougall
Front cover photograph: Portrait of Maurice Richard, *Sport. The Magazine for the Sports-Minded*,
vol. 18, no. 4, April 1955, New York, Macfadden Publications Inc., p. 48 (photo: Ozzie Sweet)
Back cover: Maurice Richard's famous backhand. Dow Breweries,
Almanach du sport, 1955–1956, illustration for December 1955.
Printed and bound in China by C&C Offset Printing Co. Ltd.
Printed on paper that comes from sustainable forests managed
under the Forest Stewardship Council
Distributed in the U.S. by Publishers Group West

Every effort has been made to trace ownership of visual material used in this book. Errors or
omissions will be corrected in subsequent editions, provided notification is sent to the publisher.

We gratefully acknowledge the financial support of the Canada Council for the Arts, the British
Columbia Arts Council, the Province of British Columbia through the Book Publishing Tax Credit,
and the Government of Canada through the Book Publishing Industry Development Program
(BPIDP) for our publishing activities.

CONTENTS

Foreword

―――――――

ROY MacGREGOR

HE IS EVERYWHERE. And if you don't believe me, come sit in the back seat as the prime minister of Canada heads for Parliament Hill.

It is November 5, 2003. I have been assigned by the *Globe and Mail* to spend an entire day with Jean Chrétien during his final week in office. He is on the verge of turning seventy and will be retiring after a full decade in the country's top job. He is leaving on his own terms after winning three successive majority governments—a feat that should have him, one would think, comparing himself to another supremely successful Liberal leader, Sir Wilfrid Laurier.

But he is not. He is thinking of a man who always said he had no political designs at all, a man known immediately by nickname or number.

The RCMP convoy is taking the MacKay Street route off Sussex Drive, and as the dark cars dart around some light roadwork, I have asked the prime minister how he himself looks back on a remarkable forty years in Parliament.

"You know," he says in that side-delivered growl so beloved by his mimics, "I am like Rocket Richard. He was maybe not the most elegant player on the ice—but he had the instinct for the net."

Why should we be surprised? As Benoît Melançon shows in his remarkable examination of the Rocket as Quebec and Canadian icon, Maurice Richard—number 9, *le Rocket*—can be a touchstone for practically anything: politics, childhood, advertising, song, poetry, theatre, art, history and, yes, even hockey. If the game is, as Morley Callaghan once wrote, "our own national drama," then Rocket Richard is the unforgettable character, even if he was never the greatest player and was actually seen to play the national game by what would today amount to a mere handful of Canadians.

But if Laurier can be on one side of the most common Canadian dollar bill in circulation, the five, then it seems only right that the Rocket should be on the other side. Check it out.

As Melançon—a self-confessed Guy Lafleur fan—writes, over the years the Rocket has become "a veritable cult." He has been credited with everything from raising the National Hockey League to major sport status to beginning the Quiet Revolution that allowed Quebec to find its own feet and voice. He sold the game, but he also sold everything from fishing line to hair colouring to beer. He became the ultimate icon and yet, mysteriously, remained very much the loner, in many ways an outsider to the very world it seemed he had himself created.

Much has been written about Rocket the player, the determined goal scorer whose very eyes looked like flying pucks. And much has been written about Rocket the accidental politician, the fiery presence who seemed, one St. Patrick's Day back in the mid-1950s, to stand up for all the repression Québécois had felt since the Plains of Abraham. How he came to become "the incarnation of Quebec nationalism" is something Melançon examines at length, with great insight, and he comes as close to separating the man from the myth as any ever has, or likely will. It is a book of endless fascination.

I did not know the Rocket, but I was the last person to see the Rocket lying in state.

This takes some explaining. When the great man died at the end of May 2000, I was in New Jersey covering the Stanley Cup playoffs and was told to leave immediately for Montreal, where Richard was lying in state at the Molson Centre prior to his funeral, which was scheduled for the next day. It would be a scramble and I would be lucky to get there before the doors closed at 10:00 pm.

I flew in and caught a cab downtown, begging the driver to hurry. But the traffic was heavy and it was several minutes past closing when I arrived. The streets were still filled with mourners—some 115,000 having passed by his open casket—but the doors to the Molson Centre were closed tight and no one was answering when latecomers pounded on them in hope of being granted an exception.

I found two men, Georges Boudreault and his son Mario, attempting a side door without luck. We talked and they told me they had raced to Montreal from their home in the Saguenay, the province's most deeply nationalistic region. They had made the drive in four hours but had come five minutes too late. The elder Boudreault said he had worshipped the Rocket all his life and had been struck with a terrible need to say thank you to him for all those years of pleasure and inspiration.

Together we went around to all the side entrances and back doors, and at the very last one an older security guard came and listened to Georges' pleas through the glass. He nodded, understanding, and with a finger to his lips quickly pushed open the door and let us in. He must have presumed I was one of Georges Boudreault's sons. Mercifully, they were not checking ID.

Telling us to keep quiet, the guard led us down a corridor and through a dark pulled curtain. The coffin was at centre ice, surrounded by flowers and bathed in a rather ethereal light.

Georges made Mario remove his cap, and father and son moved quickly toward the coffin with heads slightly bowed, as if moving through church for communion.

I knew I had no right to be there—an Anglo from Ontario who had just flown in from Newark—but I stayed with the two men. Georges Boudreault stopped at the foot of the coffin, stared at the Rocket lying there in his dark suit, the dark eyes closed forever, and he crossed himself.

It was only then that I realized Georges Boudreault was bawling his eyes out.

"Merci, Maurice," he kept saying over and over and over.

"Merci . . . merci . . . merci."

And now, if I may add: Merci, Benoît.

Introduction

THIS IS NOT A fan's book, not a hockey lover's book—and not a biography of Maurice Richard. I feel no particular connection with this figure from the sports world. It is altogether legitimate to admire him for his exploits on the ice, and for what he represented—and represents today—in Quebec and in Canada. It is equally legitimate to have no wish whatsoever to join in the chorus of admiration that swells up whenever his name is mentioned. Though I once had my favourite player (Guy Lafleur), though for years my spirits ebbed and flowed in cadence with the self-styled "national sport" called hockey, slowly but surely we drifted apart. The reason was simple enough. Over the years hockey had become terminally boring. (Recent seasons seem more promising, but we should be cautious about sudden bursts of enthusiasm.) Inescapably, in the pages that follow, Maurice Richard's life and career will stand at centre stage. But the elements of that life and that career that I have selected have been dictated by a specific objective.

That objective is to construct a cultural history of Maurice Richard. I intend to interpret the way Richard has been represented, from the beginning of his career in 1942 to the present day: in magazine articles and learned essays, biographies and memorabilia, short stories and novels, children's fiction and memoirs, poems and plays, songs and comic strips, sculpture and painting, film and television programs, not to mention objects signed by Maurice Richard, and in social customs. To interpret these representations, it is necessary to tell their story, and to place them in their own specific context, both in Quebec and in the rest of Canada.

Maurice Richard has, after all, a pan-Canadian following. A veritable cult, in fact.

The vital statistics tell us that the star of the Montreal Canadiens hockey team died on May 27, 2000—but the myth of Maurice Richard couldn't care less. As far as it is concerned, Maurice Richard is not dead. He cannot die. Of that, there is abundant proof.

Not a single Canadian citizen has not carried Maurice Richard in his pocket at one time or another. Few realize that it is he who speaks, indirectly, from the back of the Canadian five-dollar bill. One side depicts Sir Wilfrid Laurier, prime minister of Canada from 1896 to 1911. The other shows an unmistakably winter scene: to the left, a little girl is sliding on a toboggan, and an adult is showing a toddler how to skate; on the right, against a background of snow-covered firs, four kids are playing hockey; in the middle, beneath a giant snowflake, the (necessarily) bilingual sentences:

> Les hivers de mon enfance étaient des saisons longues, longues. Nous vivions en trois lieux: l'école, l'église et la patinoire; mais la vraie vie était sur la patinoire.
> —ROCH CARRIER

The winters of my childhood were long, long seasons. We lived in three places—the school, the church and the skating rink—but our real life was on the skating rink.

Anyone familiar with the writings of Roch Carrier will surely recognize the first sentence of his short story "The Hockey Sweater," the sweater in question being that of Maurice Richard. The little girl illustrated on the banknote stickhandling the puck is wearing sweater number 9, immortalized by the man nicknamed the Rocket.

As a country, Canada has not merely granted him pride of place on a banknote. It also issued a postage stamp in his honour to commemorate the fiftieth National Hockey League All-Star Game, in 2000. And on April 9, 2004, the Canadian Museum of Civilization inaugurated a traveling exposition, "Une légende, un héritage: 'Rocket Richard': The Legend—the Legacy." Among the many objects on display were items from Richard's personal collection acquired by the Canadian government when his heirs auctioned it on the open market. Upon his death, Quebec held a state funeral. Richard is the kind of national treasure that cannot be neglected with impunity.

Roch Carrier's story about the hockey star was written for beginning readers. First-year elementary school pupils can learn all about him from a book entitled *Maurice Richard (1921–2000)*, a small, illustrated volume belonging to a series comprising thirty-one titles, several of them still required reading in Montreal public schools in 2005. It is the only one to deal with a historical figure; no other book in the series is about sports. Clearly Maurice Richard enjoys special status in that schoolbook series, especially considering that neither young readers nor their parents could have ever seen him play.

No need to have seen the Rocket to esteem him, as the Montreal French-language daily *La Presse* revealed on October 25, 2004. Four years after his biological disappearance, Richard remained Quebec's third "most appreciated personality." Richard's "D-index"—"The D-Index equals recognition multiplied by level of appreciation," as the newspaper explained it—stood at 7.53, placing him behind songwriter

Luc Plamondon (8.07) and monologuist Yvon Deschamps (7.54), but ahead of twelve other personalities. Among them was a sole figure from the sports world, sprinter Bruny Surin, but not a single dead person. Even from the grave, Maurice Richard's image reigned supreme.

An east-end Montreal arena is named for Maurice Richard; for several years it housed a museum dedicated to him. A lake in the Lanaudière region, northwest of Saint-Michel-des-Saints, bears his name. Rocket Bay, at the eastern extremity of Brochu Lake in the Gouin Reservoir, near La Tuque, commemorates him, as do a street and a public square in the suburban municipality of Vaudreuil, and a Montreal park not far from his house, on Péloquin Street. The 9-4-10 Restaurant, in the Bell Centre, is named after him. He boasts his own bronze star, on Saint-Catherine Street in downtown Montreal, adjacent to that of songstress Céline Dion. (He also has a place on the Madison Square Garden Walk of Fame, in New York, and on Canada's Walk of Fame, in Toronto.)

When he died, there was an attempt to name Montreal's Dorval International Airport after him; instead, it honours former Canadian prime minister Pierre Elliott Trudeau. For others, it would have sufficed to give his name to the Molson Centre, to Mount Royal, Saint-Catherine, Atwater or Sherbrooke Street, or the Viau Bridge. Following the example of political (Jean Lesage) or musical (Félix Leclerc) freeways, the idea of naming Highway 50, which links Montreal with the municipality of Gatineau (formerly Hull) and Ottawa, after Maurice Richard was seriously considered. Some even suggested that Dollard des Ormeaux (that pseudo-hero of the seventeenth century) Day, the Quebec holiday that coincides with Victoria Day in English Canada, be designated Maurice Richard Day.

Montreal boasts three statues of Maurice Richard: one stands in front of the arena named after him; another at the downtown commercial building Les Ailes; the third in the Atrium of Champions at the Pepsi Forum Entertainment Centre, the former Montreal Forum, where he spent his playing career. There is also a statue to be found in the city of Gatineau, located along the Heroes' Path in Jacques-Cartier Park, on Maurice Richard Square, adjacent to the Canadian Museum of Civilization. In 1999, a junior hockey team was baptized "The Rocket" in his honour, first in Montreal (where it played in the Maurice Richard Arena), then in Charlottetown; the team played its first game on September 9, 1999 (9/9/99). Since the 1998–99 season, the Maurice Richard Trophy has been awarded to the National Hockey League's top goal scorer. Montreal's Société Saint-Jean-Baptiste periodically honours a sports personality by awarding him or her its Maurice Richard Trophy. Sports-Québec pays homage to his exploits with its "Maurice" prizes: no family name needed.

But that is not all. A toddler of the 1950s wanted Maurice Richard overalls to wear, his mother would serve him Maurice Richard soup, his father would buy a Maurice Richard transistor radio; this same toddler, now grown to adulthood, could have a glass of Maurice Richard wine.

Whichever way we turn, we'll find Maurice Richard. Over time, the hockey player has become a myth. How and why did the transformation take place? What does it mean? What were its great moments?

Time for a closer look.

Portrait of the Rocket as a Hockey Star

———

ANYONE UNFAMILIAR with the life and times of Maurice Richard should be aware of certain dates, of certain achievements. These dates and achievements are objective facts that can hardly be questioned. They are, simultaneously, the stuff of myth. The same can be said of his more narrowly defined qualities as a sports figure, though these too are open to interpretation.

The life and times of Maurice Richard

Joseph Henri Maurice Richard was born in Montreal on August 4, 1921, to Onésime Richard and Alice Laramée. His parents were natives of the Gaspé. Richard was reared in Bordeaux, a north-end Montreal neighbourhood. He was one of eight children.

In his youth he played baseball and hockey. As a hockey player, he used a variety of assumed names in order to play in several leagues at the same time. He also attended technical school, where he learned the machinist's trade.

In 1942, he became a professional with the Montreal Canadiens. He would play only for this team, from which he retired in September 1960.

At the beginning of his career he wore jersey number 15, but he traded it for number 9 in the fall of 1943: his daughter Huguette, born on October 27 of that year, weighed nine pounds at birth.

Over eighteen seasons Richard scored 544 regular-season (978 games) and 82 playoff (133 games) goals, for a total of 626 (1,111 games). He scored his first goal for the Canadiens on November 8, 1942; his last on April 12, 1960. He racked up 465 assists, 421 during the regular season and 44 in the playoffs. He received a total of 1,473 penalty minutes (1,285 and 188). In a nutshell: 1,111 games, 1,091 points and 1,473 penalty minutes.

During his eighteen seasons the Canadiens won the Stanley Cup, emblem of the National Hockey League championship, eight times, including five times consecutively from 1955–56 to 1959–1960, a record that still stands. Richard was named to the league's all-star first team eight times, and six times to the second team. He was awarded the Hart Trophy, conferred upon the outstanding player of the National Hockey League, at the end of the 1946–47 season: it was the only individual trophy he ever won. He was his team's thirteenth captain, serving from 1956 to 1960.

In January 1985, he was named to the Canadiens Dream Team, along with goalie Jacques Plante, defensemen Doug Harvey and Larry Robinson, and forwards Aurèle Joliat, Dickie Moore and Jean Béliveau. Thirteen years later, in its January 1998 edition, the *Hockey News*, in an article by Mike Ulmer, ranked him as the fifth-greatest hockey player of all time, after Wayne Gretzky, Bobby Orr, Gordie Howe and Mario Lemieux.

When he retired, on September 15, 1960, Richard held many team and league records. Among the most significant—and the one that lasted the longest (until April 2006)—was that for most overtime goals scored in playoff games. More proof, if any was needed, of one of

Maurice Richard's most widely praised qualities as a player: the ability to come through under pressure.

After his playing days had ended, Maurice Richard worked as a sales representative for several companies. He owned a tavern and an electronics store. For varying lengths of time, he was employed by the Canadiens and by the Molson Brewery, as "ambassador." He also wrote newspaper columns.

Except for a few weeks in 1972, when he was coach of the Quebec Nordiques of the World Hockey Association, Richard took no active part in hockey after his retirement. Playing an honorific role was enough, participating on old-timers' teams or refereeing friendly games.

In 1942 Maurice Richard married Lucille Norchet. They had seven children. She died in 1994. Sonia Raymond was Richard's last love.

He died in Montreal on May 27, 2000, at 5:00 PM, from respiratory failure. He was also suffering from stomach cancer and Parkinson's disease. He was given a state funeral at Montreal's Notre-Dame Basilica on May 31, 2000.

The player

From a sports perspective, how can we best describe Maurice Richard's style of play? What can be said about a right-winger who shot left-handed, stood 1.78 metres tall and weighed, for most of his career, approximately 89 kilos? How can we explain the impression he made on so many hockey lovers? Most eyewitness accounts agree on several key points: it was not the grace of his skating style that set him apart, nor his ability to keep the opposing team from scoring; not the power of his shot on goal, nor the accuracy of his passing game. Nor did he change the way the game was played in any significant way, something Jacques Plante (as a goalie), Bobby Orr (as a defenseman), Guy Lafleur (as a winger) and Wayne Gretzky (as a centre) were to do. So what was it that made him a player whom fans loved and still love, a player whose accomplishments they still praise? There are four answers to these questions.

Maurice Richard was a man with one sole idea: to score goals. He never hid it. "The other team's goal always attracted me like a magnet, and I headed for it with everything I had. All I wanted to do was score, score, score," *La Presse* reported on March 15, 1995. Playwright Jean-Claude Germain, in *Un pays dont la devise est je m'oublie* [A Country Whose Motto is "I Forget"], in 1976, imagined similar words when he put Richard on the stage:

> Me, when I hits the ice, ain't no foolin' around. I'm there to score! That's all I'm thinkin' of! Score! However I can, whenever I can. Score! On me knees or standin' up, from the red line, the blue line . . . score, score! Wid' me gloves! Me head! Flat on the ice, wid' me skates, wid' me stick, SCORE, SCORE! So I haul the whole other team by me shirt or me shorts, or stickin' to me pads . . . score, score! Nuthin' but score!

At the heart of any discussion of his style of play lies the Rocket's obsession.

The second, recurring image is that of a man, Richard, whom nothing could stop once he skated into the opposing team's zone. Between the blue line and the adversary's goal, he was the most determined, the strongest, more powerful, no more stoppable than Niagara Falls, according to one of his most detested opponents, Ted Lindsay, in an interview for the *Hockey News* in 2000. In the language of the man on the street, it was expressed as follows: Maurice Richard could score sitting, standing, lying down or kneeling, with a player or two on his back. From the mouth of academic, novelist and essayist Gilles Marcotte, in response to Pierre Popovic, it came out as:

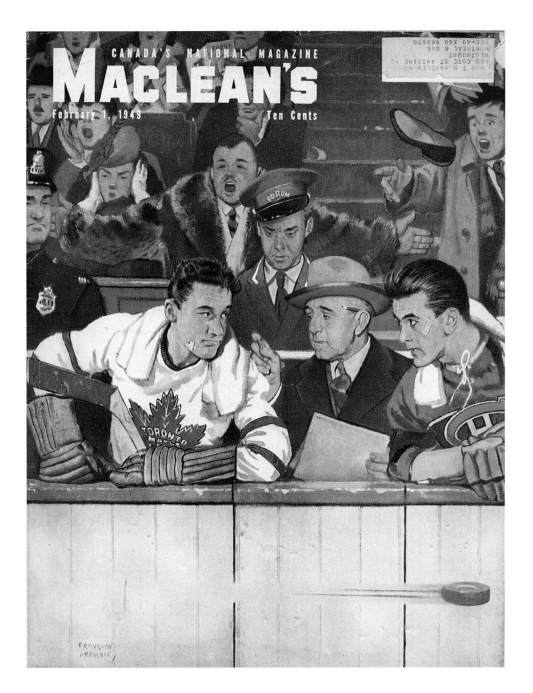

Bill Ezinicki and Maurice Richard in 1949.

Did you ever see Maurice Richard, crushed by two exceptionally husky defensemen, not only on his knees but face down on the ice, successfully, against all odds, in an effort that demands a supreme expenditure of human strength, lifting the puck and sending it past a stupefied goalie? Well, that's hockey.

It was a bad idea to get in Richard's way when he was hell-bent on a goal. But the Rocket himself sustained serious injuries: fractures to both ankles, a fractured wrist, a severed Achilles tendon, fractures of the facial bones, an injured elbow. Those injuries could halt him only temporarily—but they did so frequently. Altogether, he missed 160 games because of injury, over and above the total of 1,111 in which he played. (Ironically enough, Richard was rejected for military service twice for medical reasons.)

The obverse of that determination was violence. Though we might want to downplay it today, it was very real. First, however, came the violence that was used against him. Because he was his team's leading scorer for many years, it was considered normal that other teams did everything they could to stop him; that was the way the game was (and is) played. If we are to credit eyewitnesses, there was nothing subtle about the tactics used to try to stop the Rocket. He could be hit, hooked or tripped. It was an open secret that when it came to "ethnic" slurs, he had a very short fuse: whoever called him a "frog," the deprecatory epithet used to designate French Canadians, would pay a painful price. Opposing teams were all too ready to use such tactics, since Richard would give as good as he got. Only four other players were penalized more during their careers in Montreal: John Ferguson, Chris Nilan, Shayne Corson and Lyle Odelein.

Violence against other players could take several forms: punching, slashing with his hockey stick, shouting matches with referees. Richard, with his "Gallic" (Ed Fitkin) or "volcanic" temperament, participated in numerous brawls: he was being violently attacked, he reasoned; it was his right to hit back. We know that he was a trained boxer, and his pugilistic exploits on the ice still provide grist for the journalistic mill. And if his fists weren't enough, the Rocket would use his stick. In *The Flying Frenchmen: Hockey's Greatest Dynasty*, the book he co-authored in 1971 with Stan Fischler, he admits to having no regrets about using his stick in fights. Richard's relations with the officials were as tumultuous as they were with his opponents. Doubly victimized, in his opinion, by the violence of the players and the laxity of the referees, Richard made repeated efforts to set right a situation of double jeopardy. He made no bones about it: "Yes, I was violent. But I wasn't vicious," he wrote in *La Presse* on March 15, 1995.

The circumstances leading to the Montreal Forum riot of March 17, 1955, provide an eloquent example. On March 13, in the Boston Garden, on the Bruins' home ice, Richard was injured by a blow from Hal Laycoe's stick. He defended himself first with his fists, then with his stick. He struck the official who attempted to restrain him, and plunged back into the fight against the Bruins players. Hard on this chain of events, league president Clarence Campbell suspended Richard for the final games of the season as well as for the playoffs. Hockey fans know these basic facts. What is less well known is that in March 1955 Richard was experiencing problems with an official for the second time that season: on December 29, 1954, in Toronto, he had attacked a linesman.

In any discussion of Maurice Richard's style of play, a final question never fails to arise: Did he ever give conscious thought to what he was doing? Or, to put it slightly differently, was he totally governed by instinct? Richard himself was self-contradictory. He would claim that he was always improvising when he was closing on the opponent's goal: if he himself didn't know what he intended to do, how could the goalie? But he would also explain that he never employed the same maneuvre twice against the same adversary. It is hardly surprising that the commentators are also divided on the question. But we would be well advised to take their attempts to depict Maurice Richard as a player of spontaneous reflexes instead of rationality with a grain of salt. George F. Will (1990) has demonstrated that racism often lurked behind such simplistic opposites: would Willie Mays have been called a baseball "natural" if he had not been African American?

Obsessed by scoring goals, determined and fearless, explosive, unpredictable: such was the Maurice Richard who terrorized opposing teams (and the authorities of his chosen sport).

The twelve labours of number 9

Myths are the stories drawn from great events. Twelve such events constantly recur in the writings of those who remember Maurice Richard.

Bill Stern, in his 1952 comic book, *World's Greatest True Sports Stories*, relates the night of December 28, 1944.

April 8, 1952:
The Rocket and
"Sugar" Henry
shake hands.

Four of them took place during the 1944–45 season; Richard was then twenty-three years old.

MARCH 23, 1944. During the playoffs, held at the Forum, Richard scored five goals against the Toronto Maple Leafs: the five goals scored by his team in its 5–1 victory. He was awarded all three game stars. Camil DesRoches, a Canadiens press agent, declared in Gilles Gascon's documentary *Peut-être Maurice Richard* [Maybe Maurice Richard] (1971) that the Forum received "thousands of phone calls every year" from people who wanted to confirm the results of that game.

DECEMBER 28, 1944. In Montreal, in a 9–1 win over the Detroit Red Wings, Richard scored five goals and three assists. Before the game, he had warned his teammates and his coach that he was exhausted; he had spent the entire day moving house, carrying furniture up and down stairs. The Historica Foundation of Canada's heritage minutes series selected the event when it added Maurice Richard to its roster in 1997.

FEBRUARY 3, 1945. Richard scored a goal while carrying Detroit Red Wings defenseman Earl Seibert (95 kilos) on his back. Former referee Red Storey described the incident in the 1999 docudrama *Maurice Richard: Histoire d'un Canadien / The Maurice Rocket Richard Story*: "Earl Seibert jumped on his back. Jumped on his back! Put his arms around him. And his legs around him. The Rocket never broke stride. He went in, deked the goalkeeper, scored a goal, and shook Seibert and threw him in the corner." It happened in Montreal.

MARCH 18, 1945. Boston. Richard scored his fiftieth goal of the 1944–45 season, the first time in National Hockey League history that a player had scored fifty goals in as many games. It was thirty-six years before the record was to be equalled, by Mike Bossy of the New York Islanders.

JANUARY 6, 1951. By scoring his 271st goal, Richard became the leading Canadiens scorer of all time; when he retired, he had scored 544 regular-season goals. Guy Lafleur scored 560 goals during his career, but "only" 518 with the Canadiens.

MARCH 27–29, 1951. At the Detroit Olympia, the playoffs between the Canadiens and the Red Wings, the strong favourites, had just begun. The first game, on March 27, lasted 121 minutes and nine seconds, instead of the regulation sixty minutes, with the Canadiens winning 3–2 at the beginning of the fourth overtime period. The second game, two days later, lasted 102 minutes and twenty seconds, as the Canadiens won 1–0 with a goal at the beginning of the third overtime. Maurice Richard scored both crucial goals. (The series was also marred by violent confrontations between Ted Lindsay and the Canadiens star.)

APRIL 8, 1952. In the third period of a crucial playoff game at the Forum, Richard scored what proved to be the winning goal of the game and the series, against Jim "Sugar" Henry of the Boston Bruins, after almost being knocked unconscious earlier in the game. For Jack Todd, writing in 1996, it was "the greatest [goal] in the history of the game"; for Roch Carrier, in 2000, "the most beautiful [goal] in the history of the world." Nothing less. The moment was immortalized in the photograph showing a bloodied Richard shaking hands with a bowing Henry.

November 8, 1952. With his 325th goal, Richard overtook Nels Stewart to become the leading all-time scorer in National League history. The goal was scored ten years to the day after his first NHL goal. In a 1954 television interview just after he notched his 400th, and later incorporated into *Maurice Richard: Histoire d'un Canadien,* Richard recalled how "nervous" he had been during the 1952 season. The tension is visible in the film of the November 8 game: Richard scores his goal, then skates up to the net to collect the puck, bounces it violently off the ice as if to get rid of it once and for all, before picking it up again.

APRIL 16, 1953. At the Forum, the Canadiens defeated the Boston Bruins 1–0 to win the Stanley Cup. Elmer Lach scored the winning goal during the first overtime, with an assist from Richard. Photographer Roger Saint-Jean missed the goal, but his photo of Lach and Richard leaping into one another's arms became famous. When the Montreal daily newspaper *Le Devoir* selected eight photographs "recognized by a great majority of Quebeckers" and devoted an article to each one in a series called "One Photo Is Worth a Thousand Words," the first published, in the September 25–26, 1999, edition, was Saint-Jean's. When Richard died, in May 2000, the same newspaper published the same photo on its front page, along with the same article. (Trivia buffs will recall that Richard broke Lach's nose when he leaped into his arms.)

MARCH 13–18, 1955. On the 13th, Richard fought Hal Laycoe of the Bruins, and struck one of the officials, linesman Cliff Thompson. On the 16th, Clarence Campbell suspended him for the remaining three regular-season games and for the playoffs. On the 17th, rioting broke out in Montreal over the suspension. On the 18th, Richard appealed to his fans for calm.

JUNE 13, 1961. Richard was admitted to the Hockey Hall of Fame one year after retirement. According to regulations, players are admissible only five years after the end of their career.

MARCH 11, 1996. During the ceremony that marked the closing of the Forum, Maurice Richard was selected as one of the players invited to pass on the torch representing the Canadiens' tradition. Introduced

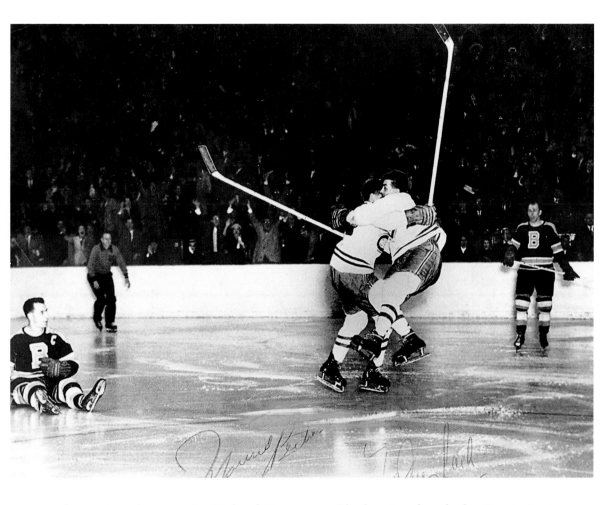

by master of ceremonies Richard Garneau as "the heart and soul of the Forum," he was given a thunderous ovation, whose length varied according to the source: seven, eight, nine, ten, eleven, even fifteen minutes. Maurice Richard wept.

Elmer Lach and Maurice Richard celebrate the Canadiens' Stanley Cup victory, April 16, 1953.

I. *The Icon*

WHEN THE EYES SPEAK...

"You've beautiful eyes, you know."

—JEAN GABIN, *Quai des brumes*, 1938

IN THE APRIL 3, 2004, edition of *La Presse*, Jean-François Bégin offered readers a composite portrait of the ideal hockey player: "The ultimate Canadien" would have "Guy Lafleur's hair," "Serge Savard's nose," "Claude Lemieux's mouth," "Patrick Roy's shoulders," "one of Chris Nilan's arms" and "one of Émile 'Butch' Bouchard's arms," "Jean Béliveau's hands," "Larry Robinson's hips," "Yvon Cournoyer's skates"—and "the eyes of Maurice Richard."

"Génétique 1" is a poem published by Bernard Pozier in his collection *Les poètes chanteront ce but* [The Poets Will Sing That Goal] (1991). In it, the author paints a composite picture of his all-time hockey all-star. In North America as in the USSR, he admires "Wayne Gretzky for his peripheral vision" and "Phil Esposito for his pranks," "Valery Kharlamov for his ankles" and "Vladimir Petrov for his smile." But former Canadiens players have a special place in his heart: "Denis

Savard for his feints," "Guy Lafleur for his slap shot," "Jean Béliveau for his elegance," "Pierre Larouche for his character"—and "the eyes of Maurice Richard."

The Montreal Rocket junior hockey team's tricolour (blue, white and red) emblem was adopted in 1999. It bears the name of the team, a rocket outfitted with hockey sticks, the number 9—and a stylized eye: one of the eyes of Maurice Richard.

La Presse sportswriter Ronald King, on December 28, 2003, penned an article entitled "Christmas with René, Céline, Rocket and . . . Magda!" Regular readers of his column "Du revers" [Backhand] immediately recognized his parakeets René and Céline, and Rocket, his pet goldfish. (Magda is the miniature turtle belonging to a certain Mr. Czgowchwz, a neighbour of Polish origin, as his name would indicate.) The article is illustrated by a drawing by Francis Léveillé, showing an aquarium decorated with Christmas lights; in it swims Rocket wearing a Santa Claus cap—and, for the attentive observer, boasting the eyes of Maurice Richard.

François Gravel's 1996 short novel, *Le match des étoiles* [The All-Star Game], is probably the most finely nuanced work to be written about the Canadiens right-winger. In Gravel's book, where the glories of the past return to face off against the stars of the moment, the former number 9 stands out: "When Maurice Richard looks at you in anger, you know just what a show that is!" His eyes are like "flame-throwers." That same year, that same pair of eyes welcomed visitors to the Maurice Richard Arena to an exposition entitled "Maurice 'Rocket' Richard's Universe," where they could read, on a panel adjacent to the entrance, the following message:

> He looks RIGHT THROUGH the opposition! One look from the
> Rocket was enough to make opponents and admirers think twice.
> "The way he looked at them, it was as if the other players didn't

exist…as if he was alone on the rink. I played with him and, sometimes, when we were on the ice together and I saw him heading for
me with that look in his eye, I felt like jumping over the boards to get
out of his way. Just think what the opposing team felt like!
—RAY GETLIFFE, Montreal Canadiens

The year before, the creators of *Le Canadien de Montréal, 1909–
1995*, a CD-ROM that tells the story of the Canadiens, singled out the
"famous look in his eye, threatening for some, intense for others," the
"two black eyes" that "hypnotized his adversaries," the "look of determination" that "was worth a month of fancy words."

Actor Roy Dupuis played the Rocket three times: in a televised
vignette for the Historica Foundation's heritage minutes series (1997),
in the miniseries *Maurice Richard: Histoire d'un Canadien* (1999) and
in Charles Binamé's feature film *Maurice Richard*. Miniseries producer
Robert Guy Scully hired Dupuis, he said, because "he had that look in
the eye, just like Maurice." Denise Robert, the film's producer, con-
curred: "Roy and Maurice Richard are both strong, silent types. Roy
expresses everything first and foremost with his eyes."

From 1940 to the present day, the eyes of the Rocket have been a
part of the popular imagination. What does it mean?

A fiery gaze

To begin with, it could be noted that the eyes of Maurice Richard are
the outward sign of his determination on the ice, of his intensity, of
his overwhelming will to win. As we have already seen, Richard the
player had only one thing in mind (to score goals) and would tolerate
no attempt to stop him from accomplishing his mission. His obsession
may have seemed violent; it was merely the price to be paid for success.

Richard's inner flame burned in his eyes. In Gilles Gascon's 1971
film *Peut-être Maurice Richard*, two interviews emphasized the

significance of that look. Camil DesRoches, the Canadiens press agent, and the novelist Hugh MacLennan reminisced on how the Rocket's eyes terrified his opponents:

> People talked a lot about Maurice Richard's eyes. They were piercing eyes. But they were more than that. A look of his was like a flash of lightning. If I'd been a goalie, I would have been terrified to see him bearing down on me.

A flash of lightning! For others, light: in a masterpiece of oxymoronic metaphor, former referee Red Storey told CTV on March 15, 1996, that Maurice Richard was "a runaway train with black headlights": light and its absence were reconciled in a single man! Richard Garneau, in Karl Parent and Claude Sauvé's 1998 television documentary, evokes smoldering coals. Or it can be simply fire, as in Bernard Pozier's poem.

The lightning flashes, the smoldering coals and the flames foreshadow a five-alarm blaze. Richard was determined; but his determination could lead to consequences that were as dramatic for him as they were terrible for others. With him on the ice, there was a constant risk of explosion, of eruption. François Gravel puts it best: "That wasn't fire in his eyes, that was real volcanoes erupting." You never know when a volcano will start to spit lava, but you know that when it does, no one can predict what will happen.

In telling the story of Jean Béliveau in *Strength Down Centre: The Jean Béliveau Story* (1970), the English-Montreal novelist Hugh Hood set out to distinguish Béliveau from his illustrious predecessor. His method was a meditation on how the eyes of "le gros Bill" (Béliveau's nickname) had not changed over the years: "His eyes have the same expression now that they had two decades ago, nothing aggressive or frantic in them, simply good spirits and a very impressive, self-contained sureness." Béliveau's eyes transmitted self-assurance; there was no "aggressiveness" in them, nothing "frantic"; they showed "good spirits" and "sureness." Those were two traits that no one would ever have associated with Richard.

The comparison points to a potential that several writers were to exploit: his were the eyes of a man possessed. One of Richard's teammates, Ken Reardon, remembers him in these terms in the March 1960 issue of *Sports Illustrated*: "I see this guy coming at me with wild, bloody hair, eyes just outside the nuthouse." The words *wild* and *nuthouse* point to a sole reality: madness. Forty years later, in *Hockey Digest*, Wally Stanowski, onetime defenseman for the Toronto Maple Leafs and the New York Rangers, said the same thing to Chuck O'Donnell: "He had that fiery look all the time. I once heard it described as having the look of an escaped mental patient. I thought that was a good description." Al Purdy, the poet, in his "Homage to Ree-shard," 1976, uses similar terms:

> "First madman in hockey," Dave says
> not sensible and disciplined
> but mad mad I see him
> with balls shining out of his eyes
> bursting a straightjacket of six Anglos.

Mad is also the word used by the anonymous commentator quoted by Frank Selke and Gordon Green in 1962, according to whom the "Punch Line," the trio made up of Toe Blake, Elmer Lach and Richard, was a "trio of mad dogs in their savage quest for goals." In a few lines, we have a "nuthouse," an "escaped mental patient," a "madman" and a "straightjacket," not to mention a "mad dog." Madness awaits those whom their intensity would devour.

The Rocket scores against the Boston Bruins.

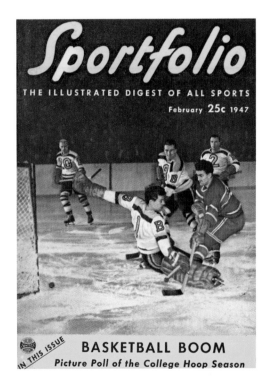

Silences

"I'd like to find the words..."
—GRATIEN GÉLINAS, *Tit-Coq*, 1948

"For beauty was in him; no power on earth could have torn from him the poignant certainty that he possessed in his heart. All he lacked were the words. And why was it that so deep, so sincere an emotion should not call forth the means of sharing it with others."
—GABRIELLE ROY, *The Cashier*, 1954

A first interpretation: fire in the eyes reflects fire within, with all the dangers it entails. A second, comparative interpretation: if so much is made of Maurice Richard's eyes, it is to draw attention away from his words, away from the way he spoke. His verbal economy was proverbial: "I don't talk for nothing," he says in one of the opening scenes of Charles Binamé's 2005 film. As though the idea was to replace Richard's silences with another mode of communication—his eyes—when he is not "speaking" with his play on the ice. For it is there that the taciturn Richard would have found the ideal form of self-expression.

The author who was to carry the idea to its logical conclusion was Gérard "Gerry" Gosselin, in his 1960 book *Monsieur Hockey*. Gosselin's elegy is rife with speculation about Richard and about language, but it also has a paradoxical side. Gosselin is constantly praising Richard's qualities to the skies, but when he quotes the star he places in his mouth convoluted utterances such as: "The fact that I managed fifty goals in a season is a disaster for me, personally. It was such an impossible objective that if I couldn't repeat it, they'd say I failed." And, to demonstrate his toughness, he writes: "You try to talk to him, but he doesn't have anything to say. His language is his game. On the ice is where he really talks, really roars, and his opponents, over the last eighteen years, have never been able to silence him." In an effort to describe his relations with the people closest to him, he likens him to:

... those eloquent orators who begin to stammer in the company of close friends. Talking with Maurice is putting him in a situation he doesn't like; making him talk about himself or about his achievements. But when he jumps onto the ice, goodbye bashfulness and timidity. Hockey transforms him into a speaker of great eloquence.

In an effort to get at the truth, he argues: "People have always attributed all kinds of feelings to him; put all kinds of statements in his mouth, while all he wants to do is work and keep quiet..." Maurice Richard's mother was adamant: "I've said it once and I'll say it again, Maurice is no talker." For his wife, he was "closed-mouthed," "taciturn." So a man of few, badly spoken words, a timid stutterer: one would have thought that, as an admirer, Gosselin might have devised a more positive portrait.

No need to agree with the author's every claim, however, to appreciate that Richard's relationship with language was never an easy one. Though we should take the statements transcribed in *Monsieur Hockey* with a grain of salt, we should not minimize Richard's difficulties either. The transcription of one of his statements for Gilles Gascon's 1971 film provides an excellent example:

> Well, I like having time on my hands I like doing what I like doing that's for sure after twenty-five years in hockey and maybe more if you count the juniors so twenty-five years I was doing what people told me to do but after twenty-five years I think you should be able to do what you like from time to time.

What could have been an expression of independence, a refusal to remain silent, is undone by the weakness of language.

There are several possible explanations for his tense relationship with speech. A man of little formal education, Maurice Richard may have hoped to avoid mistakes by speaking as little as possible. As he spoke no English when he joined the Canadiens, he preferred to keep silent. People described him as taciturn, while he described himself as timid. He played at a time and in a society that placed little value on strong speech, especially from athletes. Columnist Pierre Foglia touched on the question when he compared television hockey play-by-play announcer René Lecavalier with Richard:

> Lecavalier embodies in a troubling way Quebec's fascination, in the 1960s, with emphatic language. That fascination becomes even more troubling in that the other hero of the era, Maurice Richard, was a mute hero, a man who could not articulate.

Whatever the reasons, we must admit that they tend to explain why people have talked at such length, and so willingly, of the eyes of Maurice Richard. One has taken the place of the other.

Tears

Our eyes can speak for us. Our gaze can replace our words. We can also communicate our feelings with our eyes, with tears. Hockey may well pride itself on its reputation as a virile sport, a sport for real men; but one of its most spectacular practitioners never sought to hide his tears. Maurice Richard wept, and wept often.

There are the tears of the active player, of the competitor who collapses after the trial of strength. Among the great moments of Richard's career, the April 8, 1952, goal against "Sugar" Henry perhaps holds pride of place, thanks to the celebrated photo that shows the bloodstained Richard shaking hands with Henry, who is almost bowing before him. After scoring that goal, Richard broke down in tears in his team's locker room, beside his father. While on a visit to Prague, in 1959, where he was guest of honour at an international amateur hockey tournament, Richard first showed surprise at his reception from the public, then emotion, then broke into tears.

Maurice Richard's famous backhand.

Richard's active career ended on a tearful note as well. When he retired on September 15, 1960, his eyes glistened with tears as he spoke to journalists gathered at the Queen Elizabeth Hotel in Montreal.

Over time, the tearful stories would multiply. When the Montreal Forum closed its doors on March 11, 1996, Richard responded to the ovation with tears. When he was honoured at the Molson Centre in February 1999 for the presentation of the trophy that bears his name, and later, in October of that same year, for the launch of the television miniseries *Maurice Richard: Histoire d'un Canadien*, his reaction was the same. And when Céline Dion sang "S'il suffisait d'aimer" [If Only Love Could Be Enough] for him, on December 8, 1998, at the Molson Centre, he wept (so did she).

Charles Binamé, who directed the full-length feature film *Maurice Richard* (2005), understood that there was a double profit to be made from such behaviour. On the one hand, the reconstitution of the goal scored against "Sugar" Henry ends with a torrent of Richardian sobbing: the sign that the goal that has just been scored is unique. None of the film's other goals—and they are legion—is accompanied by such an outpouring of emotion. That goal was a mythical one. On the other hand, the moviegoer discovers his sobs at the same time as Lucille Richard, herself overcome with emotion, sees her husband from the corridor in front of the locker room door. It signifies that the great player is a family man, close to his dear ones, as when the new father takes his daughter in his arms and sheds a tear over her. This particular myth is a man, like any other.

He may be able to speak only with his eyes, words may fail him: those are secondary matters. Richard knows how to express his emotions. Giving him a human face is essential to the creation of the myth. His legendary ruthlessness as a hockey player, which can be explained by the stress to which he was subjected, gradually gives way to the gentleness of the father, then of the grandfather. His tears tell us that the coldest ice can melt.

WHAT'S IN A NAME?

"THE NAME OF MAURICE RICHARD WILL LIVE FOREVER!"
  —"Almanach du sport" [Sports calendar] 1955–56, Dow Brewery

"Our name is Maurice Richard."
—ROCH CARRIER, *Le Rocket*, 2000

Maurice Richard's relationship with his own identity was a complex one from the start. In the late 1930s and early 1940s, his passion for hockey was such that he played in several leagues simultaneously, a forbidden practice. To circumvent the regulations, he employed aliases, such as Maurice Rochon, under which he won several trophies. At the beginning of Gilles Gascon's film, filmmaker Bernard Gosselin recalls meeting his idol when he was a boy; but the idol refused to give his name. "I don't know any Maurice Richard." When he signed his autograph, he would add a number 9 in a circle between his first name and surname. He preferred to be known by the number of his hockey sweater. He could have chosen something else; the possibilities were numerous. Over the years, the man known today as "the Rocket" or "Maurice" answered to a whole list of nicknames. Considering how banal his first and last names had become, he needed every one of them.

Le Rocket

Gérard "Gerry" Gosselin entitled his 1960 biography *Monsieur Hockey*. Nothing terribly original about that: the same sobriquet was applied to Gordie Howe, another famous number 9, but with the Detroit Red Wings. Later, it would be used to describe Wayne Gretzky.

A rocket or a satellite?

In the 1940s and '50s, speed was in vogue, occasionally connected with violence. For a while Richard had been "the Comet"; there had been the "Stratford Streak" (Howie Morenz) before him, and there would be the "Golden Jet" (Bobby Hull) after him. He played for a team whose speed (and ethnic origin) were the stuff of legend: the Canadiens players were known as the "Flying Frenchmen." Hy Turkin of the New York *Daily News* dubbed Richard "the Brunette Bullet," linking Richard's dark hair with his speed and impact. Happy Day, coach of the Toronto Maple Leafs, went even farther: during World War II, German V2 rockets had inflicted heavy damage on London; on March 23, 1944, when Richard scored five goals, he was dubbed "V5." Keeping up with the headlines, the now-defunct Toronto *Telegram*, in its October 29, 1957, issue, spoke of "Sputnik Richard."

We get it: Maurice Richard had a special connection with speed, and with the heavens. He is a meteor, a Flying Frenchman, a bullet, a guided missile and a satellite (an allusion to the Sputnik launched by the Soviets in 1957). He is "the Rocket."

Anecdotal history gives several sources for his nickname. For Ed Fitkin, a *Star* reporter dreamed it up. According to Andy O'Brien, Richard had Hal Atkins to thank. Maurice Richard himself claimed Phil Watson, Murph Chamberlain and Ray Getliffe gave him the name in 1943–44. But says Jean-Marie Pellerin, backed up by the majority, the sole source of the Rocket could only have been Ray Getliffe. No matter: the nickname was there to stay. There had been attempts to give it to other sports figures, but none were quite as successful, and none had his staying power. Never will the real Rocket be confused with imitators like Roger Clemens (baseball) and Rod Laver (tennis), Pavel Bure (hockey) and Raghib Ismail (Canadian football). But what exactly did a nickname like "the Rocket" really mean?

Like other 1940s and '50s nicknames, "the Rocket" connoted speed and, more precisely, *thrust*. A rocket is not simply a fast-moving object;

it is an object that must tear itself free from the earth. The same quality could be found in "V5" and in "Sputnik." The nickname was less a celebration of the player's speed than of the difficulty in stopping him once he had wrenched himself from inertia. Unlike the comet, the rocket is an earthly body that *becomes* heavenly: it had not always been in the sky.

The connection with speed and with the heavens is self-evident; it was not lost on a single one of the Rocket's admirers. There was somewhat less interest in other aspects of his nickname.

"The Rocket" also suggests technical prowess. Though balloons have been floating in the skies since the Montgolfier brothers of the eighteenth century, and airplanes have been flying since the beginning of the twentieth century, with the Wright brothers, the invention of the rocket was contemporaneous with the rise of the Richard brothers, Maurice and Henri ("the Pocket Rocket"). Quebec in the 1940s had long been considered backward, technically and scientifically. To call someone "the Rocket" was to step, at least in the imagination, into the world of technical modernity; to consider oneself no less modern than anybody else.

For some two centuries, technical modernity had a language of its own: English. But there seems to be a curious general lack of awareness that the so-called French-Canadian national myth had an English nickname. Commentators have long noted how difficult it had been for Richard to master the language of Shakespeare early in his career, but none have noted the following: Maurice Richard may have been slow to learn English, yet he was given an English nickname; that nickname was given him by his English-speaking teammates; it was accepted by his fans, who had conflicted relations with Quebec's then-dominant English-speaking minority. Maurice Richard was not "la Fusée," despite the best efforts of the French translator of Mordecai Richler's novel *Barney's Version* and the display window designers of the Hockey Hall of Fame in Toronto; nor is he, for French speakers, "the Rocket": he is "*le* Rocket," using the French definite article. In his name, he anchored the Canadian concept of the harmonious coexistence of the two (soon to become) official languages.

We could carry the interpretation even farther. What does the word *rocket* signify, beyond speed, the heavens, technique and the English language? There is the French word *roc* (rock): Maurice Richard was as hard as a rock; some of his teammates actually called him Rock. Then there's *roquet*: since 1752, the word that originally denoted a small dog had come to mean, in a figurative sense, "an ill-tempered little runt." The first part of the definition would fit Richard perfectly; the second less so. Then, too, we have *roquette*: Maurice was given his nickname in wartime; the projectile the word denoted was in the headlines. Had he been given his nickname later, it surely would have evoked *rock,* an allusion to rock music: but it wasn't until 1957 that Denise Filiatrault sang "Rocket Rock and Roll."

It is not enough to examine only Maurice Richard's nickname; it must be compared with those of his teammates and his opponents. In so doing, we can certify that "the Rocket" did possess a mythical quality, which was not at all the case of those around him. Impossible to be a myth and be called "le gros Bill" (Jean Béliveau), Bernard "Boom Boom" Geoffrion, Émile "Butch" Bouchard, "the Pocket Rocket" (Henri Richard), "the Vest Pocket Rocket" (the nickname of a third Richard brother, Claude, who could never quite attain the sanctum sanctorum of the "Sainte Flanelle"): all that is much too familiar to elaborate on. As nicknames go, "the Old Lamplighter" (Toe Blake) and "the Chicoutimi Cucumber" (Georges Vézina) never reached beyond a restricted circle of fans.

Even the attacking trio of which Richard was the key had more symbolic impact than most: the image of the "Punch Line" (Richard, Blake, Lash) was superior to Detroit's "Production Line" (too mechanical),

Boston's "Kraut Line" (overly "ethnic"), Toronto's "Kid Line" and Chicago's "Scooter Line" (both too juvenile). Only New York's "Atomic Line" could match the "Punch Line," except for the fact that the atom, during the last half of the twentieth century, did not always enjoy good press. Between atomic energy and rocket science, the latter was less troublesome.

A deck of cards, and an ad.

The column entitled "Le mot de la fin" [The Last Word] in the April 8, 1957, edition of *La Patrie* consisted of the words "Maurice Richard..." over white space, and the following conclusion, at the bottom of the column: "...Say that name, you've said it all!" Shakespeare, known colloquially as "the Bard," had speculated on the power of a name 362 years earlier, in *Romeo and Juliet*:

> What's in a name? That which we call a rose
> By any other name would smell as sweet.
> (act II, scene II)

Unlike *La Patrie*, Shakespeare had it right: there's more to a name than white space. The same holds true for a list of nicknames.

A common name

For aspiring mythmakers, the name Maurice Richard left something to be desired; hence the nicknames. Fictional characters, however, would show no hesitation in adopting the identity of their idol. The *real* Maurice Richards had no choice.

The Forum, even though it is not identified, plays a key role in *Chien vivant* [Dog Alive], a novel by Marc Gélinas published in 2000. The principal character is an ice-resurfacing machine (Zamboni) driver called Maurice "Rocket" Tremblay.

> A name like that, it sounds almost predestined, like it was made up for some history that tells about the first thirty years in the life of an ice foreman at the Montreal arena. It's true, it was made up. Partly, anyway.

Since the novel speaks at length of hockey and of the Montreal hockey team, one might have taken it as a sign of admiration for Maurice Richard; but that is only indirectly true. The hockey player appears by name only once in the novel: Maurice Tremblay collects hockey memorabilia; he likens a recent addition to his home decor, an anonymous athletic supporter (jockstrap), to Richard's. But in the same breath he adds, "Or Gretzky's," which amounts to trimming Richard down to the level of an ordinary superstar, the Wayne Gretzky of the 1970s, '80s and '90s. As in the comic book by Arsène and Girerd, published in 1975, a future workmate gives Maurice Tremblay his nickname, with a touch of mockery: "You think you're fast on your feet, eh? Maurice 'Rocket' maybe?" His first name fares not much better: "[His parents] baptized their child Maurice, like his grandpa, like his premier..." Trapped between Gretzky and Maurice Duplessis ("his premier"), Marc F. Gélinas' Maurice Richard is a trifle drab. In Gélinas' book, the name dilemma—first name, middle name, surname—is omnipresent: depending on the time and on the speaker, the main character is called Maurice, Petit Maurice, Mo, Maurice à Théo, Zamboni, Pitou, Little Mo, Momo and Rocket. His identity is never firmly established; never is he entirely Maurice Richard, never entirely not him.

In *Rocket Junior* (2000), the complimentary references are more direct, but still ambiguous. Everything about the hero of Pierre Roy's novel for young readers predisposes him to the admiration of number 9. His first name is Richard-Maurice; his surname, Latendresse Ladouceur. His nickname is "Rocket Junior." Still, he is the first to realize just how incongruous the juxtaposition is: "You're talking about a name of player that's got to be a fighter, tough, full of energy!" His first name is inverted, while the qualities expected of a hard-hitting player are negated, including neither tenderness (*tendresse*) nor gentleness (*douceur*). Admiration for the Rocket goes hand in hand with changing values. It is as though, in sports-minded Quebec in the year 2000, some qualities were easier to defend than others.

You may be called "Rocket" or "Richard-Maurice" in a novel. But you can also be called Maurice Richard in real life. Take one of the

Rocket's sons, Maurice Richard Jr., nicknamed Rocket like his father. Take the bass player in Robert Charlebois' band, immortalized in an extemporaneous outburst in the hit song "Engagement" [Commitment]: "Hey Maurice, Maurice Richard, one hundred years playin' your bass, that's a lot! Think it over!" Take at least five other people listed in the 2005 Montreal telephone directory, not to mention the dozens who identify themselves only as "Richard, M." Take the numerous Maurice Richards interviewed by *La Presse* in May 2000, on the occasion of the hockey star's death, from one ocean to the other. Take little Maurice-Richard Boily, photographed outside the Molson Centre on May 30, 2000. Or press photographer Rocket Lavoie. There could be a less explosive name or surname to be saddled with.

SELLING A MYTH

To understand Maurice Richard's place in Quebec, and in Canada, analysis of the texts that deal with him and of the images that have represented him—to which we will soon turn—is not in itself enough. It is equally indispensable to investigate how he was used commercially. Material culture—the plethora of objects that featured the Rocket—is a gold mine of unimaginable, and scarcely exploited, richness. It was a fact that the curators of the exposition entitled "Une légende, un héritage: 'Rocket Richard': The Legend—the Legacy" at the Canadian Museum of Civilization were quick to grasp; 626 *by* 9 (2004), the catalog designed by I. Sheldon Posen, felicitously taps into the same ore-bearing lode. In a more mercantile vein, the trinket and bric-a-brac merchants who have taken over the Web are doing exactly the same thing: a brief visit to eBay will convince even the most hardened skeptics. Maurice Richard is a brand name.

Proper display of the artifacts connected with Maurice Richard presupposes a certain amount of enumeration. That accomplished, we can inquire into the target audience, and into the importance of the commercial connection in perpetuating the myth. Let us then enumerate.

Buying the Rocket

The interior decor of a Richard memorabilia collector's home would be nothing if not picturesque. Should he need lamps, he would find at least two models, one for young people: Richard, in a red uniform, is standing in front of the goal, from which the light shines. The other would be more attractive to mature buyers: it represents a beer mug topped by a lampshade, with blue the dominant colour; on the shade are the words "Watching hockey/a cool Molson" and a picture of Richard scoring a goal. The same adult who has purchased the lamp would be tempted by the Rocket ashtray, on the bottom of which are embossed a puck, two crossed hockey sticks and three stars. The ashtray itself would not be complete without the lighter emblazoned with the Richard coat of arms. Young and old alike could gather around a "Maurice Richard/9/626" transistor radio: shaped like a hockey puck, it could be easily carried thanks to its neck strap, and set up on its telescopic tripod for all to admire.

Nor would our collector's kitchen want for mementoes. There we would find a Maurice Richard mug, from which to drink the Bovril that Richard claimed to be "tasty," before adding, "Bovril scores with me every time." We would dig into a serving of Quaker Oats or enjoy a bite of "Maurice Richard" Supreme sliced bread, dipped into a bowl of "9 Maurice ROCKET Richard Condensed Tomato Soup." (In 1955, National Hockey League president Clarence Campbell suspended Maurice Richard. It was thought that Campbell, a popular brand of soup in Quebec, belonged to him. To avoid a possible consumer boycott, it was long believed, the company launched its "Maurice ROCKET Richard" label.) Later, our collector could breakfast on corn flakes from a box depicting the hockey immortal, or drink a glass of Merlot

Maurice Richard Vin de Pays d'Oc Guibaud 1999 (Société des alcools du Québec, code 00913657, $8.55).

But he would find the most exquisite treasures in his son's, and not his daughter's, bedroom: interest in distaff consumers was scanty. Our collector's pride and joy would be a shelf full of books devoted to the Rocket. He would play cards with his Maurice Richard deck, each card carrying the name of a generous sponsor. He would solve one of many puzzles: the one showing the Rocket's 400th goal (but with 500 pieces), or Elmer Lach's famous goal, on an assist from Richard, the goal that eliminated the Boston Bruins and won their team the Stanley Cup (480 pieces). He would play with his model truck painted in the colours of fuel-oil distributor S. Albert, for whom Richard worked after hanging up his skates. He would develop his muscles with the Ben Weider "wrist builder," a device for strengthening the wrist muscles: "Maurice 'Rocket' Richard says you can develop explosive hockey shooting power!" The existence of a table hockey game could have been predicted; less so, a game of bagatelle, also known as *trou-madame*, a distant ancestor of today's pinball. Canada's linguistic particularity explains why in the 1950s advertising for Bee Hive corn syrup was bilingual: in English, a player for the Toronto Maple Leafs announced that anyone who purchased a bottle would be sent, on receipt of a duly completed coupon and twenty-five cents, a novelty ring; in French, that player was Richard. From the wall would hang a Canadiens or Dow Brewery calendar, prominently featuring Richard. The lad could jot down his favourite events with his Dixon

Dupuis Frères catalogue advertisement for Maurice Richard garments, midwinter, 1951–52.

Advertisement
for Vitalis hair
conditioner,
published in
the *Saturday
Evening Post*.

pencil with the effigy of the players of the Canadiens,
including number 9, or the Maple Leafs players. In his
clothes closet he would keep his Maurice Richard garments (jacket, overalls and sweater, tie pin), garments
that he probably purchased at the Dupuis Frères department store in downtown Montreal. (Later his wardrobe
would include a Maurice Richard jacket, just like the one
his hero wore.) Before going to sleep, he could view pictures of the Rocket on his Show'n Tell machine, learning
about the rules of hockey and listening to the story of his
hero's fiftieth goal in fifty games, in 1944–45. The closet
is also the place where he would store his hockey equipment, beginning with his skates. In the 1953–54 Eaton's
catalogue—the catalogue that would play such a decisive role in Roch Carrier's story—photos of skate models
such as "the Rocket" ($10.95 or $12.95) and "Maurice
Richard" ($21.95) are accompanied by the hockey star's
picture and signature. In 1958–59 the choice is broader,
with three models available: "the Maurice Richard
Special" ($21.95), "the Rocket" ("priced low," $12.95)
and "the Maurice Richard Pro" ($43.50). These models
are shown alongside others recommended by Richard's
teammates, Jean Béliveau and Bernard "Boom Boom"
Geoffrion. Then comes the sweater. If we are to believe
young people's literature, few other objects could have
been more treasured in the 1950s. The teams imagined
by Roch Carrier (1979), Carmen Marois (2000) and David Bouchard
and Dean Griffiths (2004) are made up of players all of whom wear
sweater number 9. When he grows up and becomes a pop singer, the
lad will continue to wear the magic number, just like Robert Charlebois,
Shania Twain, Éric Lapointe and Céline Dion.

The lad matures, until one day he starts shaving. Gillette has a Rocket razor just for him. The day will come, too, when financial security will become a concern. If he has been provident, if he has not thrown everything in his room away, he can strike it rich thanks to Maurice Richard. How? By selling off the old Rocket trading cards he's accumulated in a variety of ways: by purchase, trade, through promotions, as gifts, even as bequests. There is a flourishing market for such cards, as one can attest by visiting Internet auction sites, specialty shops and collectors' conventions and by consulting the fans' bible, Beckett Media's publications. If he has been truly provident and meticulous in caring for them, our bright young man will earn hundreds of dollars for Parkhurst's Maurice Richard card RC number 4, 1951–52 series, in mint condition. If he is in a speculative mood he can hold onto the card and hope that its value will keep climbing, for it was the first official Maurice Richard card (card production was interrupted during World War II and resumed only in 1951–52) and is extremely rare. If he has been improvident, if he has discarded everything that had no (monetary) value in his eyes, the lad now become an adult will find consolation in reading young people's novels in which hockey cards play a central role, works by Michel Foisy, or by Jack Siemiatycki and Avi Slodovnick, or he can admire specimens featured in the writings of Chrystian Goyens, Frank Orr and Jean-Luc Duguay, or of Marc Robitaille. But that would be small consolation.

Advertisement for Williams shaving cream for the Spanish-speaking public.

Living in Maurice Richard's house

So numerous are the objects representing Maurice Richard that we can affirm without risk of contradiction that they will never all be accounted for. There are two explanations: first, objects bearing his likeness could not have acquired any value before the star himself became the myth he was to become. The second reason is that material culture—objects, images, products—has long suffered from lack of interest on the part of the institutions responsible for preserving and protecting the traces left by cultural memory. A museum would not think twice about conserving an early twentieth-century painting; the same considerations did not necessarily apply for such artifacts as advertising posters singing the praises in English of Vitalis hair conditioner or, in Spanish, of Williams shaving cream. As a result, many objects that once bore Maurice Richard's face have today vanished by way of the dustbin.

But one man in particular had taken an avid interest in such objects before, and more than, anyone else. His name was Maurice Richard, and he loomed head and shoulders above all other collectors.

Just how far above would be seemingly difficult to evaluate at first glance. It would be theoretically possible to scour everything written about Richard in an attempt to learn what he had to say about the cult devoted to him, and about its instruments. (There would be little to be gleaned.) We could, magnifying glass in hand, scrutinize photos of him taken at home, and attempt to isolate what within them reflected his image. (Once again, we would have little to show for our efforts.) But a more reliable source does exist: the catalogue of the "Maurice 'Rocket' Richard" collection put up for sale on May 2, 2002, by the firm Collections Classic Collectibles, designated to auction off the Rocket's personal collection. A detailed sixty-four-page catalogue, complete with full-colour photographs, printed on glossy paper, and detailed descriptions (in English only; for marketing purposes?) was published for the occasion.

The catalogue lists 289 lots, almost all of which come from the family estate (fewer than a dozen articles are labelled as being of other origin). Everything you might hope to find is there: medals and numerous trophies, including replicas of the Stanley Cup awarded to the National Hockey League's championship team; visual material (posters, charts, photographs); pieces of equipment (sticks and sweaters); numerous commemorative plaques accumulated over a long, richly rewarded career; official documents (letters of congratulation, contracts, passports, tramway passes, official dinner menus); garments; calendars and sports programs; cards of all varieties (birthday, playing, professional, post); advertising gimmicks (cigarette lighters, ashtrays, pocket knives); china; products advertised by Richard himself; books (few) and magazines. Not unexpectedly, the descriptions of these items sing their praises, the better to sell them, but even then, some of the remarks are surprising: Richard's hockey sticks are described as "the holy lumber"; one of his sweaters is compared to the holy shroud (an allusion to the Shroud of Turin). The merchants of the temple had been studying their biblical history.

As with any auction catalogue, no actual sale prices are listed; but the prices that opened the bidding are public knowledge. (Prices shown are in U.S. dollars, as in the catalogue.) The highest opening price is $5,000, for a Stanley Cup ring, for sculptures and for sweaters (including the one compared to the holy shroud, with its reputedly authentic sweat stains). At the other extremity of the commercial spectrum are articles listed at $100: a Quebec medical insurance card and motor vehicle registration documents; twelve bottles of Maurice Richard vintage wine; toys; certificates attesting that Richard was an honorary citizen of the cities of Winnipeg and Drummondville; his "vintage 'Brunswick' bowling ball."

The objects selected and the way they are presented combined to invite the reader-buyer to enter into the intimate details of the life of

GOING STEADY

Is it ruining our teen-agers?

COVER BY JOHN LITTLE
Ice-fishing at Ste. Anne de la Pérade

Toronto the Gay: fine food, a night-life boom

CLYDE GILMOUR PICKS THE BEST MOVIES OF 1958

MACLEAN'S

JANUARY 3 1959 CANADA'S NATIONAL MAGAZINE 15 CENTS

A young boy wears the number 9 sweater on an ice-fishing trip.

Maurice Richard and his family. He could purchase his idol's bedroom set (opening price: $300). He could have the front door of Richard's house on Péloquin Street, in Montreal, delivered ($200; the door from another Richard dwelling turned up on the Internet in 2005 for $5,400). The buyer of his last hockey bag would also acquire his underwear ($500). He would be able to travel with Maurice Richard's luggage ($200 or $300, depending on the model). His wife's jewellery, bearing the Canadiens emblem ($500), and a makeup kit that had been a gift to her ($300) by an unknown admirer were available, as was a tray given to the Rocket's parents in 1956 ($200). Who could doubt that wood carvings were appreciated in the Richard household: at least a dozen were available (from $200 to $2,000). Photos indicated where various objects were to be found in the house. Trophies, mirrors, wall plaques, clothing, statuettes, paintings and decorative plates had long been a part of the family's daily life.

Paradoxically, this intrusion into the private life of the Richard family was presented as an official, public visit. An "Avis important / Important Notice" had been inserted between the cover and page 1 of the catalogue. It certifies, "On April 5, 2002, the Québec Minister of State for Culture and Communications, Ms. Diane Lemieux, has issued a notice ... pursuant to the *Cultural Property Act* expressing her intention to proceed with the classification of 47 significant objects having belonged to Maurice Richard, objects which are listed in the present catalogue." The notice gave the minister the right to supervise and monitor the sale and circulation of the objects listed in it. Ultimately, the Canadian state, under the auspices of the minister of Canadian Heritage, was to purchase for $600,000 (Canadian) the forty-seven articles, which were immediately transferred to the Canadian Museum of Civilization. They are to be found in the Collections Classic Collectibles catalogue, in the showcases of "Une légende, un héritage: 'Rocket Richard': The Legend—the Legacy" and in 626 *by* 9,

MAURICE RICHARD vous recommande
d'acheter du **Sirop Bee Hive**

... *c'est la marque qu'il utilise!*

Suivez l'exemple de Maurice Richard — régalez-vous avec le Sirop Bee Hive sur du pain, des céréales et des crêpes.
Tous les Joueurs de Hockey du CANADIEN recommandent et utilisent le SIROP BEE HIVE à l'exclusion de tout autre.
ESSAYEZ la BOUTEILLE COMPRESSIBLE EN PLASTIQUE pour le SIROP BEE HIVE — se remplit à même la boîte.

PORTRAITS DE HOCKEY GRATUITS!
Dimensions 5" x 7" — prêts à encadrer. Portraits de tous les joueurs des "Canadiens". Vous pouvez obtenir n'importe lequel — ou vous les procurer tous. Envoyez une preuve d'achat de sirop Bee Hive ou 5 livres pour 2 portraits — ou le collet d'une boîte de 2 lb. de sirop Bee Hive pour un portrait — ou un collet de shortening liquide St. Lawrence ou un dessus de boîte de flocule de maïs Durham ou un dessus de boîte d'emploi Ivory, pour un portrait. Écrivez le ou les noms du ou des joueurs désirés, avec vos nom et adresse, sur un morceau de papier, et postez à la St. Lawrence Starch Company, Port Credit, Ontario.

above: Maurice Richard advertises corn syrup . . .

facing page:
. . . as well as car batteries.

the catalogue of the exposition. The transfer from the world of commerce to that of the museum has been one of the most effective vectors for the transformation of Maurice Richard as product into myth. Out of respect for the provincial motto ("Je me souviens" [I Remember]), someone must do the conserving, even if that someone is the federal government.

The salesman

Maurice Richard was not simply represented on products of all possible description, nor merely a collector of his own artifacts, some of which were later designated as cultural objects by the state. He was a businessman too.

He could frequently be seen in the role of beer salesman. He participated in advertising campaigns for the Molson and Dow breweries, and for a short time owned the 544/9 Tavern on St. Lawrence Boulevard in Montreal. He also sang the praises of fishing (Clipper fishing rods, the Club de pêche La Barrière), of fuel oil (for S. Albert and Co., then Ultramar), of consumer electronics ("Maurice Richard TV. Capri électronique. Ventes et services"), of steel (for the Lougee Steel Corporation), of life insurance (for Equitable and for Prudential Life) and of motor vehicles (for Jarry Automobile).

As he grew older, he branched out, extolling Grecian Formula 16 hair colouring liquid on television. He was hired as a spokesman for Coca-Cola, for Air Canada's Aeroplan frequent flyer program, for Fluviral influenza vaccine and for the National Bank of Canada. Thirty years after his retirement, his face could be seen, in full-page ads in the Montreal newspapers, endorsing BMW automobiles, this from a man who drove only big American-made cars. He could boast his own phone card, courtesy of Bell Canada. Immediately after his career ended, though briefly, and for a longer period at the end of his life, he served as goodwill ambassador for the only hockey team he ever played for, and for the Molson Brewery. Finally, the loving grandfather he had become handed out Sour Punch Caps candies to children.

Upon his death in 2000, things changed. A limited edition of the magazine *Les Canadiens* was published. Desjardins Financial Services, for its commemorative advertisement, used a painting that illustrated Roch Carrier's story: "We are all 'Rocket' Richard," read the caption. McDonald's used the face of a young hockey player over a particularly edifying message: "We all need a hero! Here's to you, Rocket!" The generation gap was suddenly bridged: the ad used children who had never seen the Rocket play to reach their nostalgic parents.

The Rocket's library

We know very little about Maurice Richard's reading habits.

Though occasional photographs represent him holding a book, there is little we can glean from them. With the odd exception, he is never depicted in proximity to anything but children's books. An official Montreal Canadiens photo shows him reading to his grandchildren: the book is about himself (*The Value of Tenacity*); visible on the bedside table is another book of which he is the subject (*The Hockey Sweater*). Several years earlier,

Still bridging
generations
in 1996.

THE MARK OF A LEGEND

the December 1958 issue of *Sport revue* depicted him looking on as one of his sons read *L'oie qui jouait du piano* [The Goose that Played the Piano], then helping his children do their homework, schoolbook in hand. The family man was also a reader (who liked to read aloud).

There were a few exceptions, for advertising purposes. In a 1950s photo we see him alongside one of his sons, flanked by Jean Béliveau, praising the "Collection littéraire" [Literary Collection] of the Belgian publisher Les Éditions Marabout; the combination created a bit of dissonance, as Béliveau was more readily associated with cultural pursuits than was Richard. Still, he had been photographed at the launches of books by former players like Jean Béliveau and Bernard Geoffrion, or by sports photographers like Denis Brodeur. He put his signature to the prefaces of several books, which added to their credibility: *Playing*

Better Hockey with les Canadiens, a booklet from the 1960s; Denis Brodeur's 30 *ans de photos de hockey* (1993); *Le match des étoiles*, by François Gravel (1996); *Les Glorieux*, by Réjean Tremblay and Ronald King (1996); *Yvon Robert*, by Pierre Berthelet (1999); *La carte de hockey magique* [The Magic Hockey Card], by Michel Foisy (2000).

Photos depicting Richard in the act of reading are a rarity, as are direct attestations of his reading habits. Like Montaigne's library in the sixteenth century, the walls of the Canadiens' locker room displayed, in Richard's day, a number of quotations. Some were in English ("There's always a reason"), others in Latin ("Celeritas—Auctoritas—Aeternaque" / "Speed—Authority—Eternity"). Adjacent to a phrase from Abraham Lincoln, Richard could have read Canadian officer John McCrae's exhortation, from "In Flanders Field": "To you from failing hands we throw / The torch; be yours to hold it high." What did the citizen from Bordeaux, in north-end Montreal, think of those fragments of text? We will never know.

We have no clearer idea of what he thought of the books of which he was the hero. In a column written in February 1963, for *Maurice Richard's Hockey Illustrated*, he deplored never having read a particular book about his life, even though that book had been available for a year. But in the same column he describes "devouring with his eyes" the memoirs of Frank Selke, the Canadiens' general manager, entitled *Behind the Cheering* (1962). It was quite simply "the best book about hockey I have ever read." (If it was truly the best book on hockey Maurice Richard had ever read, then we should have cause for alarm.) In 1973, Andy O'Brien related that Richard had never read his biography of him, and that he had no intention of doing so. The author of the preface to François Gravel's *Le match des étoiles* thanks the author for reminding him of such "wonderful memories." On June 21, 1998, in *La Presse*, Richard describes attending the launch of the revised edition of Jean-Marie Pellerin's 1976 book, but adds that he'd forgotten to take a copy home, and was not able to see what changes had been made from one version to another. When his family put part of the Rocket's private collection up for auction, only a few copies of magazines became available, and only a handful of books, all of which dealt with the Rocket. They had helped perpetuate his myth. He had held onto a few of them. We have nothing more to go on.

Selling himself

In attempting to draw conclusions from these facts and figures, a cultural sociologist would identify the trends indicated by the plethora of products that used Richard's image. He would classify them according to which social class (lower, middle, upper) the products were designed for. One example should suffice. Vintage Maurice Richard wine began to make sense only after the 1980s, or the 1990s, and in particular social circles at that. To lend Richard's face to a red wine would have had no impact whatsoever in the 1950s: people were simply not drinking wine back then. Selling Dow or Molson beer was the norm. Only later would the Québécois graduate to wine.

A cultural historian would single out the increasing frequency of audiovisual media. Television could not have been the main commercial vector in 1942; it arrived in Canada only in 1952. Trade in Richard began with the print media (newspapers, wrappings, catalogues) and the radio. Television finally took the lead in the 1950s, a position it would never relinquish. Not only did Richard start up an electronics business, but he became a celebrity who was a frequent guest on television talk shows. By the twenty-first century, thanks to the Internet, commercial possibilities had begun to multiply: in May 2005, parties unknown put the domain name "leRocket.com" up for sale on eBay. They hoped, at an initial price of US$75,000, to attract Net surfers fascinated by the Rocket.

Maurice Richard, one of his sons and Jean Béliveau endorse the Marabout series.

A cultural studies specialist would interpret the same development as symptomatic of capital's growing domination of sport. For him (or her), major-league sports figures could not be but paid spokespeople for the very capitalists who were simultaneously exploiting them. Commentary of this order was more prominent in the 1970s, but it can still be heard today in response to the exorbitant salaries paid to world-class athletes. In Victor-Lévy Beaulieu's 1972 profile, Guy Lafleur is presented as a young man of "proletarian origin." Though the vocabulary is no longer the same, the analytical spirit has not changed that much.

A marketing expert might term what has happened "unbundling." Children numbered among his contemporaries, as did their parents, who would be purchasing their skates and their clothing, their corn syrup, bread, soup, oatmeal, toys, books and magazines. Now those children have grown up: now they are being offered new products more in sync with their needs, from black gold to red wine. The tributes and the eulogies had awakened memories; Maurice Richard products now sought out new generations at the beginning of the twenty-first century: Rocket's first fans have grown old, but hordes of younger people have joined their ranks. The proof of a successful commercial enterprise is that as one category of consumers grows old, new replacements step forward into the breach. Maurice Richard has staying power.

The trade in Richard clearly tells us something about the man and his sport; it also tells us something about our society, and the way it has evolved. But its significance hardly ends there.

The principal impact of the trade in Richard, whatever shape it has taken, has been the transformation of Maurice Richard into a product, then into a label, and ultimately into a myth. The products and services created in his image boast of, and offer for sale, first, a hockey player and a man whose achievements have become part of the daily lives of his fans; second, the gravity of an individual who has superseded social barriers; finally, the Maurice Richard myth itself, which belongs to the ages.

The products and services endorsed by him and associated with him are less significant than Richard the public figure with whom people can identify. That figure first took shape on the hockey rink, but also—and above all—in advertising that was as dynamic as it was multiform.

THE ROCKET'S BODY

Any athlete is primarily a body, whether concealed beneath a uniform or revealed to public view. For some—weightlifters, wrestlers, shot-putters and hammer throwers, strongmen—pumped-up muscles are themselves the spectacle. Others, whose primary attribute is rapidity—gymnasts, long-distance runners, beach volleyball virtuosos, jockeys—make the most of quick muscular response. There are the hybrids, of course: hyper-developed boxers, mustachioed lady sprinters, tennis queens with sculpted muscles. The bodies of hockey players, like those of athletes in many professional sports (football and basketball, for instance), have evolved over time. Aurèle Joliat, one of the stars of the Montreal hockey club from 1922 to 1938, weighed 61 kilos and stood 1.7 metres tall; today's hockey players, more massive of body than swift of foot, would, of course, dwarf him.

Over this body, competing discourses clash. Scientific writing of a certain era speculated whether racial characteristics were a factor in estimating the potential of an athlete's body; since then, as a result of widespread doping, the athletic body has become medicalized. Sports journalism judges the body by its performance, by its successes and failures, by the extent to which it achieves the tasks assigned to it. Painters and sculptors—from ancient Greece to twentieth-century Italian futurism—have represented it in rich variety. From Pierre Popovic ("Wimbledon, P.Q.") to Courtney Eldridge (*The Former World Record Holder Settles Down*), from Harry Crews (*The Gypsy's Curse*) to Nathalie Gassel (*Musculatures*), creative minds have depicted it as an erotic object.

Though medical science seems to have been indifferent to Maurice Richard's body, painting, public praise, the press, sculpture, song and cinema have been anything but.

Strength and its weaknesses

There have been over time many attempts to depict Maurice Richard's body, in images or in words. Most chose the pointillist technique, which juxtaposes tiny dots of colour over the more traditional portrait form. A rare handful has gone against the grain. More often than not, their raw material is pain.

Serge Lemoyne's lithographs depicting the Canadiens players of the 1970s have been repeatedly reproduced. Perhaps best known among them are works representing the sweaters worn by Guy Lafleur, Ken Dryden, Bernard Geoffrion and Doug Harvey. In a 1981 lithograph inspired by Maurice Richard, *Bangkok Number One*, sweater number 9 covers a sleeping Thai girl. Louis-C. Hébert is perhaps best known for his Formula One paintings, but he has also painted Richard. Two distinct works focus, each in its own way, on the hockey star's face. In the first of them, his look is one of grim determination. In the second, belonging to Loto-Québec, which has donated it to the Bell Centre, his gaze is more at peace; but it is by no means the least interesting of the two. In 2001, Yvon Goulet created *9*, an art book. The edition, not unexpectedly comprising nine copies, is composed of three advertising hoardings in recycled corrugated plastic upon which a plethora of barely distinguishable images have been silk-screened: photos of the Canadiens, snippets of text, and a map. Maurice Richard's face barely emerges from the visual mass. Lemoyne's lithographs, Hébert's paintings, Goulet's silk screens: sweater, eyes, face. Maurice Richard cannot be captured in his entirety.

Which does not mean that no one has attempted to paint the Rocket's body. There is no lack of official portraits, both at the Montreal

Serge Lemoyne, *No. 1 de Bangkok*, 1981.

Forum and the Molson, now the Bell Centre. Many portraits are inspired by the same photograph of Richard in action, eyes popping, taken by David Bier of *The Gazette* (Montreal). It is the classic image of Maurice Richard. Depictions that stray too far from the traditional are rare. But here are two.

In *The Rocket Scores* (1998), a painting by Saul Miller, a "performance specialist," the spectators admire Maurice Richard in the country's two official languages: "Mon Dieu," "It's the Rocket," "Tabernac" (sic), "He scores." The player possesses an impossibly elongated body. Head surrounded by a halo, he is outmanoruvring the Toronto Maple Leafs' goalie as animal-headed referees and players look on, while flocks of birds rise from the ice. Miller's model is obviously Chagall.

In 1994, Montreal's Musée d'art contemporain received from Maurice Richard, in return for a tax credit of $300,000, a work variously known as *Homage to Duchamp* or *Homage to Duchamp (Tribute to Maurice Richard)*. It had been a gift from its prestigious creator, Jean-Paul Riopelle, which explains its exceptional value. The work consists of a plywood door painted on both sides, measuring 203 centimetres high and 91 centimetres wide. On the Duchamp side, a cloud of white circles speckled with blue-grey superimposed on three stacked cubes form a half-animal, half-human creature. We can recognize traces of white, blue and red; but the dominant tones are grey and brown. On the Richard side, objects stand out against a nonfigurative background: at the top is depicted a snowshoe; beneath it, a hockey stick rotated to the left, along with a goalie's stick pointing to the right face off against one another; draftsman's instruments (called ellipse templates) that vaguely resemble skate blades form the border of the elongated rectangle.

Riopelle's tribute to the hockey player is three-fold. Though the work is signed "riopelle" in the lower right-hand corner, the words "Rocket Richard" can be read alongside the player's hockey stick, in a different style of lettering; both are executed in white. Between the two sticks, which are outlined in blue, and directly beneath the snowshoe a rounded form suggests a hockey puck on which are inscribed two letters: "MR." For the crowning touch, resting upon the handle of each hockey stick the outline of a hand stands out, traced in fluorescent pink; on the player's stick the hand (right) is that of Maurice Richard; on that of the goalie, the hand (right) of the painter. The two were immortalized with spray paint on March 30, 1990, in the course of a meeting between him and Richard organized by *La Presse*. Clearly, Riopelle was no worshipper of convention. Instead of blue, white and red, we have blue, white and pink. Instead of the eyes of Maurice Richard, we see his hand. Neither high culture (Duchamp and modern art) nor popular culture (Richard and hockey) alone, the work shows the two intertwined. The artist is clearly having a good time: urban legend, as reconstructed by Riopelle, has him and Richard facing off as adolescents on the ice at Montreal's Lafontaine Park. The museum has brought them lastingly together. *Newsweek* had all but predicted it on May 27, 1963, when the weekly nicknamed the painter "Rocket Riopelle."

When it comes to putting Maurice Richard's body on display, journalists, advertisers, writers and filmmakers have been no less prolific than their colleagues the artists. Like the latter, the former have concentrated on one physical feature in particular. Unlike the artists, they have been less hesitant to bring out the physical ordeal of the body athletic.

Maurice Richard's dominant physical quality, aside from his eyes, is his strength. In *Le Rocket* (2000) Roch Carrier compares Richard to a horse, a tiger and a bull. A half-century earlier, Jeanne d'Arc Charlebois sang that he was "forceful as a bull." We are constantly reminded of how powerful his hands were: "those hands of his, that big," wrote radio host Christian Tétreault in 2005. The ultimate proof of his extraordinary strength lies in the innumerable tales of the goals scored by Maurice Richard as he carried one or even two players on his back.

Jean-Paul Riopelle, *Hommage
à Duchamp (Hommage à
Maurice Richard)*, 1990.

One of the biblical incarnations of might is Samson, whose hair was his source of strength, just as the loss of his hair signified loss of strength; it is hardly surprising to see hairiness used to depict Richard. "It must be admitted that the Richard brothers, Maurice and Henri, were as hairy as bears," related Pierre Gobeil in *La Presse*, on May 29, 2000. "Perhaps that was the secret of their exceptional strength? Like Samson, in another age." In 1973, Maurice Desjardins publicly regretted that opposing players did everything they could to stop Richard from scoring, holding him "by the arms, the shoulders, the hair, the sweater." It was somehow to be foreseen that Maurice Richard's hairdresser—they were called "barbers" back then—would appear in three films about him. In *Peut-être Maurice Richard*, by Gilles Gascon, the real Tony Bergeron appears a half-dozen times. As he is cutting Richard's hair, he relates to the camera the game in which Richard scored eight points after spending the day moving house. Behind him, at the Forum, two Anglos, a man and a woman, "around sixty-five, seventy, white-haired," were crying. "It's true what I'm telling you," he adds. In Charles Binamé's *Maurice Richard*, Tony Bergeron, played by Rémy Girard, tells Richard just what he stands for in the eyes of French Canadians. "You're not bad for a hair snipper," answers Richard, played by Roy Dupuis. In his 2005 "making of" film about Binamé's film, *Hommage à Maurice Richard*, instead of the real or an imitation Tony Bergeron, Mathieu Roy, giving the Maurice Richard myth an unexpected family fillip, interviewed the barber's son Yvon.

In 1955–56, the Dow Brewery's "Almanach du sport" extolled the "incomparable right-winger with the hair of the blue jay [sic] and the eyes of the lynx." There is not a touch of grey in his hair, and his eyes are sharp; Maurice Richard exudes youth and health.

But we remember him not only as a tower of strength. By the early 1940s, as we have seen, Richard had already suffered several potentially career-ending injuries. One of his nicknames was "Bones," suggesting their fragility. It was at that time, on his physician's advice, that he is said to have begun drinking one bottle of beer per day, to strengthen his bones. In fact, Maurice Richard suffered two bouts of serious injury, one at the beginning of his career, the other at its end. Nor did he escape entirely unscathed in between: his style of play, the attacks he suffered and the blows he inflicted all seemed to pre-ordain that he would accumulate stitches, cuts and scrapes. After he retired, he spoke openly of his insomnia and his weight problems. Filmmakers were quick to appreciate the benefits they could derive from that much-abused body, battered by the assaults of his opponents and by time itself.

With both Jean-Claude Lord and Pauline Payette in 1999, and Charles Binamé in 2005, the blood flowed freely. Nothing startling there: both still and moving images drawn from Maurice Richard's career provide ample confirmation. But the filmmakers go even farther. Lord and Payette, in the fictional segment of their docudrama, dwell on his insomnia and on Richard's efforts to conceal his injuries, even from his wife. In the documentary segment, they unabashedly depict a Richard who had slowed substantially as his career was coming to a close, in the late 1950s. Binamé ignored his insomnia and weight, bringing out Richard's internal conflicts in another way: he films Roy Dupuis / Maurice Richard not long before a game, shaking in front of his bathroom mirror, while his wife, just outside the door, asks him if he is all right. In both films we see him burst into tears after his goal against "Sugar" Henry, in April 1952. Enough is enough: he may be the darling of the crowd, his near and dear ones may love him, but pain does not spare the athlete.

The pain of the athlete, the two films also suggest, is also that of the worker who, without a properly functioning body, is nothing. In Lord and Payette's docudrama, Richard and Bernard Geoffrion explain how afraid they were of injuries during their playing days. Even in a weakened state, they stayed on the ice; had they not, they would have been replaced, perhaps permanently, entailing the loss of their livelihood. In Binamé's fictional film the work world is more at the foreground than in any other retelling of Maurice Richard's life. Between the young machinist at the start of the film and the skater of the 1950s, the link is a bodily one: to keep his job, he had to persevere in spite of physical deficiencies. The athlete's body is a wage earner's body.

Whether as an aging Samson or a wounded bull, the representations of Maurice Richard's body have ultimately helped to humanize the myth. The Rocket was a tower of strength, of course. But he paid a heavy personal price; he fell victim to his weaknesses; he suffered. In the years just before his death, visibly reduced by illness, he would make only a handful of appearances: at a press conference dealing with his health, held in 1998; at a Céline Dion concert in December of that same year; at the launch of Lord and Payette's docudrama in 1999. By the same token, he had become just like everyone else. Not only was he suffering; he was suffering alone.

Larger than life?

If the last half-century is any indication, Quebec delights in erecting statues to honour its leading political figures: René Lévesque in New Carlisle, Quebec City and Montreal; Maurice Duplessis in Trois-Rivières and Quebec City; Adélard Godbout and Jean Lesage in Quebec City; Daniel Johnson in Quebec City and Montreal; Jean Drapeau in Montreal; Pierre Elliott Trudeau in the Montreal suburb of Côte-Saint-Luc. Montreal has not forgotten its union leaders (Jean Lapierre on Papineau Street), its performing artists (Félix Leclerc in Lafontaine Park, Jean Gascon at the Monument-National, Claude Jutra in the park that bears his name, Jean-Paul Riopelle in the city's Quartier international). Sporting figures have not enjoyed quite the same profile: a statue of Jackie Robinson stands in front of an Olympic Stadium that

Statue by
Paule Marquis,
Pepsi Forum
Entertainment
Centre, Montreal.

no longer houses a baseball team; Louis Cyr stands watch over a renovation outlet in the Saint-Henri district; Ken Dryden has been relegated to Place Vertu, a shopping centre far from the downtown core. That has not stopped several sculptors from seizing on Maurice Richard's body.

Some hark back to folk art. In the early 1960s visitors to the Ville Marie Wax Museum, located at the corner of Saint-Catherine and Drummond streets a few blocks from the Forum, could contemplate "the famous MAURICE 'ROCKET' RICHARD," scoring his 500th goal against Glenn Hall of the Chicago Blackhawks on October 19, 1957. As far as we can judge from a postcard depicting the scene, the installation suffered little from excessive realism, even though the waxen Maurice Richard comes off marginally better than the goalie he is about to score against. The Maurice Richards of François Corriveau and Michel Dusablon, both later arrivals, have no particular resemblance to the player we thought we knew, but they at least convey the appearance of movement, the minimal requirement of sports sculpture.

Better-known artists also tried their hand. In the one-time Forum, since converted into a multiplex motion-picture theatre known as the Pepsi Forum Entertainment Centre, passersby can have their picture taken beside a life-size sculpture of Maurice Richard, or, behind him, next to one of his fans shown waving his hands in the air. All that remains of the former sports arena is a few rows of seats, where the

Maurice Richard stickhandling
with one hand, as imagined in
the 1960s and in 2000.

nostalgic visitor can reminisce on the Rocket's years of triumph. The statue of Richard, in sculpted cement with a metallic finish, is the work of Paule Marquis. The player is shown wearing sweater number 9, in blue, white and red, with its team captain shield, as he did in the wax museum, and in the sculptures by François Corriveau and Michel Dusablon. He is holding his stick in front of him, perpendicular to the ground. The overall impression is of a player more fragile than the man people remember: perhaps the result of the Rocket's curious haircut, which seems closer to comic book reporter Tintin's cowlick than to the fine scissor-work of Tony Bergeron, not to mention Richard's posture. The Rocket at rest is a tired Rocket, a bit low on the get-up-and-go.

When it comes to representation and posture, sculptors Jean-Raymond Goyer and Sylvie Beauchêne, the real Richard specialists, have taken different approaches. The two worked together on the statue for the Maurice Richard Arena, of which we will be speaking shortly, and also produced a bronze heart bearing the life-size imprint of Richard's hand. Together they designed a limited-edition casting for the Maurice Richard Foundation's 1999–2001 fundraising campaign. The statuette, entitled *Never Give Up*, the hockey star's motto, depicts him in full flight. Bent forward, leaning on his stick, with which he controls the puck, he looks straight ahead, head held high, his face suffused with a look of serenity. No frailty here; nothing but strength and mastery. The Rocket's fans, it seems, prefer this image to the previous one, since two monumental copies have since been cast: one located at Les Ailes, a downtown shopping complex, and another in Gatineau, not far from the Canadian Museum of Civilization. A far less monumental version, also executed by Goyer and Beauchêne, stands atop the trophy that bears Richard's name, awarded every year to the National Hockey League's leading scorer.

While perhaps the most striking aspect of these representations is the self-assurance they depict, effort and determination are the dominant features of the statue unveiled on August 4, 1997, in front of the Maurice Richard Arena, in tribute to its model on his seventy-sixth birthday. Its creators are Jules Lasalle and Annick Bourgeau, who also executed the Montreal statue of Jackie Robinson. Inspired by a statue of Maurice Richard sculpted by Marcel Choquette in 1971, it portrays the Rocket in motion, head flung back, eyes sharply focused. Of all the Richard statues it best conveys his power. It would be possible for a player to hold the position in which Paule Marquis, on the one hand, and Jean-Raymond Goyer and Sylvie Beauchêne, on the other, represented the Rocket. The same is not true of the statue at the Maurice Richard Arena: no one could hold that kind of pose. What we are looking at is

a snapshot immobilized in bronze. The position of the legs particularly reveals the player's power. Though slightly smaller than Goyer and Beauchêne's, and larger than Marquis', their 2.5-metre statue best captures Richard's playing style.

Statue by Jean-Raymond Goyer and Sylvie Beauchêne, Les Ailes shopping centre, Montreal.

The metamorphosis of the statue of René Lévesque in Quebec City must have influenced Jean-Raymond Goyer and Sylvie Beauchêne, and Jules Lasalle and Annick Bourgeau—though not Paule Marquis. Lévesque was Quebec's premier from 1976 to 1985. When he died, a bronze statue was set up in front of the National Assembly, only to be replaced a few years later by another, larger version. (Statues of) myths should be larger than life.

That obscure object of desire

In the case of the Rocket, the eroticization of the sports star's body is reflected not in statuary or in literature, but in song, motion pictures and advertising. It is also rare.

It can assume a good-natured tone, as in the song entitled "Maurice Richard," by Yvon Dupuis and Jean Laurendeau, and interpreted by Jeanne d'Arc Charlebois in 1951.

> From all across Quebec they come
> From Longue-Pointe to Gaspé
> The girls invade the Forum
> To see their man play
> Hubby they'd gladly give a miss
> Just to get a little kiss
> Maurice, of course, he'd like to please
> For him scoring goals is a breeze.

Statue by Jules Lasalle and Annick Bourgeau, Maurice Richard Arena, Montreal.

In the late 1950s, another song suggested that the Rocket's female admirers couldn't live without him: "Rocket Rock and Roll," sung by Denise Filiatrault, with lyrics by Jacques Lorrain and music by Roger Joubert. For two minutes and thirty-seven seconds the listener partakes—no surprises here—of the sadness of the girl who has lost her ticket to the Forum and cannot convince the ticket-taker to let her in.

> Mister usher, let me into the Forum tonight
> I want in
> I really, really, really want to see my superman.

The woman is on the verge of a nervous breakdown:

> Don't just stand there, I'm getting riled
> If I can't see my idol I'll go wild
>
> I'm all shook up
> I'm all wound up
>
> I'm gonna slap you
> I'm gonna scratch you
> I'm gonna roll on the floor
>
> Quit playing the clown
> I'm having a breakdown!

There's nothing for it.

> What a bummer!
>
> Missing the Rocket
> On account of a ticket!

Then, in a last-second turnabout, she finds her ticket:

> Oh mister usher, I'm on cloud nine

73

I found the ticket
Now everything's fine.

But it's too late.

Aw shucks! The game is over.

Compared with those two songs, with their timid treatment of female attraction to the Rocket, Gilles Gascon's film *Peut-être Maurice Richard* (1971) offers a thoroughly masculine take, and an ambivalent one at that. With one exception, all the interviewees are men: the sole woman, hidden behind dark glasses and not identified (the men in the film are), speaks only for a few seconds. The sexual differentiation is reinforced by speech that suggests a masculine form of eroticization. As one such "admirer," the tavernkeeper Marcel Couture, avows unabashedly in his retelling of how he followed the hockey star on the road and at home, waiting for him to score his 500th goal: "Maurice Richard gave us the shivers; I've got Maurice Richard under my skin," an unexpected adaptation of Cole Porter's 1936 hit, "I've Got You Under My Skin," and of Édith Piaf's "Je t'ai dans la peau" (1953). "Gabriel Leclerc, schoolteacher," relates the time when Richard was his pupil. He quotes Saint François de Sales—"You can catch more flies with a spoonful of honey than a barrel of vinegar"—and reveals his pedagogical secret: "You had to know how to handle him . . . Me, I handled him nice and easy, and I got what I wanted from him." Commenting on the enlarged photos behind him on the wall, a drunken customer in a tavern describes the technique of the Rocket, "a player who knows what he wants," as a "hothead" closing in on a "terrified" goalie protecting his "cage." Far from using a technical vocabulary, he eroticizes his subject: "Him, what he's lookin' for, Maurice Richard was, is the puck to stick it right where it's supposed to go, right into the goal. That's where it goes." The image of penetration ("That's where it goes") meets with the approval of the other drinkers if we are to judge by their boisterous applause, and is buttressed by a Freudian slip: our French-speaking tavern-goer uses the female article in front of a generally masculine word, changing the gender of the word in the process. In the closed universe of the Quebec tavern in 1971, to which women were forbidden entry, where men would arm wrestle to the ribald commentary of other men ("Hanky panky, wanky wanky," adds a spectator), such allusions are anything but innocent.

What makes the masculine eroticization of the Rocket even more interesting is that we tend to reduce a sport like hockey to nothing but an expression of virility. So argues Renald Bérubé in a 1973 article entitled "Les Québécois, le hockey et le Graal" [Quebeckers, Hockey and the Holy Grail].

> Perhaps we should . . . be asking ourselves: is not hockey, and more specifically the identification with Maurice Richard and the Montreal Canadiens, in Quebec, the revenge of triumphant virility over the near-institutionalized impotence of the notables (the "best people")? Does it not point to a (sublimated) cult of physical strength in a land that has long preached shame for the body?

Certainly, "virility" is "triumphant" in the way hockey lovers talk about the game, and the "cult of physical strength" is one of its components, but there may be more to it, in Gascon's film at least, than virility, than a cult seen from the viewpoint of the traditional division of sexual roles (the man is virile; the woman loves him for that reason). However, "shame for the body" was perhaps less pervasive in sports-minded Quebec of the last century than is commonly believed.

Richard himself was to play the charmer only later in life, and then with a light touch. He was fifty-nine when he recorded a series of television spots for Grecian Formula 16, a hair colouring lotion. In it, he admits concealing his grey hair for the past three years: "Look as

young as you feel with Grecian Formula 16, in cream or liquid form."
It doesn't matter if you're a father and a grandfather, you can still be
conscious of your looks: "No one even noticed." But who exactly does
he want to charm? Women at large? According to a first version of the
commercial, the answer would have been yes. "I leave just a touch of
grey; the ladies like it that way." But there was soon another take: "I
leave just a touch of grey . . . My wife likes it that way." That, at any rate,
is what Maurice Richard's wife, Lucille, told Colleen and Gordie Howe
in a 1989 interview. She preferred the second version.

Songs, motion pictures and commercials: Maurice Richard's body
proved a desirable object, one that drew men's and women's eyes to it.
Everyone could like him, on condition that they remain chaste about
it: with a few exceptions, his admirers, be they male or female, did not
kiss him, nor touch him; they could not even see him except from a
distance. Richard could upset family harmony; that would be a no-no.

COMPARING THE INCOMPARABLE

In baseball, one can hardly mention Roger Maris without speaking of
Babe Ruth: is the former's home-run record of the same order as the
latter's? When people think of Jacques Villeneuve, they automatically
think of his father, Gilles: which of the two was the better race-car
driver? The same holds true for bicycle racing: was Armstrong greater
than Indurain? Anquetil, Merckx or Hinault? We can already look forward to the day when the same kind of questions will emerge from a
recreational activity like beach volleyball. Put succinctly, the sports fan
loves to compare, evaluate, weigh and ponder. For him, sports stars
are not like lovers: they are never unique in the world. They come in
clusters: today's sports figures and those of yesteryear are matched
against their contemporaries, those of today and yesterday commin-
gled and assessed. It becomes even more entertaining, and instructive,

to remove them from their particular sporting discipline and compare them with individuals from other sectors of human activity, or with animals; we need only reflect for a moment on the legions of colts, tigers, bulls, bears, blue jays and lynx, to name but a few, that we've encountered earlier. Certain comparisons are enlightening; others are completely off-the-wall. But all of them have a story to tell, about the man and about the myth.

Just another athlete?

For Maurice Richard, the comparisons begin with his career in sports.

Was he his team's greatest player? It should come as no surprise to find out that opinions differ. Many felt that he was too brittle to last; he had suffered several serious injuries during his first seasons. It was far from clear that he could survive the hits that were bound to come his way. There have been allegations that during his first seasons the over-all quality of play was inferior, a result of World War II and its impact on signing players. The only reason Richard shone, some maintain, was that he was surrounded by mediocrities. Others conclude that Richard appeared to be such an excellent player because he played on an undistinguished team; he was the best of a bunch of journeymen. Those arguments were not to last long. His critics were forced to recognize that Richard was much more solid than his early injuries had led them to believe. He did play from 1942 to 1960, after all. They were forced to admit that he continued to stand out even after the hockey players in uniform had returned from the front. They were obliged to accept the fact that Montreal's lean years had come to an end: the team he led would stand astride the world of hockey for nearly two decades. One by one, Maurice Richard reduced his detractors to silence.

Was he the best attacker in the Canadiens' history? Great stars like Newsy Lalonde, Aurèle Joliat and Howie Morenz had come before him. One by one, he beat his precursors' records, and kept right on playing.

In any event, Lalonde, who scored 266 goals for Montreal, Joliat, with 270, and Morenz, with 257, played at a time when the rules of the game were not at all those of modern hockey. Howie Morenz played fourteen seasons in the National Hockey League, twelve of them in Montreal, but he died at age thirty-four; Richard played eighteen seasons and remained a presence on the Montreal sports scene until his death, in 2000. When he retired, he still held many Canadiens records: most goals during a regular season; most goals scored during playoffs; most penalty minutes during a regular season; most goals in a single season, most overtime goals during playoffs, etc. For at least a dozen years, he was the Canadiens' best player; of that there can be no doubt. For many years, no one even came close to him; no doubt about that either.

Was he the greatest NHL player of his era? Was he Mister Hockey, or was it the younger Gordie Howe of the Detroit Red Wings? Can we compare, as did Louis Chantigny in a *La Patrie* article first published in 1963 and reprinted in 1974, the romantic Richard with the classical Howe, "with all that the term implies"? Or can we make do with the compromise dreamed up by Bill, the hockey player invented by Jacques Poulin for his novel *Le coeur de la baleine bleue/The Heart of the Blue Whale* (1970) in a passage comparing the respective merits of a select handful of players: "Richard was more spectacular; Gordie Howe's a more all-around player." Were they "the two greatest players in the world"? Or must we make do with Michael Davey's granite puck, carved on one side with Richard's eye, and on the other, Howe's elbow (Howe was not nicknamed "Mister Elbows" for nothing)? The answer to the question "Who was the greatest?" can only be subjective. A more legitimate question would be "Who was more popular? Who did people turn out to watch play?" Judged by that standard, no one could equal Richard. Hockey fans turned out in their multitudes to see him play, both in Montreal and on the road. You never knew where or how far the fire in his belly would carry him: to the opposing team's goal or to the penalty box. What everybody did know was that there would be fire in the belly to spare. Satisfaction guaranteed.

Was he the greatest sports figure of his era? In the 1940s and '50s in Quebec few sports could compare with hockey. Bicycle racing was all but unknown. Automobile racing was something that happened far away. Beach volleyball did not yet exist. There remained (Canadian) football, wrestling and baseball, three sports that were well known to Quebec fans, assuming wrestling can be considered a sport, of course.

In comparing hockey with football, the names of Maurice Richard and Sam Etcheverry, the Montreal Alouettes quarterback, were often mentioned in the same breath; but the argument is unconvincing. When we contrast the two men, we are measuring two accomplished athletes, and attempting to prove that they reached the highest levels of achievement in their respective disciplines. However, their two sports did not enjoy the same symbolic status: football was never the national sport of Canadians, from coast to coast, even though it did play a role in forging and keeping alive a Canadian national identity; but it is not as deeply rooted in the country's DNA as hockey.

The career of Yvon Robert, a French-Canadian wrestler, is often compared to that of Maurice Richard. Indeed, the two men had much in common. They were almost the same age: Robert was born in 1914, Richard in 1921. They drew crowds, both in Canada and in the United States. They had to overcome the language barrier (English) to succeed. They were represented primarily as family men. In the preface to Pierre Berthelet's biography of Yvon Robert, published in 1999, Maurice Richard states not only that he and Robert were close friends, but that the wrestler had been his boyhood "hero," a "god," he added. And yet, "the Lion of French Canada" never achieved Richard's mythical stature. We can enumerate at least four reasons why he did not: the wrestler, who died in 1971, did not have the hockey star's longevity. Wrestling, like football, did not enjoy the same stature as hockey in the

French-Canadian imagination. Robert's memory could not draw upon the same diversity of resources as Richard's, which was kept alive by journalism, literature, popular music, motion pictures, sculpture and portraiture. Most of all, Robert's life was never marked by a catalytic event, like the riot of 1955 in Richard's career.

As for baseball, two names stand out. The first is that of Babe Ruth: everybody compares him to the Rocket. Yet he was a man of excess, on the field and off. Where Richard personified family values and modest social pleasures, Ruth was a womanizer, a boozer and a trencherman. In fact, his image as a bon vivant is what his admirers best remember about him. One example should suffice. In *High Midnight*, a detective novel by Stuart Kaminsky (1981), Ruth is heard to complain: "Stomach . . . Gone bad on me after all I did for it, all the good times I gave it, all the gals who admired it. Is that fair, I ask you?" Though the two men were radically different in their off-field behaviour, they strongly resembled one another in their determination on the diamond and on the rink, in their flamboyant style of play, in their ability to come through in the clutch and in the records they set, which were long (and mistakenly) believed to be unsurpassable.

The second baseball star who is often compared to Richard is Jackie Robinson, the first African-American player of the so-called "modern" era to play in the major leagues. For sportswriter Renald Bérubé, writing in 2000, the similarity between the two men was plain for all to see: "In one short season, Jackie Robinson became, in Montreal, P.Q., Maurice Richard's brother." There is more substance to this comparison than to the preceding one. Robinson and Richard were contemporaries: the former born in 1919, the latter in 1921. Robinson played for the Montreal Royals, the Brooklyn Dodgers farm team in the International League, in 1946, while Richard was starring for the Canadiens. Both personified the possibility that minority groups could succeed in North America: the African Americans with Robinson, the French Canadians with Richard. Both were known for their fiery temperament. Both were the subject of a wide variety of cultural discourses, from song ("Did You See Jackie Robinson Hit That Ball?") to journalism and literature: there even exists a *Jackie Robinson Reader*, published by Jules Tygiel in 1997. The two men kept company, if we are to believe Maurice Richard's May 26, 1996, *La Presse* column: "I remember him well. I often went to see him play. In 1946, he played softball with the Canadiens players." Both men were given the highest honours: their numbers (42 and 9) were retired, and both were elected to their respective halls of fame. At first glance, everything seemed to bring them together. Closer up, things became more complicated.

There are at least two reasons. Firstly, though French Canadians had long been treated as second-class citizens even in Quebec, their social status had never been determined by an institutionalized racialist discourse. Secondly, their social and biographical paths diverged. It was no accident that Branch Rickey, the general manager of the Brooklyn Dodgers and mastermind of Robinson's entry into the world of "white" professional baseball, had been so determined to make Robinson the symbol he was to become. Rickey had selected him because he was more than a simple baseball player: the man who would be transformed into an icon of social integration had earlier been a student at UCLA, and a lieutenant in the United States Army. As a student he had learned to master the weapon that Richard never would: language. As a military man, he fitted right into the revolution then sweeping the imagination of America: any man who could fight for his country could play baseball in the same league as everybody else, and not in the Negro League, where Robinson had begun his career. One man became a hero because he had been chosen for the role, and had possessed the necessary qualities; the other became a myth without ever really understanding why.

Finally, was Maurice Richard the greatest sports figure in Quebec history? We can attempt to answer the question by referring to a play by Jean-Claude Germain, *Un pays dont la devise est je m'oublie*, first produced in 1976.

Germain's "great epic jig" in eight scenes and two epilogues constructs a dialogue between Berthelot Petitboire and Épisode Surprenant, traveling players specializing in "winter sketches" and "historical tableaux." From New France to the Quebec of the 1950s, they restage the key events in the emergence of a nation. The final two tableaux and the second epilogue bring together a strongman and a celebrated hockey player, Louis Cyr and Maurice Richard, in a state of utter anachronism: Louis Cyr, known worldwide for his prodigious strength, died in 1912, nine years before the other man's birth.

The dramatist first places in Louis Cyr's mouth a soliloquy about his hard life as a living legend (seventh tableau). We then hear the recording of an interview with Maurice Richard by sports commentator Michel Normandin, followed by a long monologue by Richard, furious at his double status, as a god when he is on the ice, and as a "retard" as soon as he leaves the rink (eighth tableau). Germain finally sets up a meeting between the two national legends, Cyr and Richard (second epilogue). Cyr is made to feel obliged to assure Richard just how precious he is, and to explain his place in Quebeckers' imaginations. To a comment from his interlocutor—"I ain't half sure I'm even a memory"—Cyr answers:

> A memory, youse? Even if you wanted to, get all nice and warm, with all your washed-out photos and clippings... you ain't no memory and you never will be! You're Mau-ri-ce Ri-chard! Never was... never will be! Got it? Once and for all!

Maurice Richard would have no reason to be concerned about history: his mythical stature would perpetuate him in an unchanging present ("Once and for all!"). Louis Cyr may eventually disappear; in fact, he had all but vanished before Paul Ohl's book about him was published in 2005. Maurice Richard has never disappeared; he can never disappear. Comparisons can unite, but they also make it possible for us to make distinctions.

Today the hockey rink, tomorrow the world

Newsy Lalonde, Aurèle Joliat, Howie Morenz, Gordie Howe, Sam Etcheverry, Yvon Robert, Babe Ruth, Jackie Robinson, Louis Cyr: those names could be expected. Others, less so: the names of people who expressed themselves off the ice, often in the most prestigious of venues.

Let us leave aside, for the time being at least, the mythological and biblical comparisons: Maurice Richard as Icarus (according to Louis Chantigny), as Hermes / Mercury (in Roch Carrier), as Achilles (thanks to a tendon injury) and Hercules (for Réjean Tremblay, in Parent and Sauvé's 1998 film). A Toronto Maple Leafs defenseman, Babe Pratt, said of Richard that he was "surely one of Samson's cousins"; he was not the only one. Richard's birth, as versified by Camil DesRoches on radio station CKAC, January 14, 1945, resembles that of a legendary hero ready to conquer the world from his first cries:

> When he was only hours old,
> He began to cry, his parents told.
> Mommy asked him was he sick,
> "No, I want a hockey stick."

Let us also put aside comparisons with modern mythological heroes, such as Superman; they can be found, but in no significant quantity. Perhaps we can conclude that a man like the Rocket could fly even faster than a superhero fleeing a speeding kryptonite bullet.

Let us turn our attention to religious comparisons, and settle

Maurice Richard as Superman, by Henri Boivin.

on two. Both are visual rather than textual, and both call for a bit of imagination.

The first is local. It was said that Maurice Richard, that devout Catholic, appreciated the resemblance between himself and one of Quebec's most prominent twentieth-century religious personalities, Paul-Émile Cardinal Léger (1904–91). In some photographs, the faces of Léger and Richard are virtually interchangeable. In the Radio-Canada documentary *Maurice Rocket Richard*, filmmakers Karl Parent and Claude Sauvé and one of their guests, Pierre Létourneau, agree that what Richard and Léger had in common was the look in their eyes. The same analogy pops up in Jean-Claude Lord and Pauline Payette's 1999 docudrama. In it, Émile Genest describes, in both men, eyes like "lumps of coal." In Duplessis-era Quebec, the aspergillum was never far from the hockey stick.

Our second iconographic comparison goes deeper and is more eloquent. The April 1955 issue of the American magazine *Sport* carries a photo of Richard that is quite different from the standard image. One shoulder lowered toward the ground and the other pointed toward the skies, holding his hockey stick as if to protect himself and yet also pointing heavenward, face covered with a fine film of sweat, this Maurice Richard bears a striking resemblance to the Saint Sebastian of Luca Giordano, the seventeenth-century baroque painter. A closer look at the similarities between Richard as seen by *Sport* and *The Martyrdom of Saint Sebastian* reveals that the position of the shoulders is the same; in both, the neck is extended, the eyes have rolled upward; both bodies stand out against a black background; where one has an arrow in his side, the other holds fast to his stick. To these purely visual coincidences is added another, historical one: though the photo appeared in the American magazine in April 1955, it could be seen on the walls of the Montreal Forum as of March 17 of that year, as part of an ad for the magazine ("Read in this month's *Sport*, 'Montreal's Flying Frenchman,'" the "Montreal Flying Frenchman" being none other than Richard). Sebastian was a Roman soldier who lived at the end of the third century and was put to death by the emperor Diocletian for his Christian convictions. Maurice Richard was not a victim of his religious views, but like Sebastian, he too was a soldier of God, an uncommon being and a martyr. Digging a bit deeper, one has to take into account that the participants in the March 17, 1955, riot already had before their eyes the image of the martyr Richard was to become that very evening.

Moving on to another medium, Gilles Gascon's film *Peut-être Maurice Richard* literally pullulates with similitudes. Many are purely sports-oriented, which should come as no surprise: Richard and boxer Joe Louis, Richard and Howie Morenz, Richard and Gordie Howe. However, one hardly expects to find Richard's name associated with that of John F. Kennedy and John XXIII. That particular connection is the work of PR man Camil DesRoches:

> I've always believed that, in every field, there were men with a supreme calling, if you'd like; Maurice Richard was such a man, a man in the sports world like Pope John XXIII had been in his, or as John Kennedy had been in politics. The kind of man that counts, that springs up at a particular time and who appears once in a hundred years. There are bound to be others.

Number 9, Pope John XXIII and the thirty-fifth president of the United States have this much in common: they are the "kind of man that counts"; each one in his field, emerging "once in a hundred years."

It is tempting to ascribe juxtapositions of this kind to sheer enthusiasm. But that would be forgetting just when DesRoches drew up his list of illustrious names. The film dates back to 1971, a time when Quebec's nascent national identity was searching for historical underpinnings that it could call its own, and that would be second to none. Maurice

Richard is a historical figure *like* John Kennedy and John XXIII; ergo, Maurice Richard is a historical personage *as great as* John Kennedy and John XXIII. Similar historical parallels had been suggested before. We need only think back to André Laurendeau's editorial, "On a tué mon frère Richard" [Richard, My Brother, Has Been Killed], in *Le Devoir* four days after the riot of 1955. In it, Laurendeau draws a connection between Métis leader Louis Riel and the Canadiens hockey star. Few were to go farther than DesRoches, at least in the early 1970s.

It was at the same time that another kind of parallel began to emerge: Maurice Richard and artistic figures. We find three examples of it in Gilles Gascon's film. Actor Jean Duceppe—on the set of one of the classics of Quebec cinema, Claude Jutra's *Mon oncle Antoine*—novelist Hugh MacLennan and hockey broadcaster René Lecavalier all use the language of art in speaking about the Rocket. Duceppe describes the "stage settings" against which the Rocket "rehearsed" his moves. MacLennan concludes that "you couldn't tell where his art ended and his life began." Lecavalier compares him with painters and poets.

Over the following decades, this complex of meanings was to develop and ramify. Quebec's sense of its own identity came, in the process of self-definition, to depend increasingly upon its cultural icons: needed were significant historical figures and great creative minds. If there was to be a true Quebec identity, then it was to be found among the creative and the cultured. Two cases stand out in their eloquence: the chansonnier Félix Leclerc, who died in 1988, and the painter Jean-Paul Riopelle, dead in 2002. Both were given state funerals, just like the Rocket. Both were recognized as having stood for, each in his field, Quebec culture and the forces of nature. What could have been more natural than to associate with them another force of nature in the person of Maurice Richard. The daily *La Presse* would see to that. In 1983, it set up a meeting between Richard and Leclerc, and then, in March 1990, with Riopelle. Both conversations were good-natured

Luca Giordano, *The Martyrdom of Saint Sebastian*, seventeenth century.

Sport. April 1955.

and masculine. Leclerc arm wrestled with Richard and penned a poem about the Rocket:

> When he shoots, North America roars,
> When he scores, the deaf can hear the cheers,
> When they send him to the penalty box, the switchboards light up,
> When he passes, the new guys dream.
> He's the wind on skates,
> He's all of Quebec on its feet.
> Terrifying, alive . . .
> He's the blizzard!

Leclerc's poem went on to an illustrious career; not only frequently quoted and translated, a passage appeared in the closing credits of Charles Binamé's 2005 film. We've already seen how Riopelle drew upon his visit with Richard to complete his *Homage to Duchamp (Tribute to Maurice Richard)*. Photographers immortalized the meetings of the three artists: one who wielded the spoken word; the other, with a paintbrush; the third, with a hockey stick.

With his book *Le Rocket* (2000) Roch Carrier emerged as the uncontested champion of Richardian comparison, with animals (horse, cobra, snake, bull, tiger) in particular. He also drew up his own list of artistic parallels: with Homer, Leonardo da Vinci, Shakespeare, Balzac, Jules Verne, the signatories of the Quebec artistic manifesto *Refus global*, Picasso. (Not to mention Genghis Khan and Jesus.) What more could one possibly add?

Associations of this variety have been relatively recent. In the field of the Quebec novel, it was only after the Quiet Revolution of the early 1960s that the first halting attempts were made to resolve the latent conflict between artistic activity and concrete action. Before then, as André Belleau has so convincingly demonstrated in his study *Le romancier fictif* [The Fictional Novelist] (1980), the characters in a novel had only two choices: either create or act; they could not do both at once. Ten years after the Quiet Revolution, much had changed: one could have one foot in the artistic world and the other in the material world; Maurice Richard, for the individuals interviewed in *Peut-être Maurice Richard*, could be considered an artist. Likewise, the following year, the novelist Victor-Lévy Beaulieu depicted the young Guy Lafleur as a hockey player and author. "In the solitude of his Longueuil apartment, Guy Lafleur dreams, listens to music, writes," or so claims Beaulieu, writing in *Perspectives* magazine. This Lafleur of his keeps a diary, writes poetry and states: "For me, hockey is my way of expressing myself, like a musician." Twenty years after the Quiet Revolution, Maurice Richard had become an artist who could stand shoulder to shoulder with Félix Leclerc and Jean-Paul Riopelle. The appreciation of the artist that emerged from the Quiet Revolution and its aftermath was echoed in the world of professional sports, where men of action metamorphosed into veritable creative geniuses.

But instead of stopping here, instead of being content with sports figures of every description, with the odd cardinal or saint, a pope, a politician or a score of art-world luminaries, let us raise the bar a notch. Let us compare the Canadiens' number 9 with Nobel Prize winners. Though it seems inconceivable, someone has conceived it.

In the early 1980s, Grolier published the ValueTales series, comprising popular children's books published in both French and English illustrating the "Value of X," with a different "X" featured in each volume. In the book on Maurice Richard, entitled *The Value of Tenacity: The Story of Maurice Richard* (1983) and written by Ann Donegan Johnson, Richard rubs elbows with the best and brightest. The enumeration may run on a bit, but it is worth exploring:

Hans Christian Andersen (originality), Beethoven (giving), Alexander Graham Bell (discipline), Ralph Bunche (responsibility), Cochise (truth and trust), Christopher Columbus (curiosity), Confucius (honesty), Marie Curie (thirst for knowledge), Charles Dickens (creativity), Terry Fox (challenge), Benjamin Franklin (saving), Elizabeth Fry (kindness), Thomas Jefferson (foresight), Helen Keller (perseverance), Paul-Émile Léger (charity), Abraham Lincoln (respect), the Mayo Brothers (sharing), Margaret Mead (understanding), Louis Pasteur (believing in yourself), Jackie Robinson (courage), Eleanor Roosevelt (caring), Albert Schweitzer (dedication), the Wright Brothers (patience).

The list includes creators of classical dimensions: Andersen (and his tales), Beethoven (and his music), Dickens (and his novels). Great figures from the past meet: Columbus and Cochise, Confucius and Lincoln, Franklin and Jefferson. Inventors and scientists were by no means forgotten either: Bell, Curie, the Mayo brothers, Mead, Pasteur, Schweitzer, the Wrights. Women who have had to overcome a multiplicity of trials, which never stopped them from persevering against all odds: Fry, Keller, Roosevelt. Canadians are rare: when they are not inventors (Bell) or serving humanity (Léger), they have been chosen for their physical prowess (Maurice Richard; Fox, and his attempt to cross Canada running on his one remaining leg). Sports figures are few: aside from Richard, there is only Jackie Robinson. And three Nobel Prize winners: Ralph Bunche (Nobel Peace Prize, 1950, and athlete of distinction), Marie Curie (two Nobels, for physics, in 1903, and chemistry, in 1911), and Albert Schweitzer (Nobel Peace Prize in 1952).

Maurice Richard can stand proudly alongside the composer of the Ninth Symphony, the inventor of the telephone, a great Chinese philosopher, the man who discovered America, two presidents of the United States—and three Nobel Prize winners (but no beach volleyball all-stars). Being in the company of people like that tends to make you stick out. Alongside them, the Lalondes and the Joliats, the Morenzes and the Howes, even the Ruths and the Cyrs, simply don't cut the mustard. Maurice Richard is no longer just another hockey player. He is a great man among great men. The comparison has radically transformed him. That is why Richard is a myth: he has been extracted from his social context and elevated to the uppermost reaches of society, culture and history. And young readers ought to know it.

Maurice Richard has been compared to many people and things, most of them commonplace. But a few of them are striking, not only because they bring together two names that would seem, at first glance, to be worlds apart. In these rarest of cases, it is as though fresh light is being shone on a subject previously thought to be unknown. In only its second year of publication, in 1955, *Sports Illustrated* commissioned William Faulkner to attend a game between the Rangers and the Canadiens in Madison Square Garden, in New York, and to share his impressions with the readers of the newly founded American sports weekly. Starting with the title, Faulkner presents himself as a neophyte: "An Innocent at Rinkside." He is struck by the grace and speed of play, by its impenetrable logic. Among the players milling on the ice, three stand out: Bernard Geoffrion, the precocious lad; Edgar Laprade, the elegant veteran; and Maurice Richard. At first, unable to distinguish between the three, Faulkner points to their fluidity and their rapidity: they are "as fluid and fast and effortless as rapier thrusts or lightning." Richard, in particular, appears to him to have "something of the passionate glittering fatal alien quality of snakes." It takes a Nobel for literature to string such adjectives together, to create an image of such a disconcerting power; it takes a great writer to transcend the clichés of the sportswriter's trade.

MAURICE RICHARD AS TOLD TO CHILDREN

"[Mr. Deslauriers] is an old man, and the stories he tells are old stories. Old stories, but very fine old stories. His finest old stories are his old hockey stories, and his finest old hockey stories are his stories about Maurice Richard."
—MARC ROBITAILLE, *Des histoires d'hiver, avec des rues, des écoles et du hockey* [Some Winter Stories, with Streets, Schools, and Hockey], 1987

Ever since the 1940s, Maurice Richard had been the subject of articles, biographies, novels, poems, plays, essays, songs, films, radio and television programs, tableaux, sculptures, and more. It should come as no surprise that there was also a Maurice Richard as told to children, a Maurice Richard who is part of a family, a role model, a living legacy.

facing page: One of the best-known photos of Maurice Richard, by David Bier.

A holy trinity

In the beginning, there was the son, i.e., the child. So begins Michel Forest's short schoolbook biography of Maurice Richard, in the Célébrités canadiennes [Canadian Celebrities] series, published by Lidec (1991): the flyleaf features a photo of the hockey star with his father. For Roch Carrier, both are "men of few words," which does not mean they do not communicate: on April 8, 1952, after his dramatic goal against "Sugar" Henry, "the greatest hockey player of modern times is a frightened child crying in his father's arms." The Rocket's father has the leading role in the ValueTales publication, *The Value of Tenacity: The Story of Maurice Richard* (1983); in it, the young Maurice is close to his father, and to his mother. If he had not been a dutiful son, and his brother Henri like him, his mother would certainly not have been named "Hockey Mother of the Year" in February 1956—not in Montreal, but in Boston, the hometown of the "Big Bad Bruins"—less than a year after the events of March 1955.

Then came the husband and father. Having become the star of the Canadiens, Richard was to rapidly occupy significant media space. Journalists and commentators sang his praises. He became a regular in feature stories and promotional articles. Unsurprisingly, his family pitched in. His parents were recruited, as we have already noted. His wife, Lucille, was regularly interviewed. In his anthology *Remembering the Rocket: A Celebration*, Craig MacInnis reproduces one such interview, in two installments: "When Maurice Met Lucille: Lucille and Her Mom Chat about the Rocket, as Told to June Callwood, May 9, 1959" and "Rocket in Repose: At Home with the Maurice Richards, by June Callwood, May 9, 1959." The biographies emphasize the head of the family: that of Gérard Gosselin ("Un père de famille exceptionnel") [An Exceptional Family Man] and those of Jean-Marie Pellerin ("L'homme et sa famille") [The Man and His Family] and Chrystian Goyens, Frank Orr and Jean-Luc Duguay ("Familles, je vous aime") [A Simple Family Man].

Photos of the Rocket surrounded by his children are seemingly innumerable. One example should suffice, the article by Dick Bacon, "Mr. Hockey"—another of the Rocket's nicknames—published in the magazine *Hockey Blueline*, in May 1958. The photographs (seven of the eight depict at least one child) and the cover drawing (the Rocket with one of his sons) sum up in visual terms the content of the article: "It is probably safe to say that Richard is just as much a devoted father as he is a dedicated hockey player"; "Next to goals, or perhaps on a par with scoring, Richard is a sucker for children. He will referee a kids game at the drop of a hat if he's available and he willingly and eagerly makes hospital appearances whenever he can." When, in December 1999, *La Presse* asked its readers to share their "best sports memory," many were eager to corroborate the journalist's claims. Richard could just not say no to a child.

Those qualities were rewarded in 1959, when the hockey star was nominated "Big Brother of the Year," the same prize that future

The Rocket on the cover of *Maclean's* in 1959.

The Value of TENACITY

The Story of Maurice Richard

A ValueTale BY ANN DONEGAN JOHNSON

Maurice Richard as
grandfather and reader.

Canadian prime minister and Nobel Peace Prize winner Lester B. Pearson had received. "The annual Big Brothers Association trophy is awarded to a Canadian citizen who can be held up as an example to youth, as an ideal citizen," explained Jean-Marie Pellerin in 1976. No one has gone quite so far in linking the role of the father with that of the goal scorer as Ken Dryden, the former Canadiens goalie during the 1970s and author of that great book *The Game* (1983). In a posthumous tribute published in *Time* magazine in June 2000, he did not shrink from writing:

> On his goalward mission, he seemed past distraction, outside pain, like a father trapped with his child under the wheels of a car who finds a desperate strength to lift that dreadful weight. Such was his need.

Eventually, it was grandfather time. With retirement, Maurice Richard had continued to embody the caring father; now he was given a new role: that of grandfather. Not *a* grandfather, but *the* grandfather. Whom did Quebec choose, in 1994, to represent the ideal patriarch for the International Year of the Family? Maurice Richard, photographed alongside his granddaughter for newspaper ads under the slogan "Family: a place for warmth and togetherness." Togetherness, as exemplified by the photo ("Claudia Richard and her grandpa Maurice"), can also be found in the photo showing the grandfather sitting on the bed beside his two grandchildren. They are reading *The Value of Tenacity*: "Stick to it, Grandpa. If Maurice was a proud papa, he became an even more attentive grandpapa, doting on a third generation of Richards. Here, he and the grandkids read about Grandpa in a book extolling the Richardian trademark tenacity," argue Goyens, Orr and Duguay, who reproduce the photograph in *Maurice Richard: Héros malgré lui/Maurice Richard: Reluctant Hero*.

The attentive reader will find much to appreciate: Maurice Richard is reading a book about Maurice Richard to Maurice Richard's grandchildren. A closer look at the photograph reveals the presence of another book on the night table: Roch Carrier's *The Hockey Sweater*. It's a small world, if you're Maurice Richard!

Setting an example

"The hockey rink is a great school of life."

—MAURICE RICHARD, 1996

Maurice Richard's older fans saw him play in person, and kept track of his accomplishments by radio or television; they purchased products in his likeness. His new fans discovered him from the mouths of their elders, in television miniseries, in song. They also came to know him through reading books, from the most serious to the most superficial, and from film.

We can learn a lot with the Rocket. READING: in 2000, Graficor, a schoolbook publisher, brought out a reader entitled *Maurice Richard (1921–2000)*, in its primary school series Tous azimuts: 1er cycle du primaire; Mini-série 2. The publishers were following the lead of Les Éditions Marabout, which, in the 1950s, hired Maurice Richard and Jean Béliveau to promote their books: "Read the Marabout Marabout Marabout Marabout novels literary collection." WRITING: to explain the numeral determiner, the grammar book by Roland Jacob and Jacques Laurin (*Ma grammaire*, 1994) features an illustrated text entitled "Hockey's Gentleman" devoted to the Canadiens' number 9. BEHAVING PROPERLY ON THE ICE: in the novella *Rocket Junior*, by Pierre Roy (2000), the ghost of Maurice Richard appears to Richard-Maurice Latendresse Ladouceur, "Rocket Junior," to scold him ("No, I'm not proud of you at all!") and to guide him back to the true values of sport, which the young player's father has pushed aside: "Play for the love of sport, with your team!" RESIGNING ONESELF IN THE FACE OF ADVERSITY BY DOING AS MOTHER SAYS: in Roch Carrier's famous story, everyone seems in league against the narrator of "The Hockey Sweater" (1979), from the other boys on the team to the vicar-referee, simply because, following an error by Eaton's, he is forced to wear the shameful Toronto Maple Leafs jersey against nine "Maurice Richards in blue, white and red." LEARNING FROM GRANDPARENTS: young Alexandre Gagné, hero of Henriette Major's *Comme sur des roulettes!* [Without a Hitch!] (1999), will have the good fortune of playing the role of Maurice Richard, a "hockey player from the good old days," using the very toys that Grandpa and Grandma, "roller skating champion of the Rue Garnier in 1955," used when they were kids.

Much has been made of the determination and perseverance that were Maurice Richard's greatest qualities. Such is the lesson that Slapper, his hockey stick, drums into the young Maurice in *The Value of Tenacity*: "It was always through Slapper that he heard the voice of his own basic toughness and determination." By persevering, he would lift himself up to the same level as the great individuals profiled in the ValueTales series. We find the same lesson in a young people's novel entitled *La carte de hockey magique*, by Michel Foisy (2000). Maxime Laforest has been handicapped ever since the automobile accident that cost his parents their lives. From his uncle he inherits a curious kind of time machine. Thanks to this strange device, he can hear advice from beyond the grave, from his father and from Maurice Richard ("If you stick with it, your dream will come true one day . . . perhaps"). It works. In the last chapter, "My Life's Greatest Triumph," Maxime's wish comes true, and he is able to play hockey, at which he immediately (and miraculously) excels. In Foisy's next book, *La carte de $1,000,000* [The Million-Dollar Card] (2003), wearing sweater number 9, he will become "the little Rocket" of Rosemère, the Montreal suburb where he lives. The plot of Gaël Corboz's 2006 novel, *En territoire adverse* [In the Opposing End], hinges on a towel claimed to have absorbed Maurice Richard's sweat. The "magic towel," "the shroud of the Rocket," symbolizes the unstoppable desire to surpass oneself.

Comic books have proved an effective way of influencing and shaping young minds. In 1975, *La Presse* cartoonist Girerd, illustrating a storyline by Arsène, brought out *Les enquêtes de Berri et Demontigny:*

"*RICHARD'S REAL TRADE AND HOBBY IS TOOLMAKING. ONE EVENING BEFORE THE '50-'51 STANLEY CUP PLAYOFFS, MAURICE ENTERED HIS SHOP AND WENT TO WORK...*"

Maurice Richard at his lathe, from *World's Greatest True Sports Stories: Bill Stern's Sports Book*.

On a volé la coupe Stanley [Berri and Demontigny—Private Investigators: The Mystery of the Stolen Stanley Cup]. Though the book is not directly about Maurice Richard, his name appears several times. A Richard poster decorates the walls of the room where the hero, Louis Joseph Napoléon, mockingly nicknamed "Rocket," was born, on January 13, 1947. Alongside it are a calendar and a portrait of Pope Pius XII. Three times in the comic book, an old man in a wheelchair reminisces that he took part in the 1955 riot. The two investigators unearth, in an antique shop, a pair of skates that might have belonged to Richard.

Two decades before Arsène and Girerd, *Babe Ruth Sports Comics*, published in the United States, related the Maurice Richard story ("Hockey's Battling Terror") in three pages. In the winter of 1952, Bill Stern picked Richard's as one of his *World's Greatest True Sports Stories*. "The Man They Call the Rocket . . . Maurice Richard," a six-page, full-colour comic strip, enumerates the principal attributes of Richard's personality and playing style: determination, refusal to be pushed around, impetuousness (up to and including the risk of injury), speed, agility, modesty and violence. What makes this comic book stand out is that Richard is depicted in his workshop, at the lathe: "Richard's real trade and hobby is tool-making." It had occurred to no one before Stern, or after for that matter, to represent the Rocket in similar circumstances.

Role models, as we know, are not entitled to many defects. For Richard to attain such lofty status, it was necessary to overlook some of his character traits and to rewrite several episodes of his career. His violent nature has been attenuated, to put it euphemistically. The man who was never known for his softness ("la tendresse") or his gentleness ("la douceur") guides a lad named Richard-Maurice Latendresse Ladouceur, the hero of Pierre Roy's novel, back to the straight and narrow. The man whose hardness toward others and toward himself has never been disproved becomes a soft-touch grandpa: "Loving families!" The man who occasionally talked *with* his stick—he would be suspended by Clarence Campbell in 1955 following a slashing incident—now talks *to* his stick, Slapper, which provides him with judicious advice. The man who would never hesitate to drop his gloves now becomes "hockey's gentleman," according to Roland Jacob and Jacques Laurin: "After an eighteenth season and eight Stanley Cups with the Habs, Maurice Richard retired with the reputation of a gentleman who never went looking for a fight." In 1969, George Sullivan avoided the question altogether: there is not a word about the 1955 riot in his chapter on Maurice Richard in his *Hockey Heroes*.

Nor is there any violence in the film *Life after Hockey/La vie après le hockey* by Tom Radford (1989). The film's main character has no first name: he calls himself Brown (the film's script was written by playwright Ken Brown) and is nicknamed "the Rat," or "the Rink Rat"; his source of inspiration is Maurice Richard. In the opening scene, a man is flooding an outdoor skating rink under a full moon; we can barely distinguish his features, but the alert viewer will identify him as Maurice Richard. The first words of the film provide us with another hint: "Maurice Richard gets the puck . . . He shoots, he scores!" we hear from a radio or television recording. And at the end, back to Richard: we find him on the ice at the outdoor rink, along with the Rat. Wearing his red sweater with the number 9, he glides effortlessly over the ice, explaining to the Rat how to correct his backhand, the shot that was his specialty. He even informs his buddy that he intends to return to active play, to beat Wayne Gretzky's records, and asks him to play on his line. The last words of the film, those of the Rat, are: "And we'll win the Stanley Cup next year."

Between the two scenes, the Rocket makes numerous appearances in the film: as the mysterious "rink foreman" (as he is identified in the credits); as a goal scorer: many archive shots show him scoring, particularly his 500th goal; as an icon: the Rat's mother knits him his hockey sweaters, all with a number 9. He owns a Rocket hockey card;

Maurice Richard, as seen by Arsène and Girerd (1975) . . .

. . . and by *Babe Ruth Sports Comics* (1950).

on a visit to the Montreal Forum in 1976, he will see the huge portrait of his idol. Last but not least, the Rocket functions as an adviser. The Rat writes an imaginary letter to "Dear Number 9" to ask him how to improve his backhand shot (hence the final scene), to know what to do in a game situation, to ask about the meaning of life. (The Rat speaks instead to Wayne Gretzky in the play from which the film is derived.) In a film that sings the praises of dreams and the importance of child-hood memories, Maurice Richard never lets the Rat down. He accompanies him through life and reminds him that he must always keep in shape, which the Rat never fails to do: the example comes from high up, after all.

Legacies

Every myth leaves behind it a legacy, be it personal or collective. Accordingly, more than a few have sought to bequeath Maurice Richard to their successors, children or otherwise.

Marc Robitaille's *Des histoires d'hiver, avec des rues, des écoles et du hockey* (1987) is made up of short chapters, in which a boy of ten relives the winter of 1966–67. Maurice Richard, who has only recently retired, enters the story through the agency of a neighbour: "Monsieur Deslauriers told me that one of these days he'll take me with him to watch Maurice Richard play in the Old Timers' because even if he's gotten older, he's still got those eyes of his, and his hair still blows in the wind." It is from this album of childhood memories that François Bouvier drew the inspiration for *Histoires d'hiver* [*Winter Stories*], the feature-length film he directed and wrote along with Marc Robitaille.

Martin Roy, age twelve, is the only son of Jacqueline and Hervé Roy, a couple with cultural pretensions. The father, who works in an accounting firm, doesn't like hockey; at home, they listen to the opera; the mother paints, first by numbers, then without. It seems unlikely that they will be able to slake Martin's passion for hockey, the passion of a player, of a television viewer, of a card collector. He will turn to his father's elder brother, Maurice, an auto mechanic, smoker and bon vivant who hangs around a woman named Corinne, a bit of a loud-mouth who wears her skirts up high; he lards his conversation with English slang—and he adores hockey. He gives Martin a rocket-shaped portable radio purchased in Florida so he can listen to all the games in his bedroom. François Bouvier and Marc Robitaille (MR) bring Martin Roy (MR), Maurice Roy (MR) and Maurice Richard (MR) together in two key scenes.

Both are set at night. In the first, Martin is about to go to bed when Maurice gives him the portable radio. The boy asks his uncle: "Hey, Uncle, tell me about the Rocket," even though his favourite player is Richard's brother, Henri. Uncle Maurice goes on to recount the story of Richard's goal against "Sugar" Henry. The story breaks off; it resumes when Maurice, who has suffered an "infractus" (sic), is in hospital. His nephew is lying on his hospital bed while he picks up the tale of "one of the most beautiful plays ever seen in the Stanley Cup finals." Martin and Maurice not only share a moment of closeness; they are carrying on a conversation they have already had several times before. In fact, Martin easily completes his uncle's narrative: proof that he's heard it before, that he's committed it to memory and that he has not grown tired of it. Maurice goes on to die the day after Martin's first Canadiens game at the Forum, a 1–4 defeat by the Toronto enemy. Little matter: "He had kept me company on my journey, and he will always be with me."

Familiarity with the Richard myth is no less obvious in Jack Siemiatycki and Avi Slodovnick's *The Hockey Card* (2002). Maurice Richard's son Maurice Richard Jr. endorsed the book: "It is with great pleasure, and as executor of the estate of Maurice Richard Senior that I authorize the use of his name in the book entitled *The Hockey Card*." The book's illustrator, Doris Barrette, dedicated the book to "My brothers Mario,

François, André, Benoît, Christian, Yvon and Ugo," and publisher Alison Fripp, not to be left out, dedicated it "To my mother, with love and thanks." For the authors, the book was part of family memories:

> Jack Siemiatycki and Avi Slodovnick are brothers-in-law. They were inspired to write *The Hockey Card* by their admiration for the hockey heroes of their youth and their fond boyhood memories of collecting and playing with hockey cards. Even before the story was published, it was already a family favourite.

The plot line underscores how much the family has made the myth its own: after revealing how he drew upon the magical powers of a hockey card representing Maurice Richard, the narrator's uncle gives it to him as a birthday present.

And thus are myths passed on from one generation to the next. From the Richard family, the Barrette family, the Fripp family, the Siemiatycki and Slodovnick families, to the narrator's family: *The Hockey Card* is a story of handing down, of hanging on to the past. Often that which is handed down takes the least-expected paths. In writers as diverse as Bouvier, Siemiatycki and Slodovnick, in Roy (*Rocket Junior*) and Michel Foisy (*The Magic Hockey Card*), the vector of transmission is not the father but an uncle. For *La Presse* columnist Stéphane Laporte, writing in 1998, there are two uncles, Jacques and Yvan: "My uncles' memories have become my own." *That's Hockey/Ça, c'est du hockey*, by David Bouchard and Dean Griffiths (2004), takes only minor liberties with the model. In the country, Étienne introduces Dominique to street hockey. All the players wear the same sweater. "The sweater with the nine on it. Like Maurice Richard, you know, the Rocket..." At the end of the game, Étienne gives Dominique his sweater; at the end of the book, Dominique—whose sex we then discover—hands the sweater on down to her daughter: "But mommy, I never played street hockey!" "With this sweater, darling, you'll do just fine." Memories are for sharing.

But legacies can be a risky business, for those who receive them, and for those who leave them.

Roch Carrier is the author of *Le Rocket / Our Life with the Rocket*, published in 2000. Who is telling the story? "The old child I've become still needs his hero. A fearless hero wipes away the child's fears. If his hero is fearless, the child makes his way confidently through life." Carrier mingles his own memories with those of Maurice Richard. He relives his "childhood emotions" and his school days. He recalls Quebec as it was at the end of World War II. He revisits the achievements of his idol. He also explains how he came to write his best-known story, and how he was caught up by the myth according to which Maurice Richard and the Canadiens had won all their games against the Toronto Maple Leafs:

> I wrote a story called *The Hockey Sweater*. In it there's a sentence that echoes the memory of that fine certainty: "The Toronto team was always being beaten by the triumphant Canadiens." It was neither a charming irony, as some people said, nor an athletic tease. It was an absolute conviction. I was remembering indisputable facts.

But the facts were not "indisputable" and Carrier, in an act of false contrition, is forced to own up: the Maple Leafs frequently defeated Montreal. Did he lie? In the eyes of history, perhaps. Not where myth is concerned: "Such was the Rocket..." This is the Richard he wants to hand down as his legacy.

Denis Diderot, the eighteenth-century French writer, devoted much thought to the question of what posterity should remember of great men. In *Rameau's Nephew*, his protagonists speculate about Jean Racine. The alternatives presented are these:

Which of these two options would you prefer—that Racine had been a good man, known for his business, like Briasson, or for his yardstick, like Barbier, getting his wife regularly pregnant every year with legitimate children, a good husband, a good father, a good uncle, a good neighbour, an honest merchant, but nothing more— or that he had been deceitful, treacherous, ambitious, envious, and nasty, but the author of *Andromache, Britannicus, Iphigenia, Phèdre,* and *Athalie*?

In other words, should one be good to one's family and friends, or be a great creator? That was not Maurice Richard's way into the hearts of posterity in Quebec. He was both a family man and a genius on the ice. The little ones will never forget him.

11. *The Riot*

COMMEMORATIONS

T HE FIRST commemoration of Maurice Richard did not take place when he died, in May 2000.

Throughout his playing career, there had been ample occasion to celebrate his exploits. No sooner had he broken a record—which he did quite often—than there was a rush to pay him tribute. On January 7, 1951, for example, Richard scored his 271st goal, beating the record held by Aurèle Joliat for most goals scored by a player wearing a Canadiens uniform. In honour of the event, February 17, 1951, was proclaimed "Maurice Richard Night" at the Montreal Forum. In the presence of the prime minister of Canada (Louis Saint-Laurent) and the Quebec premier (Maurice Duplessis), the mayor of Montreal (Camillien Houde), the team's owner (Senator Donat Raymond) and the president of the National Hockey League (Clarence Campbell), Richard and his wife were presented with a trophy, an automobile (a DeSoto with license plate number 9) and an impressive array of gifts (a watch, silverware, a refrigerator, a sewing machine, a vacuum cleaner, flowers and shares in a country club). Despite its symbolic dimension, as represented by the guests of honour, the tribute was primarily a tangible one.

But Maurice Richard was also commemorated in powerfully symbolic ways. Among them, the ceremony marking the close of the old Forum and the opening of the new Molson Centre, in March 1996, stands out. Maurice Richard was one of those who had been called upon to "throw the torch," figuratively as well as literally: he had been pressed into service to smooth the transition from one place to the other, from one era to another. On March 11, at the Forum, the crowd rose to the occasion and saluted him with a monumental ovation.

Among these symbolically charged events, there stands out a moment in Maurice Richard's career, and in the history of contemporary Quebec, that the media (newspapers, radio and television), singers, authors, playwrights and filmmakers cannot tear themselves away from. That event is the Riot. Though the daily press spoke of it rarely before 1980, it gradually emerged into the full light of public consciousness. By way of example, *La Presse* readers were directed, beginning with the March 14, 1995, issue, to a series of articles on "The Forum Riot: Forty Years Later." The introductory story began with these words: "Forty years ago began one of the most dramatic episodes in the history of Quebec, and of hockey." Ten years later, on the anniversary date, the same newspaper headlined: "Riot at the Forum: Fifty Years Ago. Special Sports Section. Full Size." And on page A2, the following explanation:

> Attentive readers will have noticed that the *La Presse* logo on the front page has been slightly modified today, inspired by *La Presse* in 1955: our way of harking back to the Forum Riot of March 17, 1955, an event that was to leave its mark on modern-day Quebec.

The same day's edition of *Le Journal de Montréal* was no less effusive, dedicating six pages to the same event. *Le Devoir*, the most "serious" of the three Montreal dailies, restricted its coverage to two stories.

The Riot is one of the pillars of the Maurice Richard myth. In the very Forum where he had been so often hailed with adulation, violence had broken out, violence that later spread into the streets. Maurice Richard's role in the events of that day was peripheral, but those same events had a lasting impact on people's recollections, and on the stories they would go on to tell. Had there been no Riot, it is doubtful there would ever have been a Maurice Richard myth.

MARCH 4, 1951

To say that Maurice Richard enjoyed strained relations with hockey officialdom would be to understate matters. In reality, he was involved in frequent altercations, and not all of them verbal at that.

In his *Fire-Wagon Hockey* (1967), Andy O'Brien suggests that Richard, toward the end of World War II, had attacked an official during an exhibition game in Quebec City. Jeanne d'Arc Charlebois sang, rather complacently, about such behaviour in 1951:

> Maurice shoved the ref
> And he paid the fine
> Let him do it again,
> Our old number 9.
> Five hundred bucks he needs?
> Let him back in the fray
> And score five more points
> The very next day.

Yvon Dupuis, who wrote the words to "Maurice Richard," stops just short of transforming Richard's attitude toward authority into an article of faith:

Those Canayens are dinks
An NHL ref thinks
So he plays the big shot
But when Maurice gets hot
He won't turn his back
Just goes to show
In Montreal, better go slow.

I. Sheldon Posen, in his 2005 article on songs dedicated to the Rocket, connects the lyrics to an event that took place in New York on March 4, 1951, shortly after the celebration of his 271st goal at the Forum. In the lobby of the Piccadilly Hotel, Richard had had an altercation with referee Hugh McLean, whom he had accused of unfair decisions a few days earlier during a game at the Forum. He was slapped with a $500 fine for his action, just as Jeanne d'Arc Charlebois describes it. It was the stiffest penalty ever imposed by the National Hockey League.

But Maurice Richard's problems with authority were not to end there.

MAURICE RICHARD'S WRITINGS

Over the years, Maurice Richard's byline had become familiar. Of course he was not the author of the numerous articles that appeared under his name. Victor-Lévy Beaulieu (1972) has revealed that the young Guy Lafleur kept a diary and wrote poetry. Ken Dryden, in *The Game* (1983), produced a work of sports ethnology; instead of studying the great apes, he attempted to understand the curious specimens who inhabited the Canadiens' locker room along with him in the 1970s. Maurice Richard lacked their ambition; writing in the daily press, both in Quebec and in the United States, was enough for him.

Richard also lent his name to prefaces and epilogues: to a pamphlet entitled *Jouez du meilleur hockey avec les Canadiens / Playing Better Hockey with les Canadiens* (in the early 1960s), to the photo album *30 ans de photos de hockey* by Denis Brodeur (1993), to young people's fiction, including François Gravel's *Le match des étoiles* (1996) and Michel Foisy's *La carte de hockey magique* (2000), as well as Réjean Tremblay and Ronald King's compendium *Les Glorieux* (1996) and the biography of the wrestler *Yvon Robert: Le Lion du Canada français*, by Pierre Berthelet (1999). He is listed as co-author, with journalist Stan Fischler, of *The Flying Frenchman: Hockey's Greatest Dynasty / Les Canadiens sont là! La plus grande dynastie du hockey* (1971), to which he contributed the second section, "My Life with the Canadiens." In it, he settles old scores with several people, former teammates and opponents, and laments how low hockey has fallen. And yet, "Despite all these grumblings from this particular grey-beard, the hockey picture is not at all bleak ... By now you may find this hard to believe, but I really do love the game of hockey." But the bulk of his prose offerings are to be found elsewhere, in his weekly column in *Samedi-Dimanche* [Saturday-Sunday] (under the title "The Hat Trick," 1952–54) and *Parlons sport* [Let's Talk Sports] (in the early 1960s), in *Dimanche-Matin* [Sunday Morning] (throughout the 1960s, '70s and '80s), in *La Presse* (1985–2000) and in an ephemeral New York publication called *Maurice Richard's Hockey Illustrated*.

In his columns, Richard delivered what had come to be expected of those whom we could define as player-reporters: he proffered personal news spiced with greetings to friends, congratulations, good wishes and intimate details ("We're going to call my great-grandson Maxime"); he offered his insider's views about his sport ("I've always believed that whether a hockey team wins or loses depends 75 percent on its goalie"); he mingled memories of his own career with opinions about developments in the sports world (he continued to be adamantly

PLAYING BETTER HOCKEY
with les Canadiens...

MONTREAL CANADIENS — N.H.L. CHAMPIONS — 1961-62

by
MAURICE
Rocket
RICHARD

opposed to European players in North American professional hockey). His style was unpretentious, full of homely turns of phrase drawn from everyday speech. Richard's "views" were of the as-told-to variety, involving a journalist who would hammer them into shape: Paul de Saint-Georges at *Samedi-Dimanche*; Alain de Repentigny and Ronald King at *Dimanche-Matin*; Pierre Nadon (briefly), Alain de Repentigny again and André Trudelle at *La Presse*. What really counted were the byline and the photo that headed the column.

Richard's writings rarely generated controversy, with two notable exceptions.

On December 6, 1952, in *Samedi-Dimanche*, he sharply criticized Quebec City hockey fans, particularly from the Saint-Sauveur district, whom he labelled "hoodlums" for the way they had treated his brother Henri, who had yet to become "the Pocket Rocket." The affair quickly took a political turn when the elected representative for Saint-Sauveur, Francis Boudreau, raised the matter in the Quebec Parliament. The Quebec City council demanded a retraction. Richard stood his ground in capital letters, writing on December 20:

> I will not retract a word of what I said two weeks ago about certain Quebec City gangs, except the word "hoodlum." My "ghostwriter" has courageously admitted that it's one of his favourite insults, and that he uses it frequently when he gets angry, without implying that whomever he calls a "hoodlum" is necessarily a murderer or a highwayman.
>
> EVERYTHING ELSE THAT WAS PUBLISHED WAS DICTATED BY ME...

For Quebec City residents, Richard's wrongs were considerable. Not only had he insulted some of their reputedly ill-mannered spectators, he had attempted to deprive them of their hockey star, Jean Béliveau, whom Richard had invited to join him in Montreal, instead of continuing to play with the hometown Aces. It was a case of one number 9 attempting to lure another away.

In the same weekly, in early 1954, following the suspension of Bernard "Boom Boom" Geoffrion, our commentator zeroed in on a bigger target. He had made up his mind to take on the authority of the president of the National Hockey League, whom he suspected of reverse ethnic favouritism: Geoffrion was depicted as the victim of Clarence Campbell's anti–French Canadian feelings.

> According to more than a few friends who have been observing President Campbell during the games at the Forum, in his private box on the south side of the arena, His Excellency has demonstrated clear-cut partiality in the way he reacts to the game; he smiles and displays his pleasure when the opposing team scores against us; it is well known that on several occasions he has taken decisions against Canadiens players . . . In my opinion, Mr. Campbell may well be partial.

Downplaying the fact that his teammate, ostensibly in self-defence, had injured a player of the opposing team, Ron Murphy of the New York Rangers, with his stick, Richard lashed out at Campbell, the "dictator" whom he challenged openly, adding insult to injury: "If Mr. Campbell would like to kick me out of the league for daring to criticize him, well, let him do it!" "That is my frank opinion, and if it earns me disciplinary measures, well, that's just too bad! I'll walk out on hockey; I've got an idea that there are plenty of other players on the Canadiens who feel just like me, and would do the same thing!"

Unkept promises. The league called upon him to retract, leading to the following letter, dated January 14, 1954:

> Since hockey has been so good to me, I submit my most humble apologies to President Campbell and the Governors of the League,

not because I have been forced to do so by my own club, but because it is the honourable and sportsmanlike thing to do.

I realize full well that my accusations were unfounded, and I wish to establish beyond any doubt that I was not casting doubts upon Mr. Campbell's integrity, nor upon the honourable nature of the sport.

Should you be disposed to accept this retraction, I would be relieved of a weighty responsibility.

A newspaper cartoon showing Maurice Richard as a disobedient student and Clarence Campbell as schoolmaster (and Nazi, on the blackboard).

The column that touched off the controversy was to be the last for several years. So claimed Richard, who was also taking pains to protect himself:

> As proof of my good faith, I am depositing a cheque, in the amount of one thousand dollars, as confirmation that each word of this letter says exactly what it means.
>
> If I do not keep my promise, I will lose one thousand dollars. If you find me worthy of your indulgence, I am confident that these monies will be reimbursed when my playing career has come to an end.

The appeal to caution, to say the least, had been heard.

But the polemics were to resume two days later, in Richard's last column for *Samedi-Dimanche*. Abandoning the contrite tone of his letter, he brought his relationship with the newspaper to an end in these terms:

> I regret to say that this is my final column as a journalist, for I have enjoyed the opportunity to express my personal opinions on hockey-related matters.
>
> I have been *denied* this right. *Freedom of speech* is no longer mine to enjoy. As a hockey player, I am obliged to obey my employer's orders. I make no judgment about their decision. That I will leave to my friends.
>
> Perhaps later, when my hands are not tied behind my back, I will return. Perhaps sooner than anyone thinks.

Richard the "journalist" styles himself a devoted employee, all the while suggesting that he does not entirely share his employer's views. There is something to be said for his claim to be a martyr for freedom of speech, even though others shared his interpretation of events, both at the time and later on.

From New York to Montreal, and from English to French, Maurice Richard's pen now seemed to have been dipped in prudence. Clear-cut opinions would be permitted, perhaps even a touch of audacity; but it would not be in his best interests to lay down a direct challenge to authority. The future was to remind him that discretion was the better part of valour. Our revolutionary would have to learn to keep his head down.

DECEMBER 29, 1954–MARCH 18, 1955

"Admirers are rarely rioters..."

—JEAN BARBEAU, *La coupe Stainless* [The Stainless Cup], 1974

On December 29, 1954, the Canadiens were playing in Toronto. During the game, Richard came to blows with Bob Bailey of the Maple Leafs. As he was leaving the ice after the fight, Richard leaned toward his coach, Dick Irvin, who spoke to him, then turned on his heel. Rushing back on the ice, he attacked linesman George Hayes, who had stepped between Richard and Bailey. He was assessed a $250 fine and reprimanded by the National Hockey League authorities, who were determined not to tolerate any violence toward their officials.

A few weeks later, on March 13, 1955, during one of the last games of the 1954–55 regular season, in the Boston Garden, the Bruins' home ice, Richard was wounded by a blow from the stick of Hal Laycoe; stitches were needed to close the cut. Blood pouring from his face, he fought back with fists and sticks: after having broken his on an opponent's back, he went looking for a second, which he proceeded to use as a weapon. Some accounts, including Clarence Campbell's, speak of a *third* stick, which Richard was emphatically to deny on March 20, 2000, in *La Presse*. Whatever the case, as linesman Cliff Thompson was restraining him, Richard struck Thompson in an attempt to

free himself to continue the brawl with the Bruins. As a result he was
expelled from the game by referee Frank Udvari, and threatened with
arrest by the Boston police.

The altercation in a New York hotel lobby in 1951; the two polemics touched off, in 1952 and 1954, by Maurice Richard's articles; the
Toronto donnybrook of December 29, 1954; the events of March 13,
1955 in Boston: by the time Richard appeared before Campbell in
Montreal on the morning of March 16, 1955, the adversarial relationship between the two men that had been building over four years cast a
long shadow on the proceedings.

Richard was accompanied by his coach, Dick Irvin, and a former
teammate who had become a member of Canadiens' management,
Ken Reardon. Campbell listened to the three men, as well as to Laycoe,
Thompson, Udvari, Sammy Babcock (the second linesman in the
March 13 game), Lynn Patrick (the Bruins' coach / general manager)
and Carl Voss (the league's chief referee).

That afternoon Campbell, who had served as a prosecutor for
the Canadian War Crimes Comission at the Nuremberg tribunals,
announced the sentence. Having outlined the facts and described the
incident of late 1954, he concluded as follows:

> I have no hesitation in coming to the conclusion on all of the evidence
> that the attack on Laycoe was not only deliberate but persistent in
> the face of all authority and that the referee acted with proper judg-
> ment in accordance with the rules in awarding the match penalty. I
> am also satisfied that Richard did not strike linesman Thompson
> as a result of a mistake or accident as suggested . . . Assistance can
> also be obtained from an incident that occurred less than three
> months ago in which the pattern of conduct of Richard was almost
> identical, including his constant resort to the recovery of his stick to
> pursue his opponent, as well as flouting the authority of and striking

officials . . . Consequently, the time for probation or lenience has passed. Whether this type of conduct is the product of temperamental instability or willful defiance of the authority of the game does not matter.

Campbell's conclusion dwelt much more on the failure to respect authority than on the brawl with Laycoe. The reasons for Richard's lack of respect are, he writes, of little concern to him, whether it is a matter of "willful defiance of the authority" or "temperamental instability."

As punishment, Maurice Richard was suspended for the final three games of the 1954–55 season, as well as for the playoffs. He ended the season with thirty-eight goals and thirty-six assists, and was slapped with 125 penalty minutes, a career high. No sanctions were brought against Laycoe. The details of the decision were immediately broadcast by the media, and first among them by radio.

The next evening, on March 17, the Canadiens were playing at the Forum. Throughout the day there had been calls for Campbell not to attend, out of concern that fans might overreact. As for the fans, they deplored—to put it mildly—the fact that Campbell's decision would deprive Richard of what might well have been the scoring championship, and feared that the team, without its star player, would not be able to win the Stanley Cup. They were right on both counts. At the time of his suspension, Richard was leading the league in scoring, but he would be overtaken, amidst a chorus of boos, by his teammate Bernard Geoffrion, who would also win the bonus for leading the league in goals. The Detroit Red Wings would go on to win the Stanley Cup in seven games against the now Richard-less Canadiens.

The game began on time, at 8:30. The Red Wings, locked in a battle for first place with Montreal, jumped into an early lead. During the first period, as the Red Wings increased their lead, Campbell wound his way toward his customary seat, escorted by his secretary Phyllis

March 18, 1955: *The Gazette* (Montreal) depicts Maurice Richard atop a pedestal and reminds readers that Clarence Campbell had been a prosecuting attorney at Nuremberg.

King (who would later become his wife) and two other young women. His appearance was often interpreted, then as now, as a provocation. On the following day, Montreal mayor Jean Drapeau would criticize Campbell for attending. He had received death threats only a few hours before the face-off; he must have known that he would be given a rude reception. But could he have anticipated what happened then?

The spectators quickly singled him out for attention, although accounts differ considerably. He was bombarded with programs, bottles, galoshes and overcoats, fruits and vegetables, eggs (fresh and rotten), sacks of peanuts, ice cubes, bags filled with water, coins and pickled pigs' feet. A man (his identity was still being debated in 2006) tried to get close enough to punch him in the face. A photo, reproduced abundantly ever since, depicts Campbell protecting himself, hat in one hand, program in the other, as the ushers grapple with his would-be assailant. (Maurice Richard had a framed reproduction of the same photo. It was sold at auction along with the rest of his collection, in 2002.) A few moments later, another spectator crushed a tomato (or perhaps two) on Campbell. One thing was certain: the situation was getting rapidly out of hand, as still and motion pictures of the event depict.

At the height of the melee, a tear gas bomb exploded. The game was brought to a halt. Campbell withdrew to the trainers' room, where he encountered Richard. Though he was not in uniform, the star of the team was on hand to urge on his teammates. In the pandemonium created by the acts of violence against Campbell and by the tear gas bomb, the Montreal fire chief decided to evacuate the Forum, which took place calmly. (If we are to believe Sidney Katz, writing in the September 17, 1955, issue of *Maclean's*, the Forum organist accompanied the evacuation with a rendition of "My Heart Cries for You.") Detroit, which was leading 4–1 at that point, was declared the winner; the home team had been unable to ensure the safety of the visiting team.

Among the evacuees were the players of both teams, Forum staff, journalists and photographers, and thousands of nameless spectators. Some were not to remain entirely nameless, among them: Jean-Claude Lord, who went on to direct the docudrama *Maurice Richard: Histoire d'un Canadien/The Maurice Rocket Richard Story* in 1999; Donald Cuciolleta, who was to investigate the parallels between Jackie Robinson and Richard; and one of the Rocket's eventual biographers, Andy O'Brien. Hugh MacLennan, the author of the classic novel about the ties between Canada's two founding peoples, *Two Solitudes* (1945), was there, as his *Saturday Night* article "Letter from Montreal: The

Explosion and the Only Answer" would attest. Quebec nationalist historian Lionel Groulx was also in attendance, according to his niece and collaborator, Juliette Lalonde-Rémillard. It's tempting to dream about the conversation MacLennan and Groulx might have had on that fateful night. Would what they saw have confirmed their theses on the uncomfortable cohabitation of Canada's two linguistic communities, or would it have shed some light on the concerns those two communities shared?

The Riot, strictly speaking, did not take place in the Forum. The explosion came a few minutes later, outside the building, on Saint-Catherine Street, after the fourteen- to sixteen-thousand spectators had cleared the building. Groups of demonstrators had begun to form even before the game, to express their anger at the league president's decision. They brandished picket signs: "Richard is being persecuted," "Outrageous decision," "Injustice against French Canada," "Injustice against sports fans," "Campbell" (with drawings of pigs or ... pears), "Stupid puppet Campbell," "Vive Richard," Vive le Rocket," "We want Richard," "No Richard, no Cup," "Down with Campbell," "Campbell go home," "I'm not going, are you?" "All sins are forgiven, Campbell. Long live Richard," "Our national sport destroyed." An immense effigy of Richard, which had been used in happier times, such as his 400th goal at the Forum, had been set up on the back of a truck. The people streaming out of the Forum joined the demonstrators.

Violence had begun even before the start of the game: objects had been thrown through the Forum windows, and a crowd had gathered in Cabot Park, just across the street. After the evacuation, the violence exploded, taking multiple forms. Automobiles were overturned. Streetcars were stopped in their tracks. Fires were kindled on the street. Display windows were shattered. Telephone booths and newsstands were vandalized. Shops, particularly jewellery stores, were looted. Police and demonstrators were injured (no one seriously). From the Forum the crowd surged eastward, along Saint-Catherine Street. On the morning after, damage was estimated at $100,000 before falling to a more modest $30,000; there had been several dozen arrests and charges laid for an event that lasted between five and seven hours, depending on the account (at the most, from eight at night until three in the morning). Maurice Richard saw none of what would later be known as the Maurice Richard Riot: after leaving the Forum, he would learn from the radio that a riot was underway and keep track of its progress.

The following morning, from the Forum, Richard made a public statement on radio and television, in both French and English:

> Because I always try so hard to win and had my troubles at Boston, I was suspended. At playoff time it hurts not be in the game with the boys. However, I want to do what is good for the people of Montreal and my team. So that no further harm will be done, I would like to ask everyone to get behind the team and to help the boys win from the New York Rangers and Detroit. I will take my punishment and come back next year to help the club and the younger players to win the Cup.

In the short term, that was where things stood. Which did not mean that the story would be buried. Song, radio, the novel, the theatre, television, the cinema and the press were to feed on the events of that night for more than a half-century. And there is no reason to believe that a vein of such richness is likely to be exhausted any day soon.

IN SONG

The Riot immediately found its way into song, in both French and English. In 1955, Oscar Thiffault sang "Le Rocket Richard," and Bob Hill and his Canadian Country Boys, their "Saga of Maurice Richard." Almost a half-century later, they would be joined by Robert G. Anstey.

I. Sheldon Posen, in 2005, noted how alike were Thiffault's and Hill's songs. Both were written quickly, which would explain why their melodies are drawn from the folk tradition. Thiffault sings about the Riot to the tune of the traditional French-Canadian ditty "C'est l'aviron qui nous mène," while Hill uses the nineteenth-century Irish soldiers' shanty "Abdul Abulbul Ameer." Both composers seem more interested in the duel of hockey sticks than in the quarrel with the referee. In so doing, they totally invert the official version as found in the Campbell decision. Thiffault tells his listeners: "Par un dimanche au soir en jouant à Boston / Vous auriez dû voir les fameux coups d'bâton" [One fine evening in Boston / You should have seen the hockey sticks fly], while Hill gives Campbell the floor: "Young man, that stick in your hand / Has put you in trouble, by gar." But first and foremost, both spring to Richard's defense.

Thiffault embeds it in the lyrics, which begin and end with the refrain: "C'est Maurice Richard qui est si populaire / C'est Maurice Richard qui score tout le temps" [Maurice Richard's the popular one / The one who scores and scores]. Richard may have been suspended, but it is only a temporary measure: "Y a été suspendu / On a été chanceux qu'il ne soit pas vendu / . . . Comme un bon Canadien y a accepté son sort / Il reviendra compter pour le Canadien encore" [They suspended him / Good thing they didn't sell him / . . . Like a good Canadian, he took it like a man / He'll be back to score again]. Resignation in the face of adversity, a "Canadian" quality, holds out the hope for Richard, and for the song's listeners, of better days to come. After all, is Richard not "one of the best goal scorers of the last few years"? In his press conference, Richard had said essentially the same thing: "I will take my punishment and come back next year to help the club and the younger players to win the Cup." In "Le Rocket Richard," Richard's defense rests upon another aspect of the song, a musical one. The words are sung by Oscar Thiffault, but are echoed by a children's chorus. Among the little children who yearn for their hero to return to the ice, and who would not be capable of adulating a violent man, hope springs eternal.

For Bob Hill, the Rocket's actions were justified in a different way. His song is far less repetitive than Thiffault's—the former contains 134 words; the latter, 321—allowing him to deliver a much more complex version of the event. The song's narrator defines himself as a Canadian when he sings of "our national sport" and, in the same breath, as a Montrealer, when he sings about "our town" and "our Forum." He reminds us of what had happened in Boston on March 13, by way of explanation of Richard's behaviour:

> One evening in Boston they struck at his head
> And cut him right over the ear
> With his temper so red, and the way that he bled
> His thinking could not have been clear
> In all the confusion before they subdued him
> He'd struck an official, I hear.

Enter Clarence Campbell: "He [Richard] trod on the toe / Of Campbell, the man without fear"; his temerity would dearly cost the man who was "quite the cream of the Montreal team."

> Says Campbell, "Young man, that stick in your hand
> Has put you in trouble, by gar
> Though you needed five stitches, you're too big for your britches
> Just who do you think that you are?
> Now you've done this before, and you've made me quite sore
> And although you are a great star
> You're through for the year, do I make myself clear
> Mister Maurice, 'The Rocket' Richard?"

Campbell's condescension perhaps best explains the rioters' call: "Off with the head / Of Campbell, the man without fear!"

On March 17, 1955, a cloud of opprobrium had settled over the town and its hockey team ("Now our town has lost face and our team [is] disgraced"), but it was to have no more impact upon them than the suspension had upon Richard:

> He will return and his legend will burn
> In the annals of sports near and far
> There was never a name of such stature and fame
> As Maurice "The Rocket" Richard.

As in Thiffault's song, the Rocket would return; a mere passing incident could not tarnish his legend, and his name would always be sung.

One song is a fine thing; many songs are better still. Unlike Oscar Thiffault and Bob Hill, Jeanne d'Arc Charlebois and Denise Filiatrault, one song about the Rocket was not enough for Robert Anstey, who went on to compose a total of twenty-seven. Though never recorded, they were brought together under the title *Songs for the Rocket* (2002), accompanied by a long introduction, footnotes and commentary. Lest we be startled by such prolixity, it should be noted that, by 2002, Anstey had already composed more than twelve hundred songs and written ninety books.

His is the work of a fan, and our prolific composer makes no attempt to conceal it. Anstey had begun to compose songs about Maurice Richard as early as the 1970s. Back then, he explained, hockey was better than it is today, and nothing better exemplified it than the excitement the Rocket brought to the game. Hence his passion for a player he'd never once seen in action. So what if Richard was violent. Other players were to blame. So what if he fought with his stick. What could have been more normal: "He was no sissy." It goes without saying that he was superior to Gordie Howe; Richard made the difference when it counted. His eyes were what set him apart: Anstey mentions them dozens of times.

Anstey is systematic: it comes as no surprise that one of his songs would deal with the Riot—it is the eighth of the series "The Rocket's Riot," written in 2000. The songwriter is full of admiration: it comes as no surprise that he springs to his hero's defense. In total chronological confusion he tells the story of the March 13 brawl, the stick blows, the attack on a referee ("The Rocket started shoving a referee"). He recalls the suspension, its effects on Richard, on the Canadiens and on the fans:

> It was the night of the Rocket's Riot
> In the city of Montreal
> Those fans could never just sit quiet
> While they watched their idols fall.

He describes the Riot itself, its shouting and its violence, inside and outside the Forum.

The composer places full responsibility for the Riot upon Campbell's shoulders. The Rocket's fans cannot bring themselves to "believe what Campbell had done." When they see him take his seat, it is as if they have seen "the smoking gun." In the commentary that follows the song, Anstey speaks of Campbell's "provocation." In the section of his introduction entitled "Campbell and the Rocket," he had already said as much. (*Songs for the Rocket* is an extremely repetitive book.) Further along, we come upon a song on "Campbell and the Rocket," which deals expressly with the league president's determination to "clip [Richard's] wings":

> Campbell tried to get the Rocket
> In any way he could.

For the true believer, what could be more eloquent than a clear-cut case of black and white, of hero versus villain? If only it had been that simple.

133

...IN PRINT AND ON THE AIR

No modern myth, in all its manifestations, can hope to survive and prosper unless the media take it up. Maurice Richard would be no exception.

The press could never get enough of him, both during and following his career; the sports pages kept track of his accomplishments on a daily basis. In 1960, a Montreal paper asked its readers if he was still capable of performing at the same level. There were two possible answers: "Keep it up, Rocket" and "Time to stop, Rocket." Whether or not the poll results influenced his decision, Richard retired that year. But he kept on making headlines, either in stories about his life as a retiree or because he soon began to contribute as a "sportswriter." At times, Richard even abandoned the sports pages for other sections of the newspaper, ranging from the gossip column to the editorial page. In like manner, the specialized publications had turned Richard into one of their pet subjects. The monthly *Sport revue*, "sports magazine of the French Canadians," devoted no fewer than thirteen covers, between June 1955 and May 1960, to Richard. Other popular press outlets also profited from his immense popularity: we find his photograph on the cover of the *Almanach du peuple*, published by Beauchemin, in 1952, 1956, 1957 and 1959.

Without minimizing the importance of press coverage of this kind, we must assign a particular preeminence to radio. In the collective memory, Maurice Richard is associated much more closely with this medium than with any other. Television had made its way into Quebec households much more rapidly than is generally believed: in 1956, only four years after its introduction, almost two-thirds (64.2 percent) of Quebec households already possessed a television set, according to Yvan Lamonde and Pierre-François Hébert. The press was far more diversified in the 1940s, '50s and '60s than it is today: there were more newspapers, both general and specialized. Yet when his fans mention the postwar Maurice Richard, when they think of the active player, when they connect their own memories with those of the Rocket, they end up with radio, and with it almost alone.

Future political dignitaries like Lucien Bouchard, Jean Chrétien, Bernard Landry and Guy Chevrette; future hockey players like Jacques Plante, Jean Béliveau, Bernard Geoffrion, Guy Lafleur and Serge Savard; the future trade unionist Gérald Larose; the future sports journalist Réjean Tremblay; the future photographer Denis Brodeur and the future actor Stephen McHattie (who would play Dick Irvin in the film *Maurice Richard*, in 2005) all discovered Richard by radio. Roch Carrier frequently sang the praises of his idol in several texts. In *Le Rocket* (2000), that "ode to Maurice Richard," radio is the medium that keeps popping up. The title of the hockey poetry anthology published by Bernard Pozier in 1991 says it all. It borrows its title, *Les poètes chanteront ce but* [Poets Will Sing That Goal], from the radio; those were the exact words used by sports commentator Michel Normandin in February 1945 to describe the goal scored by Maurice Richard with Earl Siebert "hanging from his neck." The first image to appear on the screen in Charles Binamé's film *Maurice Richard* is that of a radio set. In the fictional portion of Jean-Claude Lord and Pauline Payette's 1999 film, the Richard family gathers around a radio set to listen to the exploits of Howie Morenz, then to follow his funeral services, before reciting the rosary in his memory. In the opening sequence of the film *Peut-être Maurice Richard*, filmmaker Bernard Gosselin describes the hockey star as an "abstraction" for the "little guys" like him from the "low-rent districts" of Montreal because they knew him only by radio.

In Richard's life story, as a man and as a sports personality, radio holds a far from negligible place. As a boy, it was on the radio, and not in newspapers, that he discovered professional hockey in general, and the existence of his future team in particular. Before signing a contract with the Canadiens, he had never once set foot in the Montreal Forum;

he could only imagine it as it was evoked on the airwaves. After having been signed, he would give numerous radio interviews, and would eventually boast his own program, "Allô Maurice Richard," on CKAC. He heard the news that a riot was taking place outside the Forum on the night of March 17, 1955, over the radio. When he addressed the public the following day to appeal for calm, he did so on the radio. Oscar Thiffault's and Bob Hill's songs were broadcast on the radio.

There are several ways to evaluate the importance of radio in Quebec during the 1940s and 1950s: by studying the work of media historians, such as Marie-Charlotte De Koninck; by analyzing the *Répertoire des œuvres de la littérature radiophonique québécoise, 1930–1970* [A Repertory of Radio Literature in Quebec, 1930–1970], by Pierre Pagé, Renée Legris and Louise Blouin; by reading Gabrielle Roy's novel *Alexandre Chenevert* (published in English as *The Cashier*), which was released one year before the Riot.

The book's eponymous protagonist, Alexandre Chenevert, is an employee of the Montreal City and District Savings Bank, and in many ways the anti-Richard. He is obsessed with money, with waste, with the cost of living. Unlike his immediate superior, Émery Fontaine, he is interested in neither golf nor hockey. He engages in no physical activity and sees no reason to take up bowling, despite the exhortations of his physician. He is the bookish type:

> You had to read. Modern man was the heir of such a mountain of knowledge. Even had he limited his curiosity to that which was pub- lished in his own day, he could never have succeeded in absorbing it all . . . And where did the truth lie in this mass of writing?

A man of few words, Chenevert spends his life surrounded by the words of others. A failure as a man of the world, he is a man of *infor- mation* about the world: in addition to its allusions to newspapers, books, encyclopedias and newsreels, Roy's novel seems constantly tuned in to the radio. It is the radio that brings boundaries into existence by suggesting that they might eventually be broken down. It is the world within—and the world without; it is Montreal and the "old globe" (Stalin, Tito, Truman, Gandhi, the Nuremberg tribunal). It is the whispering of the world.

It is hardly an accident that Claude Béland, who would become president of the Desjardins Cooperative Movement, and Aimée Sylvestre, who would become comic actress Dominique Michel, best remembered the Riot through their radio memories. Nor is it an accident that novelist Pierre Gélinas and dramatist Jean-Claude Germain, among those who sought to textualize the Riot (Eugène Cloutier, Rick Salutin, Jean-François Chassay), were closely attuned to the role of the radio in the imagined construction of the event. In that way, they linked arms with the filmmakers who collected the statements of eyewitness accounts to the events of March 1955. The story of the Riot is a story made for—and by—radio.

...IN STORY

Les inutiles [The Useless Ones] is the title of a novel published in 1956 by Eugène Cloutier. In it, two escapees from the Saint-Jean-de-Dieu psychiatric hospital set out to look for a friend who had been interned along with them, but who had been released earlier. After a series of wanderings through Montreal, Toronto and the Laurentians, Jean and Antoine, the two escapees, finally locate Julien. The final act of the tragedy takes place on a particular day, and in a particular place in the city. That day is March 17, 1955; that place, the Montreal Forum.

The thirteenth and last chapter of the novel is devoted to the Riot at the Forum. It is prefigured in the preceding chapters; one of these prefigurings provides the narrator with the opportunity to explicitly link the figure of Maurice Richard with a question that will emerge as essential in its novelistic or dramatic representation, that of time. In chatting with an usher who predicts "trouble" for the March 17 game, Jean realizes that Maurice Richard has become a part of a much larger time frame, at the very moment when short-term social upheavals have begun to occur:

> At that instant the thought that there had never been a break with the past could have gone to his head. Richard had never ceased to be the star of hockey. His exploits would continue to bring the crowds to their feet... Had that man—who had nothing to recommend him but a light-as-air fluidity of movement on the ice—not become a universal cult figure, and at the same time, a model tacitly provided for the new generations?

The continuity evoked in this passage immediately enters into conflict with the development of the narrator that follows it.

> Jean was fascinated. Sincerely fascinated. That very morning the newspapers had headlined the suicide of a young poet. It was the fifth such suicide in less than a year. And that very evening thousands of people had demonstrated in support of Richard. A new civilization was on the march, one that could not be foretold.

In Jean's mind, continuity and the idea of a break with the past are intermingled, the enduring quality of the "universal cult" now marches forward in lockstep with the "new civilization" that "could not be foretold"; myth (deep time) stands elbow to elbow with history (passing time).

At the beginning of the chapter on the Riot, the image of the "new country" reactivates that of the "new civilization," as does the book's final scene, in which Jean and Antoine make their way to the harbour, determined to leave their town for an undetermined destination, Brazil or Cuba perhaps. Individual and collective renewal rub elbows, however briefly, with a sense of solidarity, which troubles Jean: "Memories welled up in him with a newfound clarity. Suddenly, he felt he belonged to the group. The impression would not last." Solidarity, when built on foundations of "passion," quickly degenerates into violence, that of the "mob," of those "thousands of spectators," of a "mass" or of a "rushing torrent" of heads. Jean intends to take advantage of the "panic" to kill Julien, whom he accuses of surrendering to materialism, and having done with him, to break with the city of Montreal and then to flee disguised as a priest, to be followed by Antoine, who miraculously pops up amid the tumult and shouting at the Forum.

The failure of the scheme to kill Julien plays a significant role in the plot of the novel, as do comparisons of the Riot with the carnivals of Rio de Janeiro and Recife or with Iroquois tortures, but they are of secondary interest to us. Let us turn instead to the narrator's thoughts about Maurice Richard. Following a description of the panic inside the Forum, an individual looks down from the cheap seats—in total opposition to historical reality (that was not where Maurice Richard was sitting that night, but behind the Red Wings goal, close to the ice):

> In one of the last rows, up beneath the rafters, with a mixture of pride and disgust a man contemplated the spectacle. He had wanted to attend incognito this first game since his suspension. He was overwhelmed; what had begun as a brawl seemed as though it could degenerate into civil war. In deep torment, he slipped out through a secret exit. The hysterical crowd that was defending his official personification had not even recognized him in his street clothes. He was no longer a man; he had become a myth.

Solitary, anonymous, robbed of his own face, looking down on the situation from on high, "overwhelmed" by events, "in deep torment," Maurice Richard had ceased to be a man. He was now a myth: the word had been uttered in Cloutier's novel. The year: 1956.

Three years later, Pierre Gélinas published a novel, *Les vivants, les morts et les autres* [The Living, the Dead and All the Rest], in which two chapters are devoted to the Riot. Rather than taking up the mythical dimension of the event, the novelist is sensitive to what it represents for his main character and to its place in a plot line in which social and economic factors are determinant. While Eugène Cloutier prefers myth, Pierre Gélinas is rooted in history.

The hero of Gélinas' socialist-inspired novel, the young Maurice Tremblay, believes in his mission among the textile workers. Having accepted trade unionism as others accept religion, he visualizes their struggle as an existential matter and transforms it into a mechanism for arriving at truth. He dreams of swimming "along with the current of history," of reestablishing "harmony between world and self, that is to say, between man and himself." Despite his successive failures—joining the Canadian Communist Party brings him nothing but indignities and disappointments—he chooses, in spite of everything, to lend his existence a positive meaning by practising charity (which is the last word of the novel). We are not at all surprised to encounter, in a political novel dealing with social involvement in the 1950s, allusions to the Riot at the Forum, for Gélinas' prose relies on snippets of historical reality. In it we encounter the names of Stalin, Mao and Khrushchev; we are reminded of the Korean War and the Valleyfield textile workers' strike; we are provided with statistics about home ownership rates in Toronto; commercial strategies are evaluated.

The Riot enjoys a peculiar place in the structure of the novel—and in Maurice Tremblay's career. The opening of the twelfth chapter of the second part underlines its vital importance:

Of course, no one could claim that without the "Richard Riot" Maurice Tremblay's life would have taken a different course . . . Some small tragedies owe less to the incidents that make up their

backdrop, or even serve as a pretext, than to the nature of the protagonists. But, after that, thanks to what could be called "social"
events, we can freeze moments of personal tragedy in memory.

That "social" event coincides in Gélinas' "memory" with a thoroughgoing
shift in Tremblay, his "personal tragedy," while for Cloutier, it coincided
with an existential crisis and with the beginnings of a new civilization.

   The first of the two chapters on the Forum Riot takes place immediately before it starts (chapter XII). After delivering in schoolmasterly
fashion a summary of the causes that brought about the Riot, then
reproducing fragments of radio programs dealing with its premises, the
narrator points to the ruling class concealed behind the forces of law and
order as they prepare to intervene, by analyzing the actions of Clarence
Campbell and of the mayor of Montreal. The worldview of these two
members of the ruling elite is based on racial typology (British, French,
French Canadian, American, English Canadian) and on anti-nationalist
political morality. For them, the "populace" must remain silent and bend
to the will of those who know how to wield "reason" or, at a minimum,
how to shelter behind their "property instincts."

   In the following chapter (chapter XIII), the narrator relates the Riot.
Now the tone is journalistic:

> He'd happened to turn on the radio.
>   "There are reports," said the announcer's excited voice, "that hun-
> dreds of people have gathered in front of the Forum. Our mobile unit
> is on the way; we will be back to you as soon as we have established
> communication. Stay tuned . . ."

Now he adopts the guise of the historian (ostensibly, as what is being
narrated does not always correspond with contemporary accounts):

> A tear gas bomb burst at centre ice; at the same time, the spotlights
> were switched off, and it was as if the Forum had been plunged into

night... Who had thrown the bomb? Light was never shed on the matter; in all probability, a police officer stationed in the upper rows had been armed with the device, in anticipation of just such an incident. Certainly he displayed considerable judgment in throwing the bomb at that precise moment, where it helped avert a catastrophe, though the pros and cons were still being weighed the following day.

Like any self-respecting fictitious intellectual, Maurice Tremblay "had paid little attention to the sports events that had become the pretext for the riot." He remained "deaf" to the "collectivization" of anger that had swelled up "in a single wave"; he'd "felt nothing." Unlike him, before the game, "thousands of people were drawn toward the Forum in a kind of suction that each one of them had helped to create." He would follow the demonstrations on the radio and then hurry there to have a closer look at the rapidly changing situation.

Even before the game had begun, claims the narrator, "the whole affair had begun to look like a national movement"; one of the book's characters calls it "an upheaval of national indignation." But at the heart of the narrative lies an eloquent absence: amid the crowd of "malcontents," there is not a trace to be found of Maurice Richard, whose fate lay at the centre of the crisis. Indeed, the central protagonists of the chapter on the Riot are, first, Clarence Campbell and then the crowd, and not Maurice Richard, of whom not a word is spoken.

Campbell's actions are the main concern of the narrator, who considers him to be responsible for the Riot: "The game was already underway when news of his presence was transmitted to the outside; it kept the hard core of the riot, which would undoubtedly have dispersed, on the premises." He is the victim of the "claws of the howling beast" of the "crowd"; it is he who must die. Then the narrator traces with near-military precision the movements of the crowd: the rioters enter the

Forum, "just as before the war it was possible to enter Germany via Danzig, through the long corridor of Saint-Catherine Street from the natural boundary to the east, Saint-Laurent Boulevard." (We should remind ourselves that in 1956, Eugène Cloutier had already raised the spectre of "civil war.") The narrator notes with interest "the virtually chemical composition of the riot," interprets the reactions of successive waves of rioters, delves into their psychology, imagines their relation with the city and the street. Pierre Gélinas' romantic realism leaves room only for one particular myth: that of the crowd. The Forum Riot has left its imprint on the lives of several individuals, either singly or as part of a larger group, but it does not participate in a mythical narrative in which Maurice Richard plays an emblematic role.

Maurice Richard occupies several pages of Jean-Claude Germain's 1976 drama, *Un pays dont la devise est je m'oublie*. The play's seventh scene is devoted to distinguishing between a historical figure (Louis Cyr) and a mythical figure (Richard). The eighth scene, which is divided into two parts, deals with the public image of the Rocket, specifically dating from the events of March 17, 1955, in Montreal.

In the first part of the scene, the dramatist reproduces a verbal exchange between Richard and radio commentator Michel Normandin, "the bard par excellence of our national sport," "an authentic poet." Germain could have placed the dialogue in the mouths of two actors; he does not. Instead, he contrives to maintain the historical colour of the piece by using the radio. "When *Un pays dont la devise est je m'oublie* was being produced, we ascertain by reading the stage directions, the recording used . . . dates from that period and the voices were authentic." The radio commentator and the Canadiens player are talking about a goal Richard scored to fulfill a "sick child's" wish (broadcast at the end of the 1949–50 season, the interview was sponsored by Bee Hive corn syrup) and about his determination to ensure his financial future: "I've been working for Jarry Automobile for seven years now; I spend all my free time there and, two weeks ago, I was promoted to sales representative."

The second part of the scene draws on an entirely different dramatic procedure. Instead of hearing the voice of the historical Maurice Richard, of the individual being interviewed on the radio, the dramatist enters into his thoughts as the Riot is taking place, by way of a totally imagined interior monologue. Germain's introduction reads:

> Toward the middle of the interview, the scene is transformed (by lighting) into a skating rink and the theatre plunged (by the evocative magic of sound effects) into the atmosphere so characteristic of a hockey game at the Forum; the sounds and the noise of the rink become increasingly violent, until they have become those of a riot in full swing—that of March 17, 1955, the so-called Maurice Richard Riot: amidst the roar of the crowd, the scream of police sirens and the crash of breaking glass, blinded by flashbulbs and harassed by pursuing journalists, the Rocket enters the team's locker room: he is wearing the celebrated sweater number 9 and full hockey gear, as though he had just left the ice.

His first words are "LET ME ALONE! I'VE GOT NOTHING TO SAY! NOTHING!"

Jean-Claude Germain's Maurice Richard on the night of March 17, 1955, takes just as many liberties with historical reality as do Cloutier's and Gélinas'. The former has Richard wandering through the top rows of the Forum; the latter has the tear gas bomb being thrown by a police officer and exploding "in the middle of the rink"; Germain has him fitted out in full hockey gear. But beyond the benign bending of the historical narrative, his Richard is revealing in his explosion of anger: he throws the parts of his uniform to the floor (he "flings" them) and punches the lockers. Is the cause of his fury his treatment at the hands of that "old bastard" Clarence Campbell? Is it the Riot itself? Assuredly, but not only.

If Maurice Richard is so furious in *Un pays dont la devise est je m'oublie*, it is above all because of the duplicity of his supporters. He is well aware of their adulation:

> These guys, for them, when I'm on the ice . . . It's like I was a god! . . . You can feel it, up there in the cheap seats, like you was some kind of giant . . . some kind of Saint Christopher carrying all bloody Quebec on his shoulders!

The fans know exactly what he stands for:

> MAURICE RICHARD, HE'S BIG ENOUGH FOR PEOPLE TO RIOT ABOUT! BIG ENOUGH SO THAT QUEBEC MAKES THE HEADLINES AROUND THE WORLD FOR THE FIRST TIME!

But still they mock him:

> So they send me invites to their colleges and their high schools! And then what? Tell the students they gotta study, they tell me, gotta talk right! Don't be like me, I tell 'em! . . . Don't be like Maurice Richard who everybody laughs when he talks!

The theatrical version of Maurice Richard is sharper than his fans think he is; he knows they're speaking out of both sides of their mouths. But he's not as sharp as he'd like to be; he keeps on uttering the same words: "I DON'T GET IT." Still, he begins to connect the two threads of what the fans are saying:

> Maybe it's 'cause I never went to school . . . but me, there's one thing I just don't get in all those lessons of theirs! Sometimes, it's like them educated people and me . . . we don't live in the same country. They

talk better than me! They know more than me! But I bet they gave
up tryin' to score long ago!

Maurice Richard, as imagined by Eugène Cloutier in 1956, was in
"deep torment" on the night of the Riot; twenty years later, Jean-Claude
Germain's character continues to suffer, in the same circumstances,
yet something has taken shape within him, something that links him
intimately with the nation, even though he has trouble articulating it.
One "scores," the other does not (or has not yet).

Published a year after Jean-Claude Germain's, Rick Salutin's play
The Canadiens was first staged in Montreal in 1977, then in Toronto
and Vancouver, in widely varying versions. Radio still has a presence,
but what strikes the reader above all is how two strongly distinct
authors raise similar questions. One, Germain, who writes in French,
never concealed his sympathy for independence; Quebec is his favourite subject. The other, writing in English, defines himself, at least
before writing his play, as "a lifelong Maple Leafs fan"; he is looking
at Quebec from the outside. But their views on the myths surrounding hockey, and the emphasis they place on nationalism and its history,
contrive to bring them together.

When Montreal's Centaur Theatre commissioned Rick Salutin to
write a play about the world's most famous hockey team, he must have
been aware that he would be stepping into a (brief) tradition. In bringing together hockey, the theatre and politics, Jean-Claude Germain was
not his sole predecessor: *Le chemin du Roy: Comédie patriotique [The
King's Road: A Patriotic Comedy]* by Françoise Loranger and Claude
Levac (1969) and *La soirée du fockey* [Fucker's Night in Canada] by
André Simard (1974) had both attempted to combine those three elements of Quebec culture. But Salutin could not have known that an
event would soon take place that would radically modify his thinking,
both with respect to hockey and to Canadian politics. That event was

the election of a Parti Québécois government on November 15, 1976. For Salutin, the election would bring an end to the myth of the Montreal Canadiens: quite precisely what his play had set out to illustrate.

Its first act, "Survival," unfolds a panorama of Quebec history, from the British conquest of New France in 1759 to the terrorist incidents of October 1970. Its structure is quite similar to Germain's, who wrote parts for the traditional travelling players known for their "winter sketches" and their historical vignettes, from New France to 1950s Quebec. The game clock is Salutin's device for punctuating his text with an even greater number of key moments from French-Canadian history. In addition to 17:59 (1759) we find 18:85 (1885, the Riel affair), 19:09 (1909, the founding of the Canadiens), 19:16 (1916, the first conscription crisis) and 19:43 (1943, the second). Three dates commemorate Maurice Richard: 1943, 1954 and, obviously, 1955.

On a stage transformed into the Forum rink, exactly as in Germain, parade the Canadiens administration (J. Ambrose O'Brien, Léo Dandurand) and the star players (Georges Vézina, Howie Morenz). It becomes clear that over time hockey had become a symbol of national unity, but of a fragile—because artificial—national unity. English speakers and French speakers had nothing in common—except for their adulation of the Montreal team. But violence was never far away. And when Maurice Richard appears, violence breaks out.

1943. Before being identified on the scoreboard, before the public learns the name of this player without a number, Richard speaks . . . and does not mince words: "Fuck this garbage! Play hockey!" Rick Salutin's Rocket is a tightly wound ball of fury, ready to explode at the slightest provocation. The playwright paints a picture of a player obsessed with scoring goals and with winning, immune to the attacks of the opponents who pile onto his back. Nothing can stop him. He scores.

1954. A wealthy businessman enters the Canadiens locker room. He wants to purchase the team, but the players pay him no heed. For them,

the solidarity of sport has nothing to do with money. (The businessman will prevail, for $4 million.)

1955. The scene plays out under a black flag of anger: on the scoreboard, we read *"Mange d'la merde"* [Eat shit!]. To physical injury are
added ethnic insults ("Fucking frog!" for Salutin, "French pea soup" for
Germain). The problem is less the insults themselves than the fact that
Richard refuses to play along: to a referee and an English-speaking
player who attempt to explain to him that you cannot respond to all
insults, that they are meaningless and that it's normal in fact to utter
them, he insists on answering each and every one with his fists. The
English-speaking player (but not the dramatist) comments: if Richard
can't figure that out, he's "a fruitcake." Enter Clarence Campbell, "soldier, scholar, businessman, president of the NHL." The character carries realism to the point of repeating Campbell's exact words, as spoken
on March 16, 1955: Richard must be suspended for defying authority
one time too many. What's more, even if Richard is not crazy, he's an
"unstable character."

The Riot breaks out, and History accelerates. That evening, Richard hears the demonstrators insulting Campbell, he sees the tear gas
bomb explode, he observes the exodus from the Forum and the pillage
of storefronts; he looks on as the police round up troublemakers. But
above all, he becomes aware that what has just happened is "the opening shot of the Quiet Revolution and all that came after it." Against
a background of ambient sound, the scoreboard is a silent witness as
history picks up speed. Now the dates rush by at a dizzying pace: 19:62
("Thousands Protest in Front of CNR Headquarters"), 19:64 ("Bombs
in the Streets of Westmount"), 19:65 ("Protest Against the Queen
Crushed by Police"; the real date is 1964), 19:67 ("Huge Crowd Cheers
'Vive le Québec libre!'"), 19:68 ("Beatings, Arrests in Anti-Trudeau
Riot"), 19:69 ("Riot Act Read in St. Leonard"), 19:70 ("War Measures

Act Proclaimed"). Overall, the scene is pessimistic, and the first act ends with the following stage directions:

> The ARMY has moved in. The streets are quiet at last. The Forum is dark, closed. The ice is empty. The lights fade.

In a throat-gripping inversion of history, the second act ("The Day of the Game") would deal not with the violence of nationalism, as one would have expected after reading the lines quoted above, but with its peaceful triumph. The "day" in question is November 15, 1976. In the presence of the English- and French-speaking players who haven't the faintest idea what is going on, the public gathered in the Forum, instead of urging on those who had been their only standard-bearers, is carried away with joy by the election of a government that promises to promote national independence. The play makes it clear that one era has ended and another has begun. There is no longer a place for Maurice Richard in this world, despite all that he had personified up until that point: the men who now wear the Montreal uniform have no idea who he might have voted for, and his portrait has vanished from the Forum ("Where'd you go?"). Salutin's Canadiens are no longer what they used to be; they are no longer mythical figures but men just like anyone else.

The first act charted the construction of the myth; the second traces its destruction and the entry of Quebeckers into reality. The symmetry is faultless: the play begins with the British conquest, and ends with "a sort of conquest of Quebec in reverse." Instead of figurative success (hockey), Quebeckers have chosen literal success (politics). Myths are no longer of any use to them.

Starting with similar categories—myth, history—which are also those of Cloutier and Gélinas, we can now see what separates Germain and Salutin. But the two dramatists share the same conception: there is only one Maurice Richard myth, and it is national.

There is a recurring character in Salutin's play, that of a mother who cannot understand why her son is so attached to hockey and at the same time why he cannot get a handle on his political situation. She, finally converted to the "mystique" of the Canadiens, must ultimately explain to the spectators exactly who Maurice Richard is:

> Dieux du Forum,
> Forum Gods!
> Oh you, gloire à toi, Maurice.
> Oh Rocket, aux pieds longs,
> Tu es le centre de la passion
> Qui régénère notre nation,
> And you showed us the way and a light and a life.
> Oh you,
> Nous vous aimons et admirons!
> And yet Maurice, you are the one,
> Rocket, tu es le plus grand,
> Parce que tu es le centre et le centre est Québécois,
> Because you're the centre, and the centre is Québécois,
> Parce que tu es le centre et le centre est Québécois!

Her soliloquy can be interpreted in several possible ways. Its curious bilingualism—or, more accurately, its curious mix of the two languages—is immediately striking. Some lines are translated; others are in one language or the other. As in Jean-Claude Germain ("It's like I was a god! . . . some kind of Saint Christopher"), the text has a strong religious dimension: "Dieux," "Gods," "gloire à toi," "passion," "régénère" [regenerate], "and you showed us the way and a light and a life" (an allusion to the Gospel according to Saint John 14:6). The text is almost prayer-like in its use of repetition. We can also detect the ambivalence of the speaker: one speaks to an idol in the language of familiarity, as in a prayer ("Oh you, gloire à toi, Maurice"). One might even speculate as to whether Maurice Richard's "pieds longs" [big feet] are a vague allusion to the "agile feet" of Homer (*Iliad*) or Virgil (*Aeneid*).

We cannot help but note that the hero who has just stepped onto the ice to the strains of a hymn of love and admiration is a *national* hero. For it is the "nation" that must be "regenerated"; the "centre" is thrice "Québécois." Without Quebec, Maurice Richard means nothing. The playwright has made no attempt to conceal his Quebec nationalist sympathies.

More than fifty years after the fact, Jean-François Chassay published *Les taches solaires* [Sunspots] in 2006. In the final pages, Maurice Richard puts in an appearance, succeeding quite involuntarily in curing one of the characters of his "depression":

> The day after the March 1955 riot... that followed the suspension of the Canadiens right-winger for the last three games of the season and the playoffs by the horrible president of the league, Clarence Campbell, my grandfather, Jean Beaudry, was obliged to call at the police station to pick up my father, Jean Beaudry, a dedicated sports fan in general and a hockey fan in particular. At age eighteen, with the Canadiens emblem tattooed on his heart, he could not tolerate such an insult, and joined the rioters. On his way to the station-house, my grandfather breathed a deep sigh and suddenly, in his mind, everything became clear. There had been enough pining; it was time to move forward, to forget the past history of his horrible family. Thanks to you, Maurice, my grandfather's life was no longer a vale of tears.

The representation of the Rocket is here linked to collective memory, that of the family and that of the nation, and to individual memory, and through it, to identity itself. He is the "symbol of the little French-Canadian people and of their French culture that has survived in North America, despite all the obstacles"; the one who has enabled

Jean Beaudry to break with an unfortunate family history. What could be finer than a great event to pry oneself loose from the past? The Riot, arising from grave injustice to be set right, would be that event: "Thanks to you, Maurice . . ."

What are we to conclude from our cursory comparative analysis of some novels and plays about the Riot?

Telling the Maurice Richard story necessarily involves considerations of time, and through it, of memory. Whether we ponder the connections between historical time and mythical time; whether we postulate time as being pre–Maurice Richard and post–Maurice Richard; in both hypotheses the Riot looms as a pivotal event, and it cannot be made to vanish. Even children's books, although they are generally edifying and non-violent in nature, deal with it: there are allusions to the Riot in Arsène and Girerd's comic book *On a volé la coupe Stanley* (1975) and in Pierre Roy's young people's novel *Rocket Junior* (2000).

While Jean-François Chassay's novel makes the Riot the locus of a personal transformation, the novels by Eugène Cloutier and Pierre Gélinas, and the plays by Jean-Claude Germain and Rick Salutin, approach the question of memory more from a collective than an individual perspective. But all of them attempt to answer a single question: What is the function of historical and mythical time in Quebec's self-description in the 1950s, and later in the 1970s?

Eugène Cloutier attempts to articulate those two temporal dimensions, but the articulation takes place in the thoughts of a character, Jean, who at the beginning of the novel leaves a psychiatric hospital, and who, on the last page, leaves the city in which he no longer feels at home; one might have hoped that the issue could have been articulated under more favorable auspices. Pierre Gélinas believes only in historical time, that of social action, of commitment to political action and to the cause of trade unionism. For Cloutier, the figure of Maurice Richard is relegated to deep time, that is to say, of myth, even though he allows some latitude for historical time as expressed by a rapidly changing society. But for Gélinas, the same historical figure is part and parcel of a concrete reality, that of Quebec's emergence as a modern society; the author's socialist realist approach has no use whatsoever for the mythological dimension of time.

Twenty years later, the comparative positions of Germain and Salutin are no longer quite the same. The author of *Un pays dont la devise est je m'oublie* draws a distinction between the two temporal categories we find in Cloutier and Gélinas but does not believe that one can replace the other: his historical Louis Cyr is as necessary as his mythical Maurice Richard. Better still, his Maurice Richard must be embodied historically: that is the function of the monologue in which the character of Richard, in the aftermath of the Riot, begins to reflect upon his status in Quebec society. Salutin's solution is different. For him, in order to enter fully into history, the myth must be destroyed; we must move "from myth to reality." In his mind, the Riot marked a turning point:

> The Campbell-Richard riot represents the height of the identification of the cause of Quebec with le club de hockey Canadien. Yet it also represents a kind of going beyond the symbol.

In a certain sense, and with differing methods, the gap between Germain and Cloutier is gradually bridged through the interpenetration of historical and mythical time; Salutin, however, is closer to Gélinas, in that both insist that their character choose one term or the other, history or myth.

This is the version of the fictitious image of Maurice Richard—and along with it, of the Riot—that was later to reappear in the cinema and on television.

...IN PICTURES

It is all well and good to sing, to speak and to tell of Maurice Richard. How much better—at least at the end of the twentieth century and the beginning of the twenty-first—to depict Maurice Richard.

Richard was a popular television personality. He could be seen on sports programs but also on general interest shows and in commercials. And yet, whether in his appearance in a comic series like *Moi et l'autre*, on Radio-Canada television in the 1970s or in his promotion of commercial products, Maurice Richard never seemed at ease on the television screen. The same thing could be said of his television appearances at the crucial moments of his career; for example, when he announced his retirement. It might be argued that he was hardly any less ill at ease on the radio than on television. True though it may be, we would be forgetting that precisely because it is a vehicle of image, television, for those who cannot master it, is the cruelest of media.

Television programmers and filmmakers, however, came early to understand how much they stood to profit from the existence of the Rocket. From Gilles Gascon to Charles Binamé and from Jean-Claude Lord and Pauline Payette to Brian McKenna, by way of Leslie McFarlane, Hubert Aquin, Gilles Groulx, Pierre Letarte, Pierre L'Amare, Sheldon Cohen, Tom Radford, Jacques Payette, François Bouvier, John Hudecki, Jean Roy, Mathieu Roy—and the duos of Karl Parent and Claude Sauvé, and Luc Cyr and Carl Leblanc—numerous are those who have sought to exploit the riches of the myth on screen. Many would put the Riot front and centre.

Others would allude to it (to a greater or lesser extent).

When Roland Barthes wrote the commentary for Hubert Aquin's 1961 film, *Le sport et les hommes* [Of Sport and Men], he turned his attention to five activities: bullfighting, soccer, auto racing, hockey and bicycle racing. Hockey is the "national sport" par excellence. "What is a national sport? It is a sport arising out of the very elements of a nation, out of its soil and from its climate." Hockey is "a buoyant, vigorous, passionate sport," a triumph over nature, the incarnation of (regulated) speed, "an offensive game." How are these characteristics to be illustrated? By images of Jean Béliveau, Gordie Howe and Maurice Richard, and by child and adolescent players, taken from Leslie McFarlane's 1953 documentary film *Here's Hockey! / Hockey.*

Hockey is also the locus of potential "scandal":

> This scandal occurs when the men break the thin barrier between the two combats: that of sport and that of life. Having lost all form of intermediary, deprived of objective and rules, the combat between the players is no longer controlled by that element of distance without which there can be no human society. It degenerates into conflict.
>
> Sport then falls back into the immediate world of passion and aggression, drawing along with it the crowd that had come precisely to seek purification.
>
> Sport is the trajectory that separates combat from riot.

How then are we to illustrate those instances when "combat" degenerates into "riot," when sport no longer fulfills the social function assigned to it? With the image of a cyclist using his bicycle to attack a spectator who, we deduce, has caused him to fall. With images of the Riot. In both cases, only a few seconds are needed to make the point.

The bulk of Gilles Groulx's *Un jeu si simple* [Such a Simple Game] (1964) is devoted to the hockey of the 1960s. In it, players—Henri Richard, Gilles Tremblay, Phil Goyette, Jean-Guy Talbot and Bernard Geoffrion—speak for themselves. Despite the superficial differences (in the one, classical music; in the other, jazz), Groulx's perspective and that of his scriptwriter Marcel Dubé are not unlike that of Hubert Aquin and Roland Barthes. "Hockey is our national sport," declares the narrator categorically. Its rapidity makes it hard to describe: "We know everything there is to know about the game, and yet it escapes description." Both films lay heavy emphasis on the interaction between the crowd and the players, visually and textually. In both films, the images speak for themselves, and neither fears lengthy silences. A recurring leitmotif, a kind of abstract dialogue, unites both films: to Aquin and Barthes' implicit question ("What is sport?"), Groulx responds with "Hockey is such a simple game."

Though it covers the years after Maurice Richard's retirement, the film also deals with the Riot, once again from a perspective similar to that of its predecessors.

> What counts most is that passion must be sportsmanlike. But when
> it spills over the fine line that separates reality from the game, then
> it becomes riot. The Montreal Riot of 1955.

Groulx uses images similar to those of Aquin and Barthes but dwells more extensively on the nationalist dimension of the Riot. To buttress his point, he shows a picket sign displayed by a demonstrator on the night of March 17, 1955, a sign not seen in other films depicting the events of that night: "Destruction of our national sport." It also presents Richard as an "unerring sharpshooter who is leading the league in scoring" whom he quickly reduces to a single formula that is supposed to explain everything: he is "a French Canadian." The scenes of the Riot irritated National Film Board administrators, who ordered them removed from one of the two versions of Groulx's short documentary.

The two documentaries just mentioned suggest more than a casual link between what is said and what is seen. Their respective narrators have adopted a point of view on sports, one that is confirmed by images. Gilles Gascon's approach is different.

Peut-être Maurice Richard was produced by the National Film Board of Canada in 1971. Our first observation is that it must be situated in a long tradition of sports films at the National Film Board. We have already mentioned *Here's Hockey!*, *Le sport et les hommes* and *Un jeu si simple*. To the list we might well add, among other films and television programs, *Passe-partout: "Le sport est-il trop commercialisé?"* [Is Sport Too Commercialized?] by Gérard Pelletier (1955); *La lutte* [Wrestling], by a collective made up of Claude Jutra, Michel Brault, Claude Fournier and Marcel Carrière (1961), Gilles Groulx's *Golden Gloves* (1961), and *Volleyball* by Denys Arcand (1966). According to film historian Yves Lever, such productions were emblematic of Canadian documentary filmmaking: *Les raquetteurs* [The Showshoers] by Gilles Groulx and Michel Brault (1958), for example, "emerges as the manifesto of the new documentary cinema with which the French division [of the National Film Board] would go on to make its mark." In fact, there exists at the National Film Board not only a tradition of dealing with sports, but also a specific approach, whose principal trait is that of ideological critique.

In Gascon's film the critique is expressed by the choice of a tavern as the place where "Maurice" drops by for a visit, proof that the myth can be spoken to like any normal man, the kind of man you could sit down and arm wrestle with, the idea of the film being to find out exactly what the people are saying where they are saying it. It is also expressed in the editing, which juxtaposes contradictory accounts of the events in Richard's life and career. Some say Richard was aware he was an idol; others disagree. For Frank Selke, Richard's style of play was instinctive; not so for Richard himself. During the time he was an active player, Richard most certainly signed blank contracts, claims Selke; most certainly not, Richard claims with equal firmness, immediately thereafter.

Its account of the Riot uses the same approach. Richard struck the referee in Boston on March 13, 1955, because the sweaters of the officials and those of the Bruins were almost the same colour, according to journalist Charles Mayer; that would have confused the Canadiens player. False, answered Clarence Campbell. It is less important to know who is right than to see Mayer's statement as part of a wider collective effort, in the film, to defend Richard. Yes, he struck a referee. Yes, he was often involved in fights. But, say Mayer, Red Storey, Jean Duceppe and Alfred Miron, Richard was only reacting to attacks of which he was repeatedly the victim. Richard may well have been violent, but he was never the instigator of violence.

In Gascon's film, the sequences on the Riot, most of them taken from 1955 news footage, are not restricted to that sole contradiction, or to an apology for Richard.

The filmmaker dwells extensively on the financial dimension of the Riot. What seems commonplace to us today was relatively new in the early 1970s: it is as though the financial demystification of sports that has since taken place harks back to that era. By suspending Richard, Campbell deprived him of the chance to win the league scoring crown and the bonus that went with it. He also deprived the Montreal team of its chance to win the Stanley Cup; in that event, Richard would have earned a second bonus, as would his teammates.

Not unexpectedly, the film's interviewees wonder aloud if Campbell was right to suspend Richard. (Not unexpectedly, the answer, from journalist Jacques Beauchamp and from Frank Selke, is no.) Campbell, meanwhile, speaks out of both sides of his mouth. Reading from notes, he reviews the facts and deplores Richard's challenge to authority as embodied by the referees. He then speculates on what the Riot meant for number 9. It was at that moment, he suggests, that Richard realized what he symbolized for French Canadians; that discovery was a "dramatic" one.

The nationalist reading of the events of March 1955 is left to actor Jean Duceppe: Richard's suspension was, he says, "an insult to the French-Canadian nation." But a film that takes such pains to offer contrasting viewpoints raises several interesting questions. What if Jean Duceppe was wrong? What if the Riot was not simply a manifestation of French-Canadian nationalism after all? Did we, as spectators, have any say in the matter?

In 1998, nationalism was an essential ingredient in *Maurice Rocket Richard;* in 1999, in *Maurice Richard: Histoire d'un Canadien;* in 2000, in *Hockey Lessons;* and in 2005, in *Maurice Richard.* But in each case it was to be modulated in different ways.

Realizing that Maurice Richard's death was imminent, in 1998 Radio-Canada decided to honour him. As anchorman Bernard Derome remarked in the introduction to the first of the two one-hour segments of *Maurice Rocket Richard,* whatever we may think, the "immortals" are anything but. By way of tribute to this man of "a distinct race," *dixit* Derome, Karl Parent and Claude Sauvé scoured the archives of the national broadcasting network to find the footage that was to yield a two-part film, *Racontez-nous Maurice . . . : Le hockey depuis Maurice Richard* [Tell us, Maurice . . . : Hockey since Maurice Richard]. Each part is subdivided into three "chapters": "The Legend," "The Events of 1955," "The Man," and "The Hockey Player," "Modern Hockey," "The Heritage." The second chapter describes the Riot.

For former players Émile Bouchard and Elmer Lach, Richard's suspension was the result of a conspiracy hatched by the club owners, who hoped to weaken the Montreal team (a recurrent theme in discussion of the Riot). For sociologist Gilles Bourque, the Riot should be seen in the context of other roughly contemporaneous events: the Quebec artists' manifesto entitled *Refus global* [Total Refusal] (1948); the Asbestos strike of 1949; and the Radio-Canada producers' strike (1959). But we should take care not to lump all these events together indiscriminately: in the first case, we have an incident that simply "reveals a situation highly charged with social tension"; in the other three, we encounter a true desire for change and a "project". They are events that "presage social transformation." As far as the political significance of the Riot is concerned, opinions differ widely. Some—including the film's narrator, comedienne Dominique Michel, journalists Réjean Tremblay and Jean-Paul Chartrand—who describes it as the "total rebellion of the French speakers against English speakers"—see in it only nationalism. Alone in a corner where he would remain, actor Émile Genest takes vigorous exception to that vision: describing himself as an eyewitness to the events of March 1955, he refuses to pit the two linguistic groups against each other.

The 1999 docudrama by Jean-Claude Lord (for the fictional segment, one-third of the film) and Pauline Payette (for the documentary, two-thirds) *Maurice Richard: Histoire d'un Canadien / The Maurice Rocket Richard Story* has all the appearances of an authorized biography. Jean Roy, one of the film's producers, had been Maurice Richard's agent. Among its sponsors we find the Government of Canada and several crown corporations and Quebec government agencies, including Canada Post, Via Rail Canada and Hydro-Québec. The Maurice Richard family was intimately connected with its release, on October 25, 1999, at the Molson (now Bell) Centre and on the Réseau de l'Information / CBC Newsworld, another Crown corporation. The Maurice Richard depicted in the miniseries is doubly Canadian: he plays for the Canadiens; he resides in Canada. It would be illusory to expect any startling revelations: the film is the closest approximation we have of the official version of Maurice Richard's life.

Indeed, all the key elements are there, from birth to retirement, by way of the Riot. The miniseries is divided into two parts, both identified by the zodiac sign that stands for determination. "1921" opens with the words: "He knows what he wants, he is ready to pay the price, and nothing can stop him. His name? Maurice Richard"; "1951" with "He won't back down for anything, or anyone. Only the league could stop him." The film's reading of the Riot in the second segment brings together two aspects of French-Canadian history. The first, which pervades the entire film, is the language question; the second, the nationalist dimension of all that took place in March 1955. One contrives to offset the other. Conversely, the same two dimensions reinforce one another in Charles Binamé's 2005 feature.

Several times during the fictional segment of Lord and Payette's docudrama, the filmmakers remind us that in the 1940s and 1950s there existed a language barrier in the Montreal hockey club's locker room. The English speakers spoke English; the French-speaking Canadiens had to be bilingual. In *Maurice Richard: Histoire d'un Canadien*, that invisible partition is always embodied by an anonymous character, Number 19. (From the 1951–52 to the 1957–58 season, Dollard Saint-Laurent wore that number for the Canadiens.) He congratulates Maurice Richard in English before correcting himself; among French speakers, it's the least he could do. He also teaches his English-speaking teammates, gathered in Maurice Richard's apartment, to sing "Il a gagné ses epaulettes" [He's Won His Stripes]. He translates articles about sports or politics from *Le Petit Journal* or *Samedi-Dimanche*, including the one that would help touch off Richard's conflict with Clarence Campbell. He is the man who must agree to switch from a French to an English radio station on March 16, 1955, so that everyone can learn of Richard's penalty at the same time. Though he is constantly pointing to the existence of two languages in the locker room, two languages of unequal status, Number 19 never does so in a confrontational manner. Our intermediary is an apostle of the Canadian Way, and he succeeds: never are Richard's teammates found lacking in esprit de corps. A single example: French speakers and English speakers together step between Richard and the police officers who came to arrest him after the March 13 game in Boston.

In 1955, people willing to step between were in short supply. In the Richard household, tensions were running high, at least in the fictional part of the film (I will leave aside the documentary segment; it resembles most other films on the Riot). It was not the first time that the outside world threatened the family's peace and quiet. In 1952, some Quebec City residents had sent threatening messages, by telephone or mail, to Richard and his family following publication of one of his articles in *Samedi-Dimanche*. Lucille Richard, played by Macha Grenon, was on tenterhooks. But three years later, it would be worse still. She and her husband, interpreted by Roy Dupuis, do not learn of the suspension at the same time. He is in hospital for tests; she is at home with the children and the in-laws. When the news is broadcast, Richard reacts by refusing to speak and with a tormented expression; his wife weeps; his father and mother are shocked. On returning home, Richard is like a caged lion; he rips the telephone from the kitchen wall to shut off the torrent of incoming calls. In the run-up to the Riot, the makers of the miniseries choose to play the card of pathos.

After the Riot, they turn to didacticism. When one's name is Maurice Richard it is no easy matter to explain all that has happened to one's children. The dilemma is resolved by having his wife read to them, at the breakfast table, an article from the March 21, 1955, issue of *Le Devoir*, written by André Laurendeau: "Richard, My Brother, Has Been Killed." After all, she had confessed, at the beginning of the second episode: "What really makes me proud, it's that you've proved to the whole world that a French Canadian could be the best." In matters political, hers is the voice of authority. Once recovered from his surprise—did the Richard family really read *Le Devoir*?—the viewer is invited, as the Richard family is by the mother, to see the Riot as an expression of nationalism.

But our viewer must bear in mind at the same time that this particular nationalism is not the only way of representing exchanges between what have long been called "the two founding peoples." The demonstrators wished to answer, in the name of the French-Canadian nation, an alleged English provocation; true enough. Those close to Richard held the same view; also true. But there are ways of coexisting harmoniously, as illustrated by the Canadiens' locker room; no less true.

John Hudecki's *Hockey Lessons* (2000) is part of the Living Histories film series; it belongs to what might be called the oral historical tradition. In it, eyewitnesses—Jeanot Donfut, born in 1929 in Montreal; Gilles Légaré, born in 1934 in Montreal; Gérald Renaud, born in 1927 in Hull, and Jean-Paul Sarault, born in 1930 in Montreal—step before the camera to relate what hockey has meant to them. Maurice Richard is not the subject of the film, but his name pervades it. Of the film's seventy-five minutes, almost half are devoted to the Riot. Alternating, the men tell their story, and the fragments of their narrative, irrespective of the narrator, form a coherent chain. Their collective narrative has a distinctly nationalistic tone: "It was English against French," Jeanot Donfut concludes. The two groups were at loggerheads because French speakers saw Clarence Campbell as the representative of the English-speaking "establishment."

In *Maurice Richard*, released in 2005, the Riot plays an ambivalent role. Since the film ends in 1955, many had expected it to delve deeply into the events of March. Nothing of the kind happens; in fact, director Charles Binamé has come under criticism for the "omission." His film opens with a radio report of the Riot, and it ends with a sequence that ties together the March 13 brawl and the entry of the Boston police into the locker room after the match, the March 16 hearing in Montreal and the announcement of Campbell's decision (Richard learns of his suspension by radio, at the hospital). Images of the Riot ensue. Its representation is both underscored and marginalized.

Underscored, present at the beginning and at the end, it brackets the narrative. Marginalized, it accounts for only a few moments of screen time in a two-hour feature film. Why was so little prominence given to what, at first glance, would seem to be so eminently cinematographic? We might put it as follows: the Riot is of almost no use to director Charles Binamé's and scriptwriter Ken Scott's demonstration, for everyone knows that it happened, and that the events that led up to it were nothing more than yet another expression of the constant injustice of which Maurice Richard was victim. To dwell on those events would have been repetitious. The film, in a sense, argues that the Riot was foreseeable and that it was justified; there is no need to show it; to speak of it is enough. Maurice Richard was mistreated by his bosses at the factory, by the Canadiens' owners, by the other team owners, by the opposing players. His language was slighted and suppressed in the street, in the locker room, in the Montreal offices of the National Hockey League (Clarence Campbell, in one of his rare appearances, shows that he does not speak French). There could not *not* have been a riot. And indeed, a riot there would be. Enough said that it took place. Everybody knows that it was the preeminent example of the very struggle between French speakers and English speakers that the film ceaselessly puts forward. Nationalism expressed itself on March 17, 1955; it was to express itself with equal vehemence, if not more so, in 2005.

THE SEVEN FILMS we have just examined dealt with the Riot—but for them, it was not the be-all and end-all. Two documentaries appearing only months apart, one by French speakers, the other by an English speaker, give it pride of place. The differences in interpretation between the two films are not where one would have expected to find them.

The 1999 film by Luc Cyr and Carl Leblanc takes its title from André Laurendeau's 1955 article; where the journalist had written "Richard, My Brother, Has Been Killed," the filmmakers opt for *Mon frère Richard* [My Brother Richard]. The film is divided into five sections: an untitled preamble, three periods and an "overtime." The viewpoint of the narration, and of those interviewed, is clearly nationalist and pro-Richard. We are treated to a close-up examination of the events of March 16, 17 and 18, drawing on what are often new images and eyewitness reports. There lies the film's principal interest.

By-now-familiar faces speak of the Riot: Frank Selke Jr., a Montreal Canadiens PR man; Phyllis Campbell, secretary and future wife of the National Hockey League president; Red Storey, referee of the March 17 game at the Forum; Dick Irvin Jr., son of the Canadiens coach; journalist Claude Larochelle; Maurice Richard himself, but in interview sequences dating from 1978 and 1982. Several of those shown are unknown: an usher, concession stand vendors, police officers—and, above all, participants in the Riot. (It should be noted that not a single player, nor a single specialist on the 1950s in Quebec, whether sociologist or historian, is heard from.)

Participants are broken down into three categories. The eyewitness accounts of "fans" convey information on the Riot as it unfolded, both inside and outside the Forum. One relates how he headed for the Forum when he heard on the radio about a "rally." Another distinguishes the vandalism against the Forum, which he deems justifiable, from the attacks against nearby businesses, which he does not. The film interviews a "spokesman" for the demonstrators, whose version of events the narrator introduces with these words: "Montreal is getting set for a busy night. With the game against Detroit only a few hours away, the Rocket's fatherless children are preparing to swing into action. Among them, the Robinson brothers." Guy Robinson picks up the story. He and his two brothers, André and Robert, had gone to the Forum on March 17 armed with "very ripe tomatoes" with which they attempted to hit Clarence Campbell from a distance, unsuccessfully in the event. André is said to be the brother who actually got close to Campbell, fully intending to crush his last tomato on the league president's head. (In Sidney Katz's version, written in 1955, Robinson's action was far less heroic than in the documentary.) The acts of the three brothers were somehow less reprehensible than those of the members of the third category of participants, the "rioters." Tomatoes were not enough for them. Réal Arsenault smashed a jeweller's display window with a ball of lead, of unknown origin, then with a chunk of ice, before being arrested. Jacques Bibeau attacked a streetcar; he was also arrested. And there was the case of Marcel Desmarais.

Along with Robinson, his is the lengthiest account of all the participants in the Riot. He is introduced as a member of a certain "little Bonnot gang," the "Latreille gang." Édouard Latreille's auto repair shop, at the corner of Rachel and Saint-André streets in east-central Montreal, was their headquarters. The band was made up of Latreille, André Parent (the shop accountant), a man called Lacoste (the shop manager) and two younger men, André Gendron and Desmarais. Latreille, claims Desmarais, was the "ringleader" of the rioters. It was he who obtained the tear gas bomb and who, after Desmarais and Gendron drew lots, assigned Gendron the task of throwing it. But when they arrived at the Forum, Gendron backed out, and Desmarais took over the mission.

The eyewitness accounts heard in the film, from both unknown and known figures, take us forty years back in time. Furthermore, those of the rioters are uncorroborated. They must be interpreted with caution, but at least two conclusions can be drawn. The first is that the "demonstrators" and the "rioters" explain their acts by their wish to respond to an affront they saw as national in character: a nasty Anglo had abused the hero of the French Canadians, and that called for revenge. The second conclusion is that none of the participants display the slightest regret: their behaviour was justified. Myths are rare; they must be protected, in the past as well as in the present.

The other documentary on the Riot, *Fire and Ice: The Rocket Richard Riot/L'Émeute Maurice Richard* (2000), was directed by Brian

McKenna. While the film's structure is slightly less chronological than Cyr and Leblanc's, most of the events it depicts are the same. For obvious reasons the images used by the two films are often identical, whether of the Riot or of Richard's exploits on the ice. But unlike Cyr and Leblanc, McKenna reconstructs two scenes: Richard's brawl with Laycoe in Boston on March 13 and his appearance in Campbell's office in the Sun Life Building in Montreal three days later. Several of the protagonists of both films—Red Storey, Dick Irvin Jr., Guy Robinson, Phyllis Campbell, a police officer (Yvon Beaulieu)—retell the same stories. Instead of journalist Claude Larochelle, Gilles Proulx, Jean-Paul Sarault and Red Fisher are interviewed. Cyr and Leblanc spoke to neither players nor specialists; McKenna questions Ken Reardon, one of Richard's former teammates, and historian and former army officer Desmond Morton, in addition to a jazz musician, Billy Georgette. The assault by tomato staged by the Robinson brothers is related similarly in both documentaries, except for one detail: André Robinson may have needed help before taking action, and may well have found that help in a bottle of gin. The story of the tear gas bomb is totally different: in McKenna's film, there are no plotters, just a young fan who puts a homemade bomb together in his kitchen. Neither production was able to convince Richard to participate: Cyr and Leblanc use old interviews, while McKenna uses footage from Gilles Gascon's 1971 film with a voice-over recording of Richard's voice. Both filmmakers could have used Richard's radio and television broadcast of March 18: Cyr and Leblanc give us only snippets, in French, over the final credits; McKenna used snippets as well, but in English. For greater differences between these two interpretations of the Riot we must look elsewhere.

McKenna's film has the merit of saying explicitly what a substantial number of the images of the night of March 17 and the journalistic accounts of the following day reveal. More than an outburst of violence, whose dimensions cannot be minimized, the Riot was a festive occasion.

In *The Canadiens*, Rick Salutin spoke of a "street festival." Cyr and Leblanc return three times to the sequence of a man dancing in the street in front of the flames; McKenna shows the same scene twice; it had already been seen in Gilles Groulx's and Gilles Gascon's films. Each of the earlier filmmakers had included scenes of young people smiling at the camera, or enjoying themselves around impromptu campfires. Mc-Kenna goes farther, in two ways. In his voice-over narrative: "Outside the Forum, it is half-riot, half-party." And in the recollections of jazz musician Billy Georgette, who was leading a group of students that evening, and whose streetcar had been stopped in front of the Forum, where the group got off "and joined the party." Of course, things quickly got out of hand. But it cannot be said often enough: before being transformed into a tragedy by the city's best-intentioned scribes, the Riot had been a pretext for celebration. Of Maurice Richard, no less. Of resistance to perceived injustice, without a doubt. Of the simple act of raising one's head, perhaps. Of the struggle against the English? By no means certain.

The party would have turned into a riot much earlier if the people gathered inside and outside the Forum had known then what McKenna's film revealed. The filmmaker argues that Maurice Richard's appearance in Clarence Campbell's office on March 16, 1955, had been "a show trial," that "the hearing had been fixed." Campbell had already made up his mind to suspend Richard for the last three games of the regular season and the playoffs before even hearing his testimony. His ruling had, the film asserts, been transmitted to the National Hockey League owners at a secret meeting held two days earlier in New York. It is a reading corroborated by Ken Reardon, which makes it all the more convincing. He asserts that he was aware of Campbell's sentence when he stepped into his office, but that he had attended the hearing all the same, in the hope of changing the verdict. The Forum, on the night of March 17–18, was a dangerous place; it could have been worse.

McKenna differs with Cyr and Leblanc in yet another way. He gives more prominence to Clarence Campbell than they do (and, it must be added, more than do most commentators, with the exception of Gilles Gascon). As we have seen, he accuses Campbell of dishonesty. He considers that opinion, in both French and English, is unanimous in imputing a substantial part of the responsibility for the Riot to Campbell. Campbell's late arrival at the Forum, which drew the attention of the crowd and exacerbated its anger, was provocative behaviour, suggest Fisher and Irwin. Former referee Red Storey, who was also interviewed by McKenna, does not mince words: Campbell was "arrogant" and "egotistical"; he took himself for God. But the filmmaker does not stop there. He is one of the few to attempt to understand Campbell instead of simply demonizing him. His portrait is hardly a sympathetic one, but it is not a crude caricature.

Clarence Campbell, born in Saskatchewan, was "resolutely British." He had won a Rhodes Scholarship to study at Oxford, had played hockey and had been a referee. Decorated for heroism during World War II, he had been a member of the prosecutorial team at the Nuremberg war crimes trials. The film suggests that he was a solitary figure; but his solitude was not that of the Rocket, even though the film represents both men in similar attitudes: alone and erect on the Forum ice. Richard stands aloof from everyone else because he does not know how to respond to their demands: we see him twice in the film on March 11, 1996; he is unable to respond to his fans' lengthy ovation, thirty-six years after his playing career had come to a close. But Campbell's solitude was made up of superiority, of arrogance, of obsession with the rules, of the inability to reach out to the other (literally: he could not speak French). In every respect, Campbell is Richard's antithesis, and vice versa. That is one possible reading of the film. Herbert Warren Wind, writing in *Sports Illustrated* on December 9, 1954, had used the words "fire on the ice" to describe Richard. *Fire and Ice*, says McKenna: Richard is the fire; Campbell, the ice.

That, for McKenna, lay at the core of the Riot: between the two men, an explosion was bound to happen: "A confrontation is brewing. When it comes, it will shake the whole country." But there is more: behind the clash of personalities, in the background, lay an old and unsettled score that would periodically surface. French Canadians have often been accused of refusing to fight during World War II, something that former military men like Campbell and Conn Smythe, the owner of the Toronto Maple Leafs, who had recruited him, could never accept. The events of 1955 could be traced back to the Conscription Crisis of the 1940s, when thousands of young French Canadians rejected the call-up. It mattered little that Maurice Richard had been prepared to fight, and had been declared unfit on two occasions. Desmond Morton was right to liken the French to the English, with their presuppositions, not to say their prejudices. What happened in 1955—or today—was a double failure: "a failure to understand the other, and a failure to take the other seriously."

There are no fundamental differences between McKenna on the one hand, and Cyr and Leblanc on the other, in their political reading of the Riot. The language they speak plays no part in their analysis. The two films offer the same nationalist interpretation of the Riot. It is the self-same nationalist interpretation that we have seen taking shape, through its most cautious manifestations, in Aquin, Barthes and Groulx, to its most forthright, in Cyr and Leblanc, Hudecki, McKenna and Binamé, by way of the more ambivalent, in Gascon, Parent and Sauvé, or Lord and Payette. It remains to scrutinize this nationalist reading in greater depth.

ROCKET POLITICS

The most widely held interpretation of the events of March 1955, repeated time and time again for the last fifty years, predicates a good

French Canadian (Maurice Richard) whose rights were trampled by a nasty English Canadian (Clarence Campbell). His compatriots took to the streets to defend him. The riot was French Canadian in character. It was a precursor of the liberation movement of the 1960s, most probably unbeknownst to its principal protagonist.

Three examples of this argument should more than suffice. As it can be found quite literally under our noses, we have only to bend over and pick it up.

Four days after the Riot, André Laurendeau published in the Montreal daily *Le Devoir* an editorial headlined "Richard, My Brother, Has Been Killed." The title alluded to another episode in the history of French-Canadian nationalism, to Quebec premier Honoré Mercier's November 1885 pronouncement, "Riel, our brother, is dead..." Laurendeau replaces Louis Riel, the Western-Canadian Métis leader hanged for his political activities, with a French-Canadian hockey player suspended for his excesses on the ice. He well knows that the two events are far from identical:

> Today's death sentence is a symbolic one. Hardly a drop of blood has been shed. No one has been able to stir up the people's anger and fashion it into political vengeance. After all, it's only hockey...

And yet, what happened should not be minimized: "Everything seems fated to slip back into oblivion. But one brief flare-up has revealed what has been slumbering beneath the apparent indifference and the long passivity of the French Canadians."

The Riot had brought something deeply buried to the surface. Laurendeau identifies it from the outset:

> French-Canadian nationalism seems to have taken refuge in hockey. The crowd that roared its anger on Thursday night was not driven only by sporting rivalry or by a sense of the injustice committed

against its idol. It was a people frustrated, protesting against its fate.

Maurice Richard, for the *Le Devoir* editorial writer, was a "national hero," comparable to Wilfrid Laurier or to Louis Riel, but his true adversary was not Clarence Campbell. Campbell, in fact, was the personification of the English speaker, the Judge (the embodiment of rough justice), the Provocateur and the Master: "Fate had named him, on Thursday, Mr. Campbell; but he embodied all the real or imaginary adversaries that this little people has encountered." The "frustrated people" had resisted him violently for the length of a riot. The roots of their violence were historical: "The feelings that drove the crowd on Thursday were certainly confused. But are we deceiving ourselves in recognizing that the same old feelings are ever young, ever vibrant...?"

Following his prologue on the national dimensions of the Riot, Laurendeau speculated on what had driven peaceful people to acts of pillage on March 17. Violence had broken out because "when [the crowd] erupts, no matter where, it becomes aggressive and incoherent...When men are numerous and driven by a common passion, where is logic to be found?" In his attempt to fathom the rioters, Laurendeau uses a thought-provoking comparison, connecting the Forum Riot with a political rally held in 1942, at the height of the Conscription Crisis. Laurendeau thus inscribes it in the history of French-Canadian distinctiveness within the Canadian federation. At the same time, he sets in motion an entire structure of meaning whose expressions we have earlier encountered in Eugène Cloutier and Pierre Gélinas, and also in Rick Salutin and Brian McKenna: the Riot was war.

During the 1942 rally, the crowd gathered at the Jean Talon Market in Montreal had applauded an orator who had rejected the anti-Semitism expressed by the preceding speakers. But the atmosphere quickly changed:

> When the rally had ended, the crowd continued to mill around the Jean Talon Market, as if at the ready. They were in no mood to go home to bed. They were still excited, they did not want to break up.
>
> A handful of ringleaders, emerging from nowhere, stepped forward and took the lead. Marching orders were given, and a thick column headed for St. Lawrence Boulevard, onto which it turned... You can imagine what happened then. The very crowd that had unanimously execrated anti-Semitism began to throw rocks through the windows of Jewish or supposedly Jewish stores.

A "handful of ringleaders" were able to transform a group of patriots into militiamen, obeying "marching orders" and coalescing into a "thick column." We have no idea why they did: "Among those who are reading me this morning there may be some of the men who participated in the acts of vandalism, and are now asking themselves why they did it." In 1942, as in 1955, it is not easy to decipher crowd psychology. Nationalism may not always lead to violence, but it sometimes does, though we do not know why.

It would be an error to underestimate the impact of such a text. *Le Devoir* published it on March 21, 1955, reprinting it on January 29–30, 2000, and May 29, 2000. It lends its title to the thirteenth chapter of Jean-Marie Pellerin's 1976 biography, and to Luc Cyr and Carl Leblanc's film, *Mon frère Richard* (1999). It is quoted in that film, as well as in Karl Parent and Claude Sauvé's *Maurice Rocket Richard* (1998), in *Maurice Richard: Histoire d'un Canadien / The Maurice Rocket Richard Story* by Jean-Claude Lord and Pauline Payette (1999), and in Brian McKenna's *Fire and Ice* (2000). Chrystian Goyens, Frank Orr and Jean-Luc Duguay reproduce it in the French (but not in the English) version of their *Maurice Richard: Héros malgré lui / Maurice Richard—Reluctant Hero* (2000). Jacques Lamarche's album (2000) gives us extracts. It was further commented on in 1995 and 1996 by Anouk Bélanger, in 1999 by David Di Felice, in 2002 by Jean-Paul Desbiens, in 2005 by Victor-Laurent Tremblay, in 2006 by Jean-Claude Germain and Paul Daoust. Laurendeau's view of the Riot is far from unique, but its impact has been lasting.

A second example of the prevailing view of the Riot could be heard on Radio-Canada's Réseau de l'Information on October 25, 1999, from the mouth of Jean-Claude Lord:

> The events that marked Maurice's life, and particularly the Riot, and all it came to mean later on, made it something special... Looking back, you had the Riot in 1955, and the Quiet Revolution begins in 1960... It's strange, hearing him in the documentary talking about those things as if they didn't really amount to anything. Unless you hear other people talking about the same events you can't understand how it was really quite something... Looking back, at the time he was the best, and he symbolized the hopes of all the French-speaking people here, at that moment, it turned into something you couldn't overlook... We were living in what amounted to a closed space, where the clergy, the Church ran everything; politics, the whole business. So you had a gut feeling of frustration that we wanted to get rid of, we wanted to shout it out, that we could do other things too, that we needed more freedom, and suchlike... We were thirsty to open our doors to the world, thirsty for liberty, thirsty to cast off the yoke from around our necks, and I think it really left its mark on my life, and on a lot of people's lives, and Maurice Richard, even if he didn't intend to do it, also left his mark on those days, in a big way.

We can learn at least five distinct things from Lord's peroration. They constitute what can be considered as the official discourse on Maurice Richard's place in the development of Quebec society.

Richard's entire career spanned an era that has long been known as "la Grande Noirceur" (the great darkness), that claustrophobically "closed space" that was characterized by the absence of freedom, particularly religious and political freedom. It was followed by an act of collective liberation, the Quiet Revolution, with its own retinue of public agitation and new demands. Maurice Richard, at the time of the Riot, had already become the incarnation of that "thirst for liberty," though perhaps "involuntarily," without being fully aware of what was going on around him. He had personified the rejection of the "yoke" applied to one group alone, the "French-speaking people here." Finally, if Maurice Richard so well represented his people's "aspirations," it was because he was close to them. He was the man people called "Maurice."

In propounding the official version, Jean-Claude Lord enjoyed a substantial advantage over André Laurendeau: he arrived on the scene forty-four years after the fact, and thirty-nine after the start of the Quiet Revolution. But he is telling us nothing new in substance.

The same year as Jean-Claude Lord, in 1999, filmmakers Luc Cyr and Carl Leblanc carry the political reading a notch farther (a notch too far); here we have a third example of the official line. The only person in their documentary *Mon frère Richard* not to affirm categorically that the Riot was the first shot fired in the Quiet Revolution is Frank Selke Jr. For him, the Riot had been the work of vandals, and not at all that of French speakers revolting against English speakers. All other interviewees concur, to a greater or lesser extent, with the filmmakers' own diagnosis: "The Montreal Forum represented economic apartheid, the symbolic image of the Quebec of the day, with the social classes stratified by the colour of the seats, and linguistic divisions drawn according to the colour of money." In those few words, linguistic ("linguistic divisions"), social ("social classes stratified") and economic ("the colour of money") factors are combined to paint a

portrait of "the Quebec of the day" and to generate a nationalist interpretation of the Riot. High up in the cheap seats were the innocent,
oppressed French Canadians; down below, in the box seats, the nasty
English-Canadian oppressors, led by Clarence Campbell. It cannot be
denied, of course, that before the 1960s, economic power in Montreal
was in the hands of the English, as economists, historians and sociolo-
gists have repeatedly and amply demonstrated. But we should refrain
from reading onto this situation an institutionalized racism modelled
after South African apartheid. Words have a weight of their own,
which must be respected.

The three examples cited above all point in the same direction.
The dominant interpretation of the Riot is a nationalist one. Except
for Laurendeau, for obvious reasons (he is writing in 1955, after all),
those who hold the thesis posit a radical historical break. Before, all
had been repression; after, liberation had begun. Maurice Richard
had played a vital role in that liberation. So say André Laurendeau and
Jean-Claude Lord, who are then joined by Luc Cyr and Carl Leblanc,
saying what each in his own way, from Oscar Thiffault, Bob Hill and
Robert Anstey to Eugène Cloutier, Pierre Gélinas, Jean-François Chassay, Jean-Claude Germain and Rick Salutin, not to mention numerous
filmmakers, had already said. In aesthetic, social, political and linguistic terms, each of these creative individuals approached the Riot in the
way most appropriate to his talent. But there are few substantial diver-
gences in the coherence of their interpretation of the Riot.

BUT CAN MAURICE RICHARD be transformed into the incarnation of
Quebec nationalism, as many have increasingly attempted to do, even
as concrete memories of the Riot fade away? Where myth is concerned,
the answer is far from clear. To place the Riot within the context of
Richardian politics, we must make a detour by way of his own patriotic
allegiance.

If we are to believe the elder Maurice Richard, his attachment to Canada never wavered. Most commentators who have thoroughly analyzed the question concur in describing him as a federalist. Alain de Repentigny, who for many years ghostwrote Richard's newspaper column, states in his 2005 book that the former star was a federalist, but in the same breath calls him a nationalist (i.e., a "French-Canadian nationalist"). Let us attempt to solve the puzzle.

The Rocket did not disdain honours emanating from the federal capital, Ottawa. The future Queen of Canada, Elizabeth, and her husband, Prince Philip, attended a Canadiens hockey game in October 1952. They looked on as Richard scored his 322nd and 323rd goals, but not his 324th, with which he equalled Nels Stewart's record as top scorer in National Hockey League history. The Rocket would send them the puck with which he scored his 325th goal, and he later met them during a ceremony held in 1959. Prince Philip remembered well the 1952 game when, writing on the Buckingham Palace letterhead, he publicly congratulated the Rocket on the release, in 1999, of the mini-series entitled *Maurice Richard*.

Richard might very well have been a soldier in the army of the father of the future Queen Elizabeth II, George VI, had he not been disqualified for medical reasons during World War II. His potential participation should not be underestimated, as French-Canadian involvement in the war effort was by no means a foregone conclusion. Likewise, it must be noted that he was declared an Officer of the Order of Canada in 1967 (Quebec would confer its corresponding honour upon him in 1985), then Companion of the Order in 1998, in addition to being named to the Queen's Privy Council of Canada in 1992.

From World War II until the end of his life, Maurice Richard's commitment to the Canadian federation and its institutions is beyond doubt. To evaluate Richard's positions on the question of French Canada, then Quebec, let us take a closer look at his ties with one of the leading advocates of this particular variety of nationalism for more than thirty years: Maurice Duplessis, who served as premier of Quebec from 1936 to 1939, and from 1944 to 1959.

It is common knowledge that the paths of "the Chief" and Maurice Richard crossed. Duplessis, that staunch defender of provincial autonomy within the Canadian federation, attended a celebration in honour of the Rocket at the Montreal Forum on February 17, 1951, where he rubbed shoulders with other elected dignitaries, Louis Saint-Laurent, the prime minister of Canada, and Montreal mayor Camillien Houde. On December 21, 1955, he wrote to congratulate the Rocket on his 400th career goal: he began "My dear Maurice." We know that Duplessis was present when Richard scored his 500th goal on October 19, 1957. If we are to believe a column in the June 21, 1987, edition of *La Presse*, the latter had apparently visited the former "on several occasions at his residence." In *Monsieur Hockey*, Gérard Gosselin quotes verbatim (or did he invent?) a dialogue between the two men:

> Mr. Duplessis was a regular attendee at Canadiens' games on Saturday night at the Forum. He never missed an opportunity to shake Maurice Richard's hand. One night, when Maurice had been unable to score, the premier tried to console him:

> "You can't always do everything you want, isn't that so, Maurice?"

> "You should know," answered the other Maurice with a laugh.

Gosselin also claims, quoting his wife, that Maurice Richard attended Duplessis' funeral in September 1959.

It would be difficult to imagine two men more unalike. Though they shared an iron will, each in his field, it is hard to see what else might have drawn them together. Religion perhaps? Theirs (Catholicism) was that of the majority of Quebeckers before the 1960s; both practised it, as did many, if not most, of their contemporaries, Duplessis also exploiting it for partisan ends. Indifference to culture? For Duplessis, this was primarily a matter of political strategy: he knew that the French Canadians of Maurice Richard's day were little drawn to cultural activities, or at least those associated with a putative "elite" ("serious" reading, classical music, etc.). Paternalism? Duplessis was a clever manipulator, while Richard was primarily a victim, particularly in his financial dealings, throughout his active career. Baseball? Broadly (they knew that baseball is the most elegant of sports) and narrowly (we do not know whether their love of baseball brought them together at anything but the lowest level).

The politician was well aware that language can be a devastatingly effective weapon, and he was a master of it, as displayed in his oft-quoted remark about the electrification of rural Quebec: "Électeurs, électrices, électricité" ["Electors, cast your vote for electricity"]. A calculating politician, he would use his talents without hesitation to crush his adversaries; he was instinctively drawn to the spotlight. "The other Maurice," to use Gérard Gosselin's term, never saw language as a weapon; his weapons were more tangible—his fists and his hockey stick. Whether or not it was feigned, he was often credited with a sense of improvisation (on the ice) that one does not generally associate with Duplessis, who was renowned for his wiliness. Richard attempted to avoid the limelight—something the politician certainly never did.

Their differences did not stop the two Maurices from rubbing shoulders off the ice, in the political arena. Though Robert Rumilly's two-volume biography of Duplessis (1978) does not touch on the subject, Conrad Black's 1977 opus reproduces a photograph of the hockey star and the prime minister, accompanied by one of the latter's most faithful allies, Maurice Bellemare. Its caption informs us that the photo was taken on July 16, 1952, at the climax of Duplessis' election campaign. We learn that Richard was "an avowed partisan" of Duplessis' party, the Union Nationale, and that he had contributed not only to the 1952 campaign, but to the 1956 campaign as well. Maurice had lent Maurice a helping hand, and vice versa. Politics creates strange bedfellows.

In looking at the photograph selected by Conrad Black, two things come to mind. First, most commentators on the Rocket make little use of it; and when they do, it is without comment, as in the television miniseries by Jean-Claude Lord and Pauline Payette (1999), where it is shown but cropped to exclude Maurice Bellemare, as if to say "two Maurices are enough." Second, Maurice Richard offered his own reading of the 1952 encounter in his *La Presse* column on November 8, 1987. He does not deny his sympathy for Duplessis: "During the early years when I began to take an interest in politics, I was close to the Union Nationale." But he refused to interpret his meeting with Duplessis and Bellemare as political partisanship: "Once, even, Duplessis asked me to participate in a political rally for Maurice Bellemare, at Cap-de-la-Madeleine. So I went, and they took advantage of my presence to say that 'Quebec's three greatest Maurices were there in the hall.'"

Whatever the real relationship between the two men, one thing is not in doubt. When one died, in 1959, and the other retired, in 1960, two eras came to an end. Filmmaker Jean-Pierre Lefebvre was right to bring Maurice and Maurice together, at opposite ends of a rainbow, in his 1969 film *Q-Bec My Love.*

Back to the Riot.

Citizen Richard never expressed himself at any length on political issues. From him there is nothing corresponding to Jean Béliveau's declaration of federalist faith in his memoirs, *Ma vie bleu-blanc-rouge/Jean Béliveau: My Life in Hockey* (2005), a man who had been considered as a potential governor general of Canada (he or she who occupies the position that symbolizes British royalty in a country that long was, but is no longer, a British colony). That would hardly make him apolitical, however; his double allegiance to both

In 1952, Maurice Richard lends Maurice Duplessis and Maurice Bellemare a helping hand.

Canada and Quebec remained unshaken. It would make him a part of a hoary French-Canadian—later to become Québécois—political tradition embodied to perfection by Maurice Duplessis. We could summarize it thus: federalist and Canadian, autonomist and French-Canadian/Québécois; the one and the other, not the one or the other.

The hockey star's admirers would be less inclined to dual loyalties. In the transformation of the Riot into discourse, the dominant perspective is the nationalist one: French-speaking, French-Canadian and Québécois. That may be the reason why Richard always seemed ill at ease with commemorations of the Riot. After attending the premiere of Rick Salutin's play *The Canadiens*, in 1977, he admitted to the playwright that he didn't like to mix politics with hockey. It is also true that attempts to lure him into the political arena had, for several years, become increasingly insistent.

From the early 1970s on, political analyses of what had become known as "the Maurice Richard phenomenon" had begun to appear more frequently. In 1971, *Peut-être Maurice Richard*, the feature-length film by Gilles Gascon, was released as part of a series of four films based on an idea by Pierre Maheu, cofounder of *Parti Pris*, an intellectual quarterly famous for its secularist, socialist and pro-independence politics. In "Les quatre grands" [The Four Great Ones], alongside Maurice Richard we find three other Quebec idols: Brother André (*On est loin du soleil* [We're Far from the Sun], Jacques Leduc, 1970), Willie Lamothe (*Je chante à cheval avec Willie Lamothe* [I Ride and Sing with Willie Lamothe], Jacques Leduc and Lucien Ménard, 1971) and, unsurprisingly, Maurice Duplessis (*Québec: Duplessis et après...* [Quebec: Duplessis and Afterwards...], Denys Arcand, 1972). In 1971, Hubert Aquin and Andrée Yanacopoulo devoted a passage from their "Éléments pour une phénoménologie du sport" [Elements for a Phenomenology of Sport] to the intertwining of sports and "national feelings," in which they cite a classic example: "When Maurice

Richard was suspended, French Canadians felt that they had been pun-
ished, and revolted." One year later literary critic Renald Bérubé was to
publish, in *Voix et images*, an article entitled "Les Québécois, le hockey
et le Graal" [Quebeckers, Hockey and the Holy Grail]. It contains the
following passage: "One thing remains certain: ever since Maurice
Richard, the Montreal Canadiens have become in a sense Quebeckers' national team." A year before, Paul Rompré, Gaëtan Saint-Pierre
and Marcel Chouinard were to go even further in their article "Essai
de sémiologie du hockey: À propos de l'idéologie sportive" [Essay in
Hockey Semiotics: On the Ideology of Sport]:

> Maurice Richard had to be more than simply a good hockey player
> to become a mythical hero. The Quebec public had to invest him
> with "national meaning," that is to say, with the responsibility of
> representing all our frustrations. For the Quebec public, Maurice
> Richard, tenacious and indestructible, endlessly victimized by
> unscrupulous opponents, referees and the magnates of the National
> Hockey League, was the supreme symbol of resistance to Anglo-
> Saxon oppression.

The article appeared in a far-left publication called *Stratégie*, which
might explain its overtly political reading of the Rocket. Nonetheless,
we cannot overstate what had become, at least from the mid-1950s,
a fundamental article of public discourse: the existence of deep ties
between Maurice Richard and the nation.

That would be to forget that Maurice Richard was more than the
standard-bearer of French Canadians / French-speaking Quebeckers.

AN "ETHNIC DIMENSION"?

The narrator of the documentary *Mon frère Richard* does not shrink
from a certain pomposity. He can be heard to utter such pearls as

"Amplified by the whispering of the press, of the open-line shows and by word of mouth, the Richard affair quickly took on an ethnic dimension. In the city, the climate was that of a lynching." Yet despite the threats uttered against Clarence Campbell before the game, the word "lynching" seems overblown: Phyllis Campbell remembers walking to the Forum that evening alongside her future husband without being bothered. Words like "ethnic dimension" would seem to call for further scrutiny.

To call the riot an "ethnic" one, that is to say, strictly French-Canadian, is to overlook two things.

First, the Rocket had unconditional admirers among both English speakers and French speakers, a fact André Laurendeau had pointed to in his March 21, 1955, article:

> There can be little doubt that all hockey fans, whatever their nationality, admire Richard's style of play, his courage and the extraordinary soundness of his reflexes. There would certainly have been English speakers among those outraged by Mr. Campbell's decision.

Twelve years later, in *Fire-Wagon Hockey*, Andy O'Brien recalls how both Montreal's English and French radio stations were overwhelmed with virulent condemnations of the suspension imposed by Campbell. Strangely, few people wish to be reminded of those facts. Nor of the curious appeal published on March 18, 1955, in *The Gazette* (Montreal):

> An Urgent Message To
> Maurice "Rocket" Richard
>
> We're with you 100% and personally feel that you were the object of a "new deal" decision. Being unable to contact you personally at this time, we are, via this ad, offering you a bona fide position with our

firm, selling wrapping papers, twines, refrigeration and allied lines. If interested, please contact us at Giffard 1606.

CANADIAN BUTCHERS'
SUPPLY CO. CORP.
Mt. Royal Ave. at Iberville

Was it a practical joke? An attempt to capitalize on Richard's name? An exercise in irony? Whatever the case, the item appeared in an English-language daily, which at the time of the Riot was said to have been hostile to Maurice Richard and favourable to Clarence Campbell.

But there is no reason, in fact, to think that the widespread discontent was restricted to French-speaking hockey fans in March 1955. Would English speakers have accepted the suspension out of "ethnic solidarity" with Campbell? Manny Gittnick, one of the "fans" interviewed by Luc Cyr and Carl Leblanc for their 1999 documentary, describes his participation in the Riot in the same language as Campbell. While the filmmakers present his eyewitness account, they fail to draw the logical conclusion from it: among the "fans," the "demonstrators" and the "rioters" they've identified can be found people from each of the "two solitudes." To believe that there were only French speakers on Saint-Catherine Street on Saint Patrick's night, 1955, would be either naive—or all too convenient.

Paradoxically, both Rick Salutin in *The Canadiens* and Brian McKenna in *Fire and Ice* adopt the same position. Even those English speakers most concerned to find out what had happened on March 17, 1955, cannot wrench themselves free of the official version. For them too the Riot was a strictly French-speaking matter, involving "the French-speaking people here," as Jean-Claude Lord put it.

To this initial reason to beware of the putative "ethnic" character of the Riot can be added a second, historical one. From 1960 to 1966

Quebec would launch into an intense process of renewal, which later came to be known as the Quiet Revolution. Even though the expression was originally English ("There's a quiet revolution taking place in Quebec," a Toronto journalist had written), it was as though this same Quiet Revolution did not apply to English-speaking Quebeckers. The Quiet Revolution did affect them, of course, but indirectly, by depriving them of their traditional power. In other words, the Quiet Revolution was to be seen as a matter strictly for French Canadians on their way to becoming Québécois.

Ever since, historians have spared no effort to seek out antecedents to that Quiet Revolution, its precursors and its premises, even if its own instigators have often seemed to want to wipe clean the slate of the past. The implicit historical reasoning goes as follows: the Quiet Revolution broke out in 1960 with the election of the Liberal government of Jean Lesage, but its first stirrings can be found in the March 1955 riot. The two events were to mark the accession of the French Canadians / Québécois to greater autonomy. Quebec's English speakers, not being involved in any positive sense with the Quiet Revolution, certainly could not have been involved in the Forum Riot. The reasoning itself is specious, an attempt to explain an event from the past (the Riot) by an event to come (the Quiet Revolution). Writing history backward is a risky proposition.

More than French-speaking nationalists had flocked to the Forum on the night of March 17, 1955. There were also angry fans and petty criminals. They had no idea that the Quiet Revolution was on the horizon—if indeed it ever was—and they came from all "ethnic horizons." In *Le Devoir*, two days before André Laurendeau published his political interpretation of the Riot, Gérard Filion asserted that the National Hockey League, in tolerating for commercial reasons acts of violence on the ice, was partially responsible for the behaviour of its customers. Writing in *Saturday Night* in April of that year, Hugh MacLennan attempted to fathom the motives of the people he called "hoodlums, goons and punks." Sidney Katz picked up both strands of argument in *Maclean's*, on September 17, 1955, when he employed the same metaphor: that of the Roman circus. Since 1955, when Filion, MacLennan and Katz published their articles, their viewpoint has been excluded from the dominant discourse on the Riot.

It would be absurd to deny the significance of nationalism during the Riot and in its interpretation. But it might be worthwhile to ponder what lies behind the domination of the nationalist reading. Could it be the price of myth?

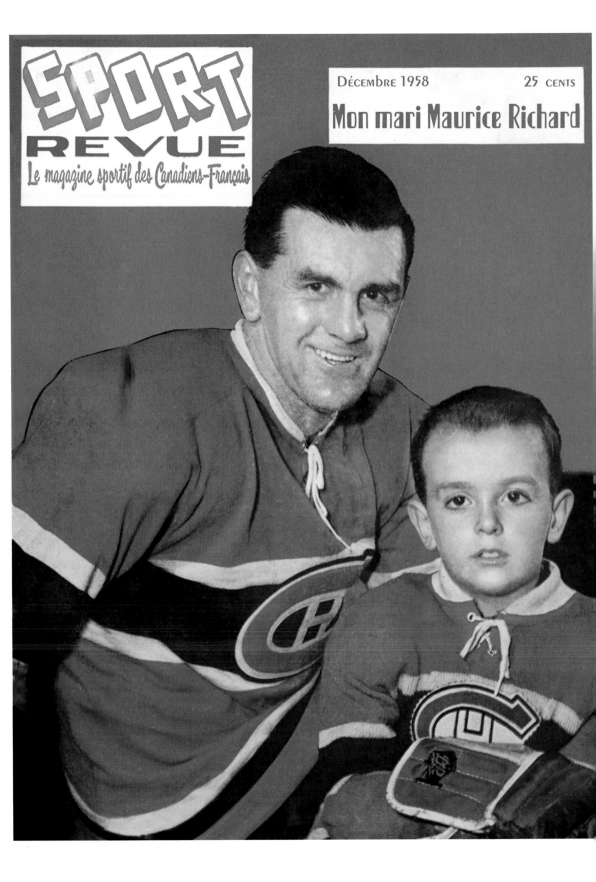

SPORT REVUE

Le magazine sportif des Canadiens-Français

DÉCEMBRE 1958   25 CENTS

Mon mari Maurice Richard

III. *A Myth*

LEGEND, HERO, MYTH

"I think I'm human, just like everybody else."

—MAURICE RICHARD, 1999

How are we to define Maurice Richard? As legend, hero or myth— or as all three at once? There is no unanimous answer to these questions, particularly since the three words, both in dictionaries and works of criticism, are intimately connected and difficult to distinguish from one another. As a matter of fact, those three words, along with several others, have been indiscriminately used to speak of Richard. Some speak of a *symbol*, or of a *monument*, others of a *god* or a *totem*. For Denis Brodeur and Daniel Daignault in 1994, and for Jean-Paul Sarault in 1996, he is one of *Les Grands du hockey* [The Greats of Hockey]. According to Daignault once more, he is a *Géant du Québec* [Giant of Quebec] (1966), then *Le plus grand héros du Québec* [Quebec's Greatest Hero] (1999) before becoming the *La fierté d'une nation* [The Pride of a Nation] (2005). For Pierre Bruneau and Léandre Normand, his name is inscribed in *La glorieuse histoire des Canadiens* [The Glorious History of the Canadiens] (2003). When Charles Mayer presented his *L'épopée des Canadiens* [The Canadiens' Epic] (1949), it ran from Georges Vézina to Maurice Richard; to speak of epics is, of course, to speak of heroes and legends. In 1976, Jean-Marie Pellerin published *L'idole d'un peuple: Maurice Richard* [The Idol of a People]; he was to update the book in 1998, and to invert the terms of the title: *Maurice Richard: L'idole d'un people*. But his perspective remains unchanged: "The birth of a legend." Several similar terms are used side by side: hero and legend (Bob Hill, 1955; Pierre Foglia, 2000); hero, legend and myth (Louis Chantigny, 1959; Jean Dion, 2000); hero, legend, myth and symbol (Lysiane Gagnon and Lawrence Martin, 2000); god, legend, myth, hero, giant, idol, star, superstar (filmmakers Karl Parent and Claude Sauvé, 1998).

But we must make every effort to distinguish between those terms if we are to understand the meanings with which Quebec and Canada have invested Richard. Put succinctly, Louis Cyr is a legend, Jackie Robinson was a hero, while Maurice Richard became and remains a myth, a myth with its own particular history and geography, which explains why it has not always meant the same thing to all people.

Legends and heroes

Louis Cyr was a legendary Quebec strongman of the late nineteenth century. As Paul Ohl relates in his recent biography, *Louis Cyr, une épopée légendaire* [A Legendary Epic] (2005), Cyr enjoyed a lengthy career on the local, national and international levels. He drew crowds in Quebec, in the rest of Canada, in the United States and in Great Britain. There may have been more carnival than sport in his feats of strength, but they possessed a physical dimension that was undeniable. Well before the Rocket, a statue had been erected in Cyr's honour, in Saint-Henri, a working-class district of Montreal. As a public figure, he was the subject of books, and of intense newspaper coverage. What was to make him a legend rather than a myth?

There are two main reasons. First, Cyr occupies only a minor place in collective memory; second, that place has shifted considerably over time. Though he was extremely well known during his lifetime, Cyr's historical star waned radically on several occasions. It is quite possible to live in Quebec today and not be aware of his name. One could have lived forty years ago and still never have heard of him. From the 1950s onward, the same thing cannot be said about Maurice Richard. Everybody knows him, or thinks they do; what is true today has been equally true for the past sixty years, without interruption.

In the search for sports figures with whom to compare Maurice Richard, the name of Jackie Robinson, as we have already noted, comes up frequently. The two men were contemporaries. Both embodied the possibility of North American success for members of minority groups. They were both known for their high-spirited play and hot temper. Both were the subject of a wide variety of cultural discourses. Yet one of them (Robinson) remains a hero, while the other (Richard) has become a myth.

It must be borne in mind that when Robinson began his career, African Americans had long been forbidden from playing in professional major-league baseball. He was the first, in the National League, to break through the barrier of segregation. He was forced to fight racism head-on. French Canadians had long been the victims of diverse forms of oppression (linguistic, economic, social and religious), but never on the basis of a presumed racial inferiority inscribed in legal and administrative texts. Maurice Richard, like the French Canadians of his day, encountered many obstacles due to his origins, as Jean-Marie Pellerin so eloquently demonstrates in his 1976 biography. But those obstacles were totally unlike the status of institutionalized inferiority to which

African Americans were subjected. Richard may well have been the target of repeated attacks on the ice, but he never had to move to the rear of the bus or quench his thirst at a separate drinking fountain because of his "race." Robinson did. He had a mission: to change the fundamental rules of American society. He forced the issue, at the cost of great personal sacrifice: he had agreed not to respond to the insults that were shouted at him, or to the blows he suffered. The constraints to which Maurice Richard was subjected were not of the same order.

Which is not to say that Richard's qualities were in any way inferior to Robinson's. Each man had his unique characteristics, created by their singular historic situations. The baseball player's behaviour was heroic by virtue of the conditions imposed upon his people at a particular time (the 1940s and 1950s) and place (the United States). Jackie Robinson was not Maurice Richard, and vice versa. As detective novel author Robert Parker put it in *Hush Money* (1999): "Nobody's Jackie Robinson."

Myths

A myth need be neither a legend nor a hero. And yet he may be more than either.

Unlike heroes, myths and legends both exist in suprahistorical time, the very long perspective: no myth can exist outside this temporal framework, in either the medium or the long term. No myth can exist strictly in the here and now; he must belong to yesterday, to the day before yesterday, to yesteryear. Myth also shares with legend the marvellous aspect of what it lays before us: there can be no myth of the banal, the small, the everyday and the mediocre. Everything about him must be larger than life, and must grow larger with the passage of time. The mythical figure draws his power from amplification and from cultural transmission, for in order to survive in memory, his exploits must be handed down from one generation to the next. The myth, like the hero and the legend, is intimately connected with collective identity: those from whom he has emerged have mandated him to represent and to defend them. Heroes, legends and myths are never alone for long.

We can then identify the four defining features of a mythical figure: he must exist in suprahistorical time; he must have a marvellous quality; he must be culturally transmitted; he must have a collective dimension. To these I would add a fifth: the myth as a malleable narrative.

A myth can be made to say much. Contradictions exist harmoniously within him. Ancient myths (Prometheus, Icarus, Antaeus) have come down to us because each subsequent era sought to reread them and to invest them with new meaning. Modern-day myths, though they lack the same historical depth, are by no means fundamentally different. If there exists a Rimbaud myth, as Étiemble (1952) has exhaustively demonstrated, it is because the figure of the French poet has, since the end of the nineteenth century, been invested with a multiplicity of meanings. When we come to Quebec, Pascal Brissette (1998) has shown how the figure of Montreal poet Émile Nelligan has been enlisted to serve contradictory ends for more than a century.

To define myth as a malleable narrative is to affirm in the same breath that his is a narrative to which belief is crucial. If we can ascribe remote meanings to Rimbaud and Nelligan, it can only be because people can be found to accept those meanings, and to believe in them. Rimbaud is simultaneously a great, iconoclastic poet, a deathbed convert to Catholicism and an arms dealer who had abandoned poetry. He is *simultaneously* chaste and debauched. Nelligan is *simultaneously* a mad poet and the prophet of a new age: so claims a book by one Nicétas Orion, patriarch of the Johannite Church (1996), according to Pascal Brissette. A mythical figure is a narrative in which truths that seem unalterably opposed are melded.

On another level, it would be wrong to underestimate, in analyzing the advent of modern myths, what can be termed the chance factor.

It alone cannot define them but it can explain their appearance and ofttimes their staying power. One fine day, Rimbaud stopped writing poetry for no apparent reason; for the last 150 years, commentators have wondered why. The Nelligan myth draws upon several causes, two of which are purely arbitrary: his birth to a French-speaking mother and an English-speaking father, and his madness. A Rimbaud who had continued to write or a Nelligan who did not go mad might have achieved the status of myth, but certainly not in the same way.

What then are we to make of Maurice Richard?

After a reading of the preceding pages, the marvellous nature of his accomplishments cannot be doubted. It little mattered that players—one or more—from the opposing team clung to him; nothing could stop him from attacking their goalie and sliding the puck behind him, for from the blue line in, no man ever possessed a fury and a determination to equal his. When the chips were down against Montreal's archrival, Toronto, Richard scored five goals and was awarded three game stars. Exhausted after a day's moving, he scored five goals and three assists. Bludgeoned by an adversary, he returned to the game not knowing where he was, driven by pure instinct toward the goal. With the game in overtime, he scored the decisive goal, as often as necessary. For myth-makers no additional feats of prowess are needed; one after the other, time and time again, they return to the tried and true.

No one could doubt that Maurice Richard had come to represent French Canadians, then Quebeckers; to defend their collective interests, in addition to his own. No study of the Rocket's life would be complete without consideration of what Richard personified on the national level. In 2000, Roch Carrier published *Le Rocket*. In English translation, the title became *Our Life with the Rocket*. "Our life" indeed! No need to seek out other examples: everyone linked Richard with his own community. But we will have to look more closely at what we mean by community: that of Quebec or that of Canada.

At the risk of oversimplification, we might venture that the transmission of Maurice Richard from generation to generation has taken two forms. On the "cultural" side, it has been taken up by the novel and the short story, by poetry, theatre, young people's literature, biography, autobiography or memoirs, schoolbooks (readers, grammars), eulogy, painting, sculpture, drawing, song, television, film, comic strips, the press, the radio, the Internet, picture books and learned discourse, particularly that of historians (of Quebec, of sports, of culture). On the "material" side, it has been represented by domestic products (soup, porridge, bread, cereal, soft drinks, fuel oil, wine), televised or print advertising, toys and games, clothing, hockey cards, autographs, national symbols (banknotes, postage stamps) and artifacts for which collectors compete fiercely. These two forms of transmission come together in the exhibitions, that of the Maurice Richard Museum and, above all, that of the Canadian Museum of Civilization. There, the "raw material" is elevated to the level of "culture." Maurice Richard has endured, and is still with us, because each of these cultural spheres, from the most official to the most marginal, has appropriated his image.

The mythical figure is a malleable narrative. His is not a discourse of unitary *truth*, but a discourse of multiple *truths*. Let us turn once more to the story of the goal Richard scored after having been knocked cold during the April 8, 1952, game. Richard had lost consciousness after being struck by a Boston Bruins player; he spent several minutes in the infirmary, and it seemed extremely unlikely that he would return to play; finally, he made up his mind to take his place on the bench, then leaped onto the rink and scored. In Gilles Gascon's film *Peut-être Maurice Richard*, press photographer Roger Saint-Jean is categorical: Richard scored the game-winning goal in the playoffs, in overtime. Tony Bergeron, Maurice Richard's barber, is no less categorical: Richard had scored the tying goal—it could not have been in overtime then—and Lach the game-winner. Camil DesRoches is no less certain (he is also right in terms of the events themselves): it was not during overtime; it was during the playoffs; it was the winning goal; it was not the final goal of the game, which the Canadiens were to win 3–1, with Richard scoring the second goal. But about that stirring deed, as about so many others, there are many stories to choose from, for each of them, when Maurice Richard is involved, possesses its own truth, contradicting the truth of its neighbour while being entirely compatible with it.

Not enough attention has been paid to the function of chance in the transformation of Maurice Richard into myth. If Richard had chosen another sport, baseball or wrestling, say, he would not have become a myth in Canada: baseball does not have the same deep roots here as it does in the United States; wrestling is not a serious enough sport (which would explain why Yvon Robert, who was so like Maurice Richard in many ways, could never have become a myth). If Richard's playing style had not been grounded in constant effort and in the spectacular demonstration of that effort, it is not at all certain that the public could have projected itself so vigorously upon him. Anyone can project something of himself onto a player who can achieve nothing without constant effort. We cannot say the same thing about players whose talent and technical skills set them far above mere mortals; think of Wayne Gretzky and Mario Lemieux in hockey, or of Michael Jordan in basketball.

Historical chance has also contributed significantly to the myth. Had Richard not begun his career with the Canadiens in 1942 it is far from certain that he would have become the myth he is today. The Montreal team was doing badly and was in desperate need of a saviour, a French-speaking saviour if possible, to replace Howie Morenz, who had died in 1937. Had Richard been preceded, like several modern hockey players (Orr, Lafleur, Gretzky, Lemieux, Lindros, Crosby) or like Jean Béliveau, by an advertising campaign that transformed him into a saviour before the fact, he would not have benefitted from the surprise that saw him come from nowhere: overnight, a player who had at first seemed fragile emerged as a goal-scoring machine. If Richard had not benefitted from the radio, it is not at all certain that he would have had the same impact on the popular imagination. Ken Dryden summed it up perfectly in 2001:

> And this was an easier time to be a hero. This was before TV. Very few people ever actually saw Richard play . . . Radio was perfect for heroes. Radio was live. Radio games offered an unknowable result. Radio meant lying in the darkness and, to the words of an excited storyteller, painting pictures of everything you heard. It meant using your own imagination. There has never been a bad game played on radio.

Had Richard not been the cause of a riot five years before the Quiet Revolution, his place in Quebec history would probably not have been what it is today. Had it happened ten years earlier, the causal link would have lost its meaning: it would have been impossible to explain the time discrepancy. Had it happened four years later, the connection would have been too obvious. Had Richard been a professional forty or fifty years after he actually was, it would have been difficult for his fans to identify with him. Today's players earn more in one game than most of their fans do in one year, making personal identification difficult. On all four levels (Canadiens history, media history, Quebec history and hockey history), Richard's timing had been perfect.

Finally, had he not been nicknamed "the Rocket" he clearly could not have been so easily elevated to mythical stature. Could we imagine a "Coco myth" (Jacques Lemaire)? A "Bionic Blueberry myth" (Mario Tremblay)? More than a few have identified "the Rocket" as a dream nickname, whose origins are unclear. There can be few finer examples of chance than when a hockey player is converted into a national myth, then transformed into a heritage to be protected and handed down to posterity.

MYTHICAL TIME

It is perhaps on the temporal level that the Maurice Richard myth is at its least clear-cut. The Rimbaud and Nelligan myths are both more than one hundred years old. The ancient myths have endured for millennia. Is it possible to speak of a myth when a person has been dead for less than ten years? When a phenomenon has existed for a mere sixty? If time were the sole criterion, we would be justified in refusing to grant Maurice Richard mythical status. However, there is more to the existence of the Maurice Richard myth than the criterion of time.

It is not enough to assert that the myth exists in suprahistorical time. We must immediately add that for the myth to exist in its temporal dimension, which is a fundamental component of the mythmaking process, what it represents must undergo a process of modification. The Maurice Richard myth is not the same today as it was fifty years ago, if it even could be said to have existed fifty years ago, nor will it be the same tomorrow. In an attempt to understand this process, let us examine three episodes of the myth's evolution more closely.

1956-60

The word *myth* was juxtaposed with the name of Maurice Richard early on. In 1956, as we have already pointed out, novelist Eugène Cloutier used it in *Les inutiles*. Richard was then thirty-five years old, and still an active player. In 1959 journalist Louis Chantigny employed the same term. It is surprising to see Maurice Richard and myth associated at such an early date.

It is all the more surprising in that the first steps toward mythical status were contemporaneous with what could be termed the familiarization of Maurice Richard. The earliest discourses on Maurice Richard are characterized by the sense of familiarity felt by his fans. Richard was not at all different from them. He was not a 2.3-metre-tall basketball player. He could not sprint a hundred metres in ten

Will Richard retire this year? asks the magazine *Hérauts* in October 1959.

seconds. He didn't like fancy words. When asked about his culinary tastes, he would respond with trivialities; for many years he had not really liked ... macaroni, Gérard Gosselin reported in *Monsieur Hockey* in 1960. By the late fifties, he had become much better known, thanks to the line of products that either displayed him or were endorsed by him, thanks to his presence in the media and thanks to a well-maintained persona as a dutiful son, an attentive husband and a caring father. Richard was a man just like everyone else, someone people could feel close to.

Except when he took to the ice. When the game began, everything changed. There was no longer the slightest hint of banality about him: he was unlike any other player. But such grandeur is not eternal. The late fifties were also the time when even his most ardent fans had to admit that his career was coming to an end. From that moment on, the question arose: How would he negotiate the passage from athletic excellence to daily life, permanently? That was what Gilbert Rogin attempted to find out in his essay on Richard, published in the March 21, 1960, issue of *Sports Illustrated*. Louis Chantigny asked the same question in an article in *Le Petit Journal*, published during the week of October 18–25, 1959, headlined "A Tragic End for the Rocket."

The article appeared several months before Maurice Richard announced his retirement. But it is predicated precisely on that very retirement, which it foreshadows and which it considers, even then, as the birth of something that will far exceed the confines of the sports world. The first sentence anchors Richard firmly in the historical time frame essential to myth: "There are men upon whom, from birth, lies the curse of greatness ..." Chantigny's text is organized around three key words, or groups of words, which lend it coherence. They paint the portrait of a lonely man, like all great men, of a most uncommon being and of someone living under a death sentence—put briefly, of a myth taking shape in front of our eyes.

On the one hand, his *grandeur* functions to distinguish the idol from the mere mortals, from the men who would like to enjoy a relationship of familiarity with him. Such is the purpose of terms such as "grandeur" (four times), "ideal" and "genius" (three times), "seeker of the absolute," "titan," "hero," "superhuman" (twice). Though perhaps not a "celebrity of the spirit," Richard is a "muscular glory" worthy of an "epic" or of a "tragedy" (four times). This incarnation of the "sublime" (twice) is expressed in the flight of the "eagle" (twice).

On the other hand, *destiny* has conferred upon Maurice Richard the status of a "legend" (three times), or of "myth," but of legend and myth that remain the playthings of forces that far exceed them. Alongside "fate" (three times) and "destiny" we also encounter the word "curse": he is the victim of a "demon"—a term that appears six times—or the "wrath of the gods," helpless against a "mysterious, supernatural power," truly a "man possessed" (twice); the solitary hero has been entrusted with a "mission," but the success of his mission can only elude him.

> Lacking true connections with their own times, almost always misunderstood by their contemporaries, [men like Richard] streak across the sky of history like meteors, shining with a fleeting but dazzling light in the darkness of their mission. They themselves do not know who they are, nor the roads their fate will follow. In the rise and dizzying fall of their lives they barely touch the real world.

Myth and ignorance, according to Chantigny, are one. Richard is a great man, but his greatness can be only partially ascribed to will. It would not be the last time an admirer of Richard was to put forward such a hypothesis.

The third recurring image is that of *bedazzlement* or *flame*. As we have just seen, Richard is a "meteor" that "streak[s] across the sky of history"; his light is "fleeting but dazzling." All is reactivated by the "lightning," the "fireworks," the "sun," the "incandescent iron," the

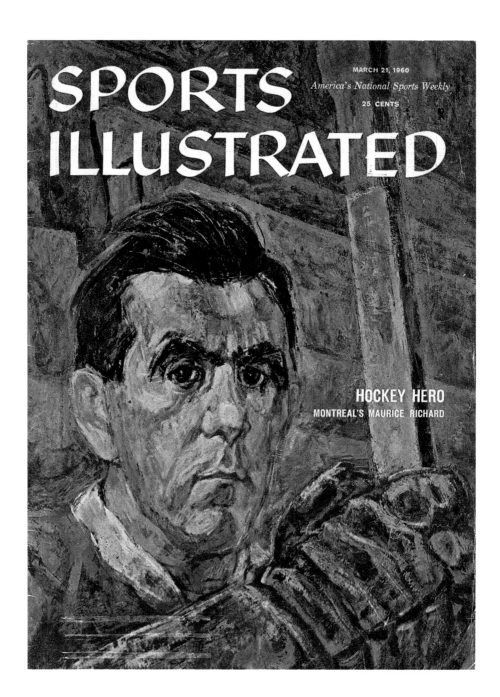

Richard, as depicted by Russell Hoban in 1960.

"dawn," the "fiery letters," the "fire of the idea"—in which the "hearts" of heroes are "consumed"—and the "strange, feverish gaze" that "shines" in their eyes. The apotheosis of the image, its culminating point, is embedded in the article's penultimate paragraph, where the author links the heavenward trajectory of a rocket to the career arc of the man nicknamed "the Rocket"—after having been called "the Comet," "V5," "the Brunette Bullet" or "Sputnik Richard"—of he who did so much to keep alive the appellation "Flying Frenchmen" to designate the Montreal hockey team:

> Yes, it would be consistent with his legend if he who was known
> as "the Rocket" at the beginning of his dazzling career would end
> it exactly like a rocket, soaring in one final blaze of glory upward
> toward the heavenly zenith before dying out, in the night of nothing-
> ness, in one last dizzying fall to earth.

Once a star in the frigid firmament, Maurice Richard has become a new Icarus.

What the article is saying, in Louis Chantigny's typically purple prose, is that Maurice Richard was not a man like all the others, that he may not even have been a mortal man. "Projected beyond their egos," those rare figures who resemble him are summoned to "triumph where all others have perished, to achieve the impossible, to accomplish what cannot be done." The "drama" of which Richard is the protagonist "has long since superseded the skating rink to encompass the universal." Maurice Richard could not be a merely national figure; he was far greater than that.

Yet it would be wrong to conclude that Richard was no longer a familiar figure, that he had been irrevocably extracted from his community. Richard was a Quebec myth. He was the man we addressed in the most familiar terms, the man we called Maurice, while at the same time we connected him with the most ancient myths. He was the man who moved house on his own, the same man who flew soaring into the starry firmament, both literally and in the figurative imagery of sports. He was the man who wept at his children's birth and who cried after having scored a goal that would soon assume mythical proportions.

In the wake of the Riot, tension would develop between the familiar and the mythic. It was not clear whether or not Maurice Richard would become (once again) a man like other men or transcend his condition to rise to a far loftier station. Would he be the identifying figure brought to light by the events of March 1955? Perhaps it would be more accurate to say that familiarity and myth had become intermingled rather than distinct.

There followed a period of ten years during which Richard, without having been pushed aside, was no longer in the limelight. On retirement, he was hired by the Canadiens to represent the team, a job he quickly tired of, so much so that he resigned his position and refused to have his name linked to the team's owners, Molson Breweries, for more than fifteen years. He plunged into sport-related activities (participating in old-timers' games, refereeing wrestling matches), into his weekly columns and into business ventures (beer, electronics, gas, heating oil) as well as into speaking engagements. The man who had seemed destined to mythical status had become a man like other men, though better known than most: Gérard Gosselin (1960) and Andy O'Brien (1961) published biographies of him; Jacques Saintonge told his story in a radio program of the Radio-Canada series *Une demi-heure avec* ... [A Half-Hour with ...] (1963); George Sullivan included him, along with Howie Morenz and Bobby Hull, in his book *Great Players* (1969). He had not been forgotten, but his rather vague presence bore no relation to what had gone before, nor to what was to happen during the decade to come.

The 1970s

At the end of the 1960s and the beginning of the 1970s, Maurice Richard's place in collective memory might not yet have appeared secure. On the first page of the May 1, 1971, issue of *The Canadian* magazine, writer Alan Walker ventured boldly: "Rocket Richard on the Brink of 50—and Oblivion." Richard himself had already been seen to wonder aloud, in Gilles Gascon's film, if one day he would not be forgotten (a prospect he found depressing):

> The day when nobody recognizes you in the street, when nobody greets you, well, then you can say that the public, people in general, have forgotten you . . . I think that ten or fifteen years from now there'll be a new generation, and I think that as time goes by they won't recognize you like they do today. I can see it coming, I accept it, but it'll be funny to go somewhere and for people not to recognize me . . . I'm not in any hurry to see that day.

In his song, Pierre Létourneau talked of Richard as though he were dead. Hubert Aquin and Andrée Yanacopoulo in 1972 labelled him as "the hero of the preceding generation." How wrong they were.

To grasp the extent of the error, we need only enumerate. 1970: novelist Jacques Poulin, in *Le coeur de la baleine bleue / The Heart of the Blue Whale*, brought Maurice Richard to life via a fictitious hockey player. 1971: Pierre Létourneau recorded "Maurice Richard," the song he composed a year before in Paris; Gilles Gascon filmed *Peut-être Maurice Richard*; Maurice Richard joined forces with Stan Fischler to co-author *The Flying Frenchmen: Hockey's Greatest Dynasty / Les Canadiens sont là! La plus grande dynastie du hockey*, in which he speaks, sometimes quite bluntly, about his use of the stick in fights, about his teammates, about Clarence Campbell, that "English Canadian aristocrat." 1972: to the strains of Pierre Létourneau's "Maurice

Richard," Pierre L'Amare directed an animated short for the National Film Board, *Mon numéro 9 en or* [My Number 9 in Gold], a florid outpouring of psychedelic art. 1973: Richard was one of Maurice Desjardins' *Surhommes du sport* [Sports Supermen]. 1974: novelist Clark Blaise published a short story entitled "I'm Dreaming of Rocket Richard"; Louis Chantigny put Richard front and centre in *Mes grands joueurs de hockey* [My Great Hockey Players]; for Trent Frayne, he was one of the *Mad Men of Hockey*. 1975: memories of the Riot can be seen in *Les enquêtes de Berri et Demontigny: On a volé la coupe Stanley* by Arsène and Girerd. 1976: Jean-Claude Germain dramatized Maurice Richard on the stage of the Théâtre d'aujourd'hui; Jean-Marie Pellerin launched the first edition of his biography; Al Purdy's poem "Homage to Ree-shard" was published in his collection *Sundance at Dusk*. 1977: it was Rick Salutin's turn to dramatize Richard, in Montreal, Toronto and Vancouver. 1978: a Radio-Canada television program, *Les coque-luches* [The Darlings], honoured Richard by way of an invitation to Pierre Létourneau, who interpreted a particular song as the song's subject looked on. 1980: Robert Tremblay began work, for a production company named Films d'aventures sociales du Québec, on a film (unfinished) entitled *Maurice Richard*, featuring Jean-Claude Germain. Many scholarly articles took up the question of hockey, and incidentally of Maurice Richard: "Éléments pour une phénoménologie du sport," by Hubert Aquin and Andrée Yanacopoulo (1972); "Essai de sémiologie du hockey: À propos de l'idéologie sportive," by Paul Rompré and Gaëtan Saint-Pierre, with Marcel Chouinard (1972); "Les Québécois, le hockey et le Graal," by Renald Bérubé (1973); "Crime et châtiment au Forum (Un mythe à l'oeuvre et à l'épreuve [Crime and Punishment at the Forum (A Myth at Work)]," by J.R. Plante (1975). Roch Carrier opened and closed the decade: in his 1970 novel *Il est par là, le soleil/Is it the Sun, Philibert?*, the eponymous hero leaps onto the ice at the Forum to avenge his idol; in 1979, with the short story

Sportorama

LA REVUE DU SPORTIF AVERTI DU CANADA FRANÇAIS   35 cents

- Rogatien Vachon, une lueur d'espoir pour le Canadien
- Un vélodrome dans la région montréalaise en 1968

Eight years after his retirement, Richard still plays for the NHL Old Timers.

"Une abominable feuille d'érable sur la glace," which would be reissued under the title "The Hockey Sweater / Le chandail de hockey," Carrier activated the process of (Canadian) mythmaking of the Rocket; the following year, he wrote the narration for Sheldon Cohen's animated short film based on his story, *The Sweater / Le chandail*.

The die had been cast.

Where Louis Chantigny's aim had been to transform Richard into a monument of universal glory, Jacques Poulin, Pierre Létourneau and Jean-Claude Germain, to name but a few, had made up their minds to fashion him into a symbol of national pride. They were simply following in the footsteps of those who, since the 1950s, had viewed him as the spokesman par excellence of the French Canadians. Their contribution to the mythmaking process came at the same time as a first wave of demythification. To represent Maurice Richard, even at that instant of discursive triumph, was no simple matter.

In *Le coeur de la baleine bleue / The Heart of the Blue Whale*, Noel, the main character, who has been given a young girl's heart in a transplant operation, is recovering slowly. His neighbour Bill is a professional hockey player, a winger by trade, who is nursing a left wrist wounded in an on-rink brawl. Brought together by Élise, Noel's wife, who will desert him for Bill, they chat: "We had long conversations about hockey." Noel is a "hockey nut," and he attempts to find out what Bill thinks about the National Hockey League players whom he has faced. The list is a long one: Bobby Hull, Yvon Cournoyer, Stan Mikita, John Ferguson, Eddie Shack, Bobby Baun, Robert Rousseau, Dick Duff and Jean Béliveau ("pure intelligence"). But two stand out: Gordie Howe, Bill's idol, who had left him with "a scar above his left eye", and Maurice Richard, whom he speaks about with less assurance ("You know, I was fairly young when Richard was at his best. So it isn't easy"). Though Bill cannot find much to say about Richard, the narrator is by no means in the same position:

Every time I spoke of Richard, heard his name, I felt something ancient move within me, like a beast that had been sleeping since the operation and now was stirring in its sleep.

For him, Richard was larger than life:

I was listening to the hockey player [Bill] but I felt like talking to him about the dazzling breakaways Richard would set up as he skated around the net, of the famous goal he scored with a player on his back, of his legendary battles, of the riot at the Forum and on rue Sainte-Catherine after President Campbell suspended him, of the sadness we felt at the sight of him dragging his leg at the end of his prodigious career.

The Rocket is connected with an individual and a collective past:

I wanted Bill to understand to what extent Richard's image was alive in the hearts of people my age and how remembering him stirred up such profound emotions they touched our deepest roots, back to the common heritage of our race.

But such things are hard to express:

I had a lump in my throat and I could feel those things churning inside me, but I couldn't explain them: on the surface there was a layer of gentleness, a sea of oil that blocked out everything.

When the narrator of *Le coeur de la baleine bleue* thinks of Richard, he thinks back over his memories, to a turning point in his life: surviving now with a heart that is not his own, he attempts to find out who he is and what is left of who he had been. But what is most striking is the collective dimension of his memories. As he strolls through Quebec City's Old Town, Noel evokes the places he had frequented, but they immediately call forth images "from the depths of my collective memory and my unconsciousness." Bringing Maurice Richard back from the past, he speaks of "something ancient," of a "fabulous" goal, of "legendary" battles, of his "prodigious" career. He would have liked for his interlocutor to grasp how "alive Richard was in the hearts of people [his] age." He goes on to speak of "our deepest roots" and of the "common heritage of our race." That particular Maurice Richard belongs to everybody; he is a shared, collective asset.

To reach a similar conclusion, Pierre Létourneau and Jean-Claude Germain would draw on a similar image. "You could have sworn he carried all of Quebec on his shoulders," sings the former; "I feel like a kind of Saint Christopher, hauling all Quebeckers on my shoulders!" the character of Richard cries out in the latter's play. It's a weighty responsibility, especially when one finds it difficult to express oneself as clearly as one would like.

Germain, in fact, draws a close parallel between the transformation of a historical figure into myth and the language spoken by that figure. His Louis Cyr had spoken at length of that relationship in the play's seventh scene. For Cyr was a master of the language, as Richard does not fail to note: "I'd have had it easy if I could talk as good as youse!"; thanks to his mastery, the strongman had come to accept his condition. He is capable of speaking "eye to eye with legend" and "eye to eye with the country." Richard, however, is "crushed by what it isn't ridiculous to call his fate," to quote from the stage directions. In Quebec, the status of myths is inextricably connected with their expression, and, indirectly, with language and its (non) mastery.

In the process, Jean-Claude Germain was contriving to kill two birds with one stone. On the one hand, the presence of Maurice Richard in *Un pays dont la devise est je m'oublie* springs from the desire to endow Quebec with myths of its own. On the other, by revealing Richard's uncertainties, the playwright joins in the (relative) demystification of those selfsame myths. Such oscillation between exaltation and criticism was typical of the Quebec of the 1970s.

Well before, at the end of the 1950s, there had been a first attempt at mythmaking, but it had no long-term impact; during the 1960s Richard's image was no longer that of the sports hero that it had once been, nor was it that of the myth that would be constructed in the 1970s. It is clear that the creation of the Maurice Richard myth was contemporaneous with the rise of a new Québécois nationalism, which was striving to ground itself in great figures. Three dates symbolize the process of renewal: in 1970, the Parti Québécois, whose program called for the secession of Quebec from the Canadian confederation, elected its first deputies; in 1976, the year in which the first version of Jean-Marie Pellerin's biography of Richard appeared and Germain's play premiered, that same party won a majority of seats in the Quebec National Assembly; in 1977, the Parti Québécois government adopted Bill 101, the "Charter of the French Language," whose first article declared, "French is the official language of Quebec." (It is essential to remember that the real Richard's political views have very little to do with the political significance his public persona was to be invested with. Maurice Richard could well have been a federalist; that would not have stopped the mythmakers from taking possession of his image.)

More than a few artists were involved in the process of sociopolitical renewal, two of whom turned their attention to the case of Maurice Richard: Jean-Claude Germain and actor Jean Duceppe, who recounts how attached he was to Richard in Gilles Gascon's documentary. At the same time, other creators were facing questions similar to those raised by Germain and Duceppe, but without referring directly to the Canadiens' number 9. First staged in 1971, *Ben-Ur*, a play by Jean Barbeau, presents the character of Benoît-Urbain Théberge, a security guard with the Brook's Agency and an avid reader of comic books. Victimized by constant sarcasm because of his name (the contraction of Benoît-Urbain into Ben-Ur), he seeks heroes in American comics (*The Lone Ranger, Tarzan, Zorro*) and regrets that Quebec can boast none of its own: even Jean Béliveau won't do, for "a hero, he lives forever..." But Ben-Ur will not have to wait too long before his dreams come true, for Quebec to acquire a mythology all its own.

The creation of the Maurice Richard myth in the 1970s can be interpreted in terms of "local" considerations: the political situation in Quebec and the role of artists in fostering it. But if we wish to understand how a newly created myth can become the object of criticism, such considerations must be put aside.

It should be remembered that sport and its ideology, at the beginning of the 1970s, had come under heavy fire in a massive campaign of demystification. In his survey of baseball player biographies, paleontologist Stephen Jay Gould identifies 1970 as the date of the radical break between biography as tribute and praise, and that which leaves nothing of a player's personal life unexamined, what he was to call "kiss-and-tell biography." That year saw the publication of *Ball Four* by New York Yankees pitcher Jim Bouton. After the "Boutonian revolution in baseball biography," wrote Gould, nothing would ever be the same again. Philip Roth's *The Great American Novel* appeared in 1973; its satire of American society as seen through its "national pastime" laid bare, in freewheeling fiction, baseball's ideological underpinnings. In 1972, the Swedish writer Per Olov Enquist, reporting from Munich, warned against the capitalist takeover of the Olympic Games:

> The Olympic Games are growing by leaps and bounds; they have become huge, spectacular productions for the masses. They have been assigned a pedagogical context: "In these Olympic games, it is more important to participate than to win," noted [an American bishop] in 1908. The words went on to assume historical status, the

motto of the Olympic ideal that was later attributed to Coubertin. The aphorism is as brilliant as it is perfectly efficient: *performance without reward*. The dream of every employer: the most important thing is not the worker's wage, but the right to work. Yet heroes have sprung up from the sports-starved masses, people who had triumphed due to their own efforts; and the pedagogy took up the refrain: those who are victorious have merited their victory. It is only just that they have attained the summit. Life is a pyramid; losers at the bottom; winners at the top. Such it is, and such it must always be.

What is perhaps most striking about this passage is its ideological interpretation of wage labour and merit, and its vocabulary—"perfectly efficient"—applied to sports.

Enquist's double-edged ideological interpretation and his choice of words also resonate, though indirectly, in Gilles Gascon's film whenever the issue of money and sports arises, as it often does. It is even more pronounced in J.R. Plante's "Crime et châtiment au Forum" and Paul Rompré and Gaëtan Saint-Pierre's "Essai de sémiologie du hockey," written with the collaboration of Marcel Chouinard. For Plante, Richard is the "ideal and avenging image of the Québécois proletarian." Rompré, Saint-Pierre and Chouinard write:

The exploitation of the hockey wage-earner / player (up to and including industrial accidents) does not call into question the alienating character of the industry. Quite the opposite, once it has been integrated into the mythical universe, the excess of labour appears as magnanimity. Far from harming that mythical dimension, it nourishes it. Here, the more the worker is alienated, the more he is magnified.

Drawing on the thought of theoreticians like Louis Althusser and Julia Kristeva, the authors are discussing the 1961 book by Andy O'Brien on

Maurice Richard. The former journalist at the *Standard* and *Weekend Magazine* would hardly have recognized himself in their analysis, but he would have concluded with pleasure that his hero had easily survived their attempt at myth deconstruction.

The turn of the century

At the end of the 1950s the process of mythmaking had swerved between proximity and distance. Proximity: Maurice Richard was a man like any other, a familiar face. Distance: Maurice Richard was different from all other players, a legend, perhaps even a myth. Later, during the 1970s, he was to be transformed into an exceptional being on several levels: a mythical figure for more and more people, the incarnation of the nation for most. Rare voices were raised in an attempt to return him to the world of mere mortals; those few commentators were wary of myths, but they could barely be heard. Between the two periods, in the 1960s, there had been a brief sojourn in purgatory; it was as if the image of Maurice Richard, seen as mired in tradition and unable to emancipate himself, had been unacceptable to the quiet revolutionaries of the day. The electoral slogan of the Quebec Liberal Party, "Maîtres chez nous" [Masters in our own house], didn't fit him, and his taciturn behaviour did not jibe with Quebec's entry into the "age of the spoken word," to borrow the title of a book of poems by Roland Giguère.

But at the end of the twentieth and the beginning of the twenty-first century things had changed. We must concede that the discourse on Maurice Richard no longer enjoys the lofty quality of Chantigny's and Germain's texts. The Rocket remains a myth, but a myth for contemporary tastes, without excessive originality. After being a neighbour of Icarus and Saint Christopher, he has now come back to Earth among his own kind. He is a Quebec myth, at once nearby and remote, familiar and extraordinary, a guy called Maurice, and a man called Mr. Richard.

For the younger generations who never saw him play, Maurice

Richard had established himself as a familiar figure: a remarkable feat. Books for young people had been written about him in the 1990s and 2000s, a clear indication that he now belonged to historical time, and of his metamorphosis into an object of edification: as a grandfather he gives wise advice to his grandchildren, while rekindling their parents' nostalgia. It can be no accident that Michel Forest (1991), Roy MacGregor (1995), François Gravel (1996), Henriette Major (1999), Michel Foisy (2000, 2003), Carmen Marois (2000), Pierre Roy (2000), David Bouchard and Dean Griffiths (2001), and Jack Siemiatycki and Avi Slodovnick (2002) all turned their attention to him at the same time.

The numerous tributes paid to Maurice Richard just prior to his death likewise contributed to the process of familiarization, and of mythmaking. Four of them were particularly significant. In March 1996 the Montreal Forum closed its doors, while the Molson Centre was inaugurated. There may have been no deliberate decision to focus the ceremonies surrounding those two events on Maurice Richard, but the focus he was, from standing ovations to parades; from tears (his own) to tears (those of his fans, of all generations). A few weeks later the exposition entitled "L'Univers Maurice 'Rocket' Richard" opened its doors at the Maurice Richard Arena; he had become a museum exhibit. At the end of the 1998–99 season the National Hockey League awarded for the first time a trophy for the top regular-season goal scorer: the Maurice Richard Trophy, which made official the Rocket's place in the history of his chosen sport, and ensured his continuing renown. Finally, when, in 1999, RDI / CBC Newsworld broadcast the miniseries *Maurice Richard: Histoire d'un Canadien / The Maurice Rocket Richard Story*, it reinforced a professionally orchestrated advertising campaign. In the presence of 104 members of his family, the show's masters of ceremonies and their invited guests repeated, in every possible way, that Maurice Richard was "someone larger than life, who never realized what an impact he made on so many people" (Marie-Josée Turcotte). Richard had been transformed into a living myth: he could not take his leave before society had declared its love for him, trumpeted the media in self-congratulatory tones.

At the turn of the century, following in the footsteps of Jeanne d'Arc Charlebois, Oscar Thiffault, Bob Hill, Denise Filiatrault and Pierre Létourneau, it was time for Éric Lapointe and Marie-Chantal Toupin to sing of Maurice Richard. In both cases, their songs were motion-picture spin-offs.

In *Les boys II* (in 2001, *Les boys III* would be dedicated "To Maurice Richard"), one of the great box-office successes of Quebec cinema in the late 1990s, Lapointe sings "Rocket (On est tous des Maurice Richard)" [Rocket (We're All Maurice Richards)]. The song, with words written by Lapointe and Roger Tabra, begins:

> We've all had our moment of glory
> We've all written a page
> In the great book of history
> Of a garage league.

Richard was close to his own people; everyman is henceforth close to him, from the Sunday hockey players whose adventures are immortalized in the *Les boys* film series to the song's listeners and the film's viewers.

For Charles Binamé's 2005 film *Maurice Richard*, Marie-Chantal Toupin sings "J'irai au sommet pour toi" [I'd Scale the Highest Peak for You]. The song's lyrics, by Claude Sénéchal, go:

> You can learn
> The wisdom of the great
> From the way they act.
> I'm not scared

Of getting hurt
Of insults thrown in my face.
I'm a big girl
And I'm proud
And so I'll be
My whole life long.

Marie-Chantal Toupin is no Gerry Boulet. Unlike the late lead
singer of the Quebec rock group Offenbach, who liked to transpose
Édith Piaf's classics, singing "I'll have my hair dyed blonde", she sings
not "I'm a big man, and I'm proud" but "I'm a big girl..." instead. Without carrying the identification as far as Boulet, she is Maurice Richard—but not exactly, and not quite.

Taken together, the two songs help us to realize where the status
of the myth stood at the turn of the century. The commonplaces of
the Richardian discourse are these: for Lapointe, violence ("checking,"
"brawl," "warriors"), nationalism ("down home guys") and eyes ("We've
got the Rocket's eyes"); for Toupin, taciturnity ("I don't say much"),
loving tenderness ("I still love you"), courage ("Even if I'm bruised and
battered / I'll never be scared"). Clearly the Maurice Richard story has
become a success story. Lapointe is categorical:

Every night's the big night
For victory is ours
The cup is full, we're going to drink
Our moment of glory has come.

Toupin is just as "big" and just as "proud":

From the way you were
I learned to win
To win in life.

A Myth

In hardship I found

The courage

Courage to give my all.

Maurice Richard is no longer the man who succeeded *in spite of* his own people, he who was bigger than them, while being all along their brother. Nor is he the man who succeeded *in lieu of* his own people, he who became a myth at the very moment that the nation was seeking one, never mind the naysayers. He is the man who succeeded *on behalf of* and *alongside* his own. "We're all Maurice Richards", sings Éric Lapointe.

The same thing would be said time and time again in the spring of 2000. The summit of the mythmaking process would finally be attained with Richard's death.

LAMENT FOR THE ROCKET

"Maurice is immortal, everybody knows that."

—RENALD BÉRUBÉ, "En attendant les buts gagnants"
    [Waiting for the Winning Goals], 2000

A man named Maurice Richard died on May 27, 2000; there is little point in denying it. But who exactly died that day?

The newspaper obituary's tone was solemn:

RICHARD, Maurice "Rocket"
1921–2000

On May 27, 2000, at the Hôtel-Dieu-de-Montréal, at age 78, died Mr. Maurice "Rocket" Richard, husband of the late Lucille Norchet. Aside from his companion Sonia Raymond, he leaves his children: Huguette, Maurice Jr., Norman, André, Suzanne, Polo and Jean, their respective spouses as well as his grandchildren, brothers, sisters, brothers-in-law, sisters-in-law, many nephews, nieces, relatives and numerous friends.

The body will lie in state at the Molson Centre from 8:00 AM Tuesday until 10:00 PM.

Funeral services will be celebrated at 10:30 AM Wednesday, May 31, at the Basilica of Notre-Dame-de-Montréal, by Jean-Claude Cardinal Turcotte.

In lieu of flowers, donations to the Centre hospitalier de l'Université de Montréal or to the Maurice Richard Foundation (1010 de La Gauchetière W., Bureau 1400, Montréal [Québec] H3B 2B2) would be appreciated.

Funeral director: Urgel Bourgie

Above the obituary, a photograph of the deceased dressed in a suit and tie, a smile on his face.

He who has just died is clearly a man of stature: the body will lie in state at the Molson Centre; a cardinal will celebrate the funeral services in a basilica; a foundation is named after him. He was a family man: one need only examine the long list of first names and relations that follows the announcement of his death. He had been sick: donations may be made in his memory to the Université de Montréal, which administers the Hôtel-Dieu Hospital. But there is no indication of what this Maurice "Rocket" Richard did for a living. Myths need no presentation: they are preceded, as are their deaths, by their aura.

Chronicle of a death foretold

It had long been known that Maurice Richard would die. On April 9, 1955, novelist Hugh MacLennan wrote of the 1954–55 season using the expression "dying years." Four years later, Louis Chantigny proclaimed "a tragic end for the Rocket." At the beginning of the 1970s, Pierre Létourneau, in his song "Maurice Richard," asked his public for forgiveness: "Forgive me today if I've talked like he was dead / 'Cause with his tricolour sweater, he was my life." In 1989, the principal character of the film *Life After Hockey / La vie après le hockey* wrote an imaginary letter to Richard: "Have you ever thought of death?" As he formulates the thought, the camera comes to rest upon a photo of the retired hockey star, as if the two were calling out to one another. Later on, newspapers and magazines kept close track of the course of his last illness. On July 4, 1998, *Dernière heure*, "The News Weekly," ran a photograph of an emaciated Maurice Richard on page 1, under the headline: "Maurice Richard: 'An Update on My Illness.' Verbatim Transcript of His Press Conference." Three months earlier, he had been pictured on the first page of *La Presse*: "I feel just fine!" read the headline. Richard described his condition (abdominal cancer), and the therapy he was undergoing. And added a confession: "It's the fear of meeting people that paralyzes me." It was as if a myth had admitted his physical decline. On September 12, 1998, once again on the first page of *La Presse*, Michel Blanchard announced that Richard's disease was in remission: "The Rocket's Greatest Victory."

And yet, he was dying.

The media had ample time to prepare. The facts (and the feats) had been assembled; the statistics collated; the stories stood waiting to be retold. The pictures—often the same ones—animated or still, were close at hand. There was no lack of sound clips. All that remained was to interview the high and mighty, and the humble, of this world, to open their pages, or their airwaves, to the public's own version, and to fling themselves into socio-mythico-historico-political interpretations of what had become by now something of phenomenal proportions. In such circumstances, the coherence of the funereal discourse was predictable. The narrative of Maurice Richard's life had already been written.

The Maurice Richards of spring 2000

More than one Maurice Richard would die in May 2000.

Even though the great majority of those who shed a tear for him had never seen him play, the funereal discourse enumerated the hockey player's exploits and his athletic qualities. The best-known stories were dusted off yet again: the five-goal game in 1944; the game after moving house, also in 1944; the goal against "Sugar" Henry in 1952; the 1955 riot; his retirement in September 1960; the ovation that followed the last Canadiens game at the Forum on March 11, 1996. Richard the player, people were reminded, existed only to score; he was at his most explosive when he crossed the opposing team's blue line; his backhand shot was devastating. He was compared to the usual great sports figures of the past, beginning with Babe Ruth, but also with the man from whom he was to be distinguished most clearly, Gordie Howe. But there was a single, recurring leitmotif: no one had ever been more determined than Maurice Richard on a hockey rink. The man who liked to claim that he was "only a hockey player" was most certainly a hockey player, but a most out-of-the-ordinary hockey player.

He was also a pioneer now lost to the nation of Quebec (to put it in media terms). In the past, he had been compared to other athletes or to political figures. Henceforth, the comparisons would become more audacious. In fact, it seemed as though everyone, from former Montreal mayor Jean Drapeau to then Canadian prime minister Jean Chrétien, from author Anne Hébert, as imagined by columnist Pierre Foglia, to Brother André, the miracle worker of Mount Royal, was fair game for comparison. Richard was still being placed alongside Paul-Émile Cardinal Léger and the other great Quebeckers of the past, but new categories had now made their appearance. Indeed, few commentators before his death would have thought to liken Richard to businessmen like J. Armand Bombardier (recreational vehicles, aircraft, subway and railway systems), Pierre Péladeau (media, printing), Paul

Desmarais (transportation, media): he had become the equal of those business empire builders (Bombardier, Quebecor, Power Corporation). The comparison to Félix Leclerc was not new, if for no other reason than the heavily publicized encounter between the two men in October 1983 that had taken place on the Île d'Orléans, Leclerc's home. The comparison was frequent in the spring of 2000, and just as frequently linked with another comparison of more recent vintage, that of former Quebec premier René Lévesque. Richard was seen as the equivalent, in sports, of the chansonnier and the politician; like them he had been an awakener and, as such, a precursor. Journalist Pat Hickey related that the player-owner of the Pittsburgh Penguins, Mario Lemieux, abstained from comparing Richard to anyone, but insisted that Richard had opened the door to French-speaking players in the National Hockey League. Whether or not the statement is arguable is beside the point, for it is entirely coherent with the media discourse of the last days of May 2000. Maurice Richard had blazed the trail.

The player and the pioneer were omnipresent. Normal enough, for in death Maurice Richard was a man who brought people together. Proof positive were the ceremonies staged in his honour. No sooner had his death been announced than the media became the spokesman for his family. They would have preferred a private ceremony, but were rapidly forced to agree to make public their mourning, so insistent was the demand. The public dimension of the mourning could be appreciated in four places.

No sooner had the news of Richard's death been broadcast than mourning fans sought out places in which to display their grief. The Forum, in the throes of its transformation into the Pepsi Centre, would never do for these early mourners, no more than did the Molson Centre, which they saw as too impersonal. Some rushed to the Hôtel-Dieu, where Richard had died, but the hospital was not closely enough connected with the hockey star for it to be suitable. The search was on

An admirer weeps in front of the statue of Maurice Richard.

for a symbolic location that could accommodate the greatest possible number. Or, in other words, where people could gather and pay their respects.

That place would be Richard's house, on Péloquin Street, in Montreal's north end. There flowers, souvenirs and farewell messages were deposited. Among the callers were many children:

> We have been your neighbours for more than nine years, and we have always admired you. Unfortunately, your death leaves a great emptiness in our Québécois heart. Francis Melanson. [Illegible] Melanson. 10884 St. Charles St.

Tears were being shed for someone close, sometimes even for a neighbour.

But not everyone knew where Maurice Richard lived. So they gathered at the arena named for him, in front of the statue depicting him. People of all generations converged upon it, to pay tribute to their hero. A Quebec flag would be draped over the shoulders of the bronze statue, along with a scarf bearing the Canadiens colours. Flowers would be laid at its feet, drawings, photos and collages, together with a motley assortment of objects (a roll of hockey tape, candles, cigars, hockey sticks). And there were messages too, dozens of them:

> Today there is one less
> Loved one on earth
> But . . . there is one more
> Star in the sky.
> Maurice CH #9

The tone of the messages, which addressed him by his first name, was familiar: "Farewell, big guy! We love you." "Maurice, to men like you we don't say farewell, we say, 'See you soon!!'" "Your memory is like a favourite book we will always read and never close. Thanks Maurice 9." "Your failing hands held high the torch; now, may they rest." "To the Rocket, be happy, and watch over me." Passersby and complete strangers traded stories among themselves or with journalists. Some even came to pray. This spontaneous altar, like that of Péloquin Street, would encounter none of the constraints of protocol of the other two official locations that were to symbolize the Maurice Richard cult. That doesn't mean they were more popular, but, clearly, people felt freer to express themselves.

On May 30 from 8:00 AM to 10:00 PM, Maurice Richard's body lay in state at the Molson Centre. Richard had never played there, but it was now home ice for the Canadiens and, as such, the obvious choice for the site of mourning. (There had been suggestions that his funeral be held there.) The casket was placed on the playing surface; the event was staged in an atmosphere of high solemnity. Richard's family stood close by. Two huge posters of the Rocket, one in black and white, an enlargement of an old photograph, illustrated the look in the star's eyes; the other, in full colour, depicted Richard wearing the red Canadiens sweater, number 9 of course, bearing a torch. The blue, white and red banner proclaiming that Maurice Richard's number had been retired never to be worn again by a Canadiens player had been lowered from the vaulted ceiling to rink level. The musical accompaniment was classical: Mahler, Gounod, Brahms, Satie, Massenet, Mozart, Vivaldi and Bach. More than 115,000 hockey devotees filed past the open casket of the idol of the house. Those who wished to do so could inscribe their testimonial in a book of remembrance located under a canopy near the Cours Windsor adjacent to the Molson Centre. The media were quick to compare the lying in state to that which had been held at the Forum in 1937 for Howie Morenz.

The following day, May 31, a national funeral service for Richard was celebrated in the city's Notre-Dame Basilica. From 1996 to 2004, in Quebec, only five other personalities had enjoyed the privilege. Before him, poet and publisher Gaston Miron (December 21, 1996) and former government minister and psychiatrist Camille Laurin (March 16, 1999). After him, painter Jean-Paul Riopelle (March 18, 2002), trade unionist Louis Laberge (July 24, 2002) and editorialist and government minister Claude Ryan (February 13, 2004). Two creative artists (one literary, the other a painter, to whom Richard had been compared), two government ministers (one pro-independence, the other federalist), a man of action who styled himself as a man of the people (Louis Laberge was known popularly as Ti-Louis): as if by coincidence, the company he kept in death defined Maurice Richard the man with surprising accuracy, right down to the contradictions.

The funeral procession arrived at the basilica after making its way along Saint-Catherine Street, that of the old Forum and of the Riot. Some three thousand people were allowed into the basilica, where his family and former teammates, political and media figures rubbed shoulders. Outside, on Place d'Armes, the ceremony was broadcast on a huge screen. Mass was celebrated by Jean-Paul Cardinal Turcotte. Paul Aquin, a close friend, one of Richard's nephews, Stéphane Latourelle, and his son Maurice Richard Jr. read the eulogies. Two passages from the Bible were read. The first, from the second Epistle of Saint Paul to Timothy (4:7–8), where the pride of having fought the good fight segues into the certainty of a reward to come: "I have fought a good fight. I have finished my course. I have kept the faith. Henceforth there is laid upon me a crown of righteousness..." The second was from the Gospel according to Saint John (14:2–3): "And if I go to prepare a place for you I will come again, and receive you unto myself; that where I am, there ye may also be." Popular vocalist Ginette Reno interpreted, as she had at her own father's funeral, "Ceux qui s'en vont, ceux qui nous laissent" [Those Who Move On; Those Who Leave Us].

(Céline Dion had been invited to perform, but declined for medical reasons: the future mother was flat on her back in a fertility clinic.) Music by Fauré, Gounod, Franck and Bach, hymns and psalms filled the air. The pallbearers were eight former Canadiens players, all of whom had played alongside Richard: Jean Béliveau, Henri Richard, Elmer Lach, Émile Bouchard, Ken Reardon, Kenny Mosdell, Dickie Moore and Gerry McNeil. Most of Quebec's French-language media outlets and several English-language television stations broadcast the entire ceremony live. In the Quebec National Assembly, debate was suspended; flags flew at half-mast.

The solemnity was equal to that of the previous day, even though it was modulated in different ways. Cardinal Turcotte, who was aware of Maurice Richard's love for the pastime, wished him good celestial fishing: "In heaven we find the apostles, who were famous fishermen . . . Fare thee well, Maurice, where the fishing is finest!" People cried out "Maurice, Maurice," using his first name without a second thought. The public applauded the closed casket, and offered him a final standing ovation, which startled English-Canadian sensibilities—but not those of Quebeckers.

From the east end of Montreal (Maurice Richard Arena) to the north (his home), from downtown (Molson Centre) to Old Montreal (Notre-Dame Basilica), Maurice Richard had brought together, in those final days of May 2000, hundreds of thousands of people, millions if we count the newspaper, radio, television and Internet reports. (Condolences could even be sent by e-mail to maurice.richard@canadiens.com.) The rare discordant voices to be heard offered no criticism of the man himself, but deplored, often with a certain lack of restraint, the unanimous nature of the discourse surrounding his demise and the extent to which it had monopolized public space. There had been no need for the death notice to introduce Maurice Richard: everybody knew him and sought to see themselves in him.

Presumed though it may have been, the identification drew strength from the fact that Maurice Richard, if we are to believe the media, had become one of Quebec's most familiar figures. Proof positive: whether they had known him or not, people called Richard "Maurice"—a Maurice who could be addressed in the most familiar tones and inflections. But what made him most familiar were the micronarratives that together shaped the overarching Richardian narrative, so reminiscent of members of a close-knit family: most of those with a Maurice Richard story to tell, and they were legion, would at the same time evoke family memories. Some of them, their numbers in steady decline, remembered having seen Richard play, and shared that memory with their children and grandchildren. Many were thus to associate Richard with their fathers or grandfathers: they had never seen him play, but they had heard what he was like. The interlocking structure of the familiar and of family memory had taken a paradoxical turn: Maurice Richard was close to everyone, a familiar face, even a member of the family, yet all the while he remained remote—those who shed tears for him had generally known him only through a third party. Reading rapidly through the testimonials of May 2000 serves only to heighten the impression of a double discourse: "I remember, because I heard the story."

The story as told was that of the hockey player, the pioneer, the man who brought people together, the man next door, the "everyman" (as radio commentator Christian Tétrault put it). But it was also that of a role model. Maurice Richard had an "inheritance" to be handed down (the word is omnipresent), a torch to be passed on (that of the photo at the Molson Centre), a message to be heard. Call him hero, legend, myth, symbol or idol, the underlying meaning, repeated in a multitude of ways, was the same: Maurice Richard cannot die; he must not die. He had been a violent player on the ice; but that only demonstrated his determination, the very determination that is called for today: the word was on everybody's lips in May 2000. He was a taciturn man; but words had little weight when measured against deeds, especially the heroic deeds uncritically attributed to him, for it is by deeds that success is henceforth to be measured, more than by words. He had been the embodiment of success for the French Canadians, then for the Québécois, even beyond their national borders; his was the example to be followed, that followed by Céline Dion, to name only her: the fighting spirits of the twenty-first century build their reputations on a global scale.

Nonetheless, a critical question looms: For whom was he a model? For French-speaking Quebeckers; for Quebeckers of all origins; for French Canadians; for Canadians? If unanimity breaks down at any point, it is here. No particular group has actually attempted to appropriate for itself and against another the memory of Maurice Richard, but from time to time tensions have run high.

French-speaking media never tire of telling anyone who might care to listen that Maurice Richard is a *national* myth, and by that they mean a *Québécois* myth. They may distinguish between *French-Canadian* and *Québécois*, but not much more. There is no question of a conflict: French-speaking commentators simply do not contemplate any other political context than that of Quebec to invest Maurice Richard with meaning. Whether in *La Presse* (Christian Dufour, Pierre Foglia, Lysiane Gagnon, Pierre Gravel, Nathalie Petrowski, André Pratte, Serge Rochon, Mario Roy, Réjean Tremblay), *Le Journal de Montréal* (Michel C. Auger) or *Le Devoir* (Jean Dion, Jean-Robert Sansfaçon), the interpretive framework is always the same. The *we* that weeps for Maurice Richard is a Québécois *we*; it is for "us" that Richard must be a model.

On the English-speaking side, the picture is more complex. Mike Keane, one of Richard's successors as Canadiens captain, when told that Rocket was a legend, an inspiration for French-speaking people, quickly begged to differ, reported Mario Leclerc of the *Journal de Montréal*: "He was a legend for the whole hockey world." Under a page 1 headline, "Au revoir, Maurice," the June 1, 2000, issue of the

Calgary Herald reported several similar statements. For commentator Don Cherry, among others, the Rocket was also a hero, beloved of all Canadiens, and not only of the Québécois: "People in Quebec loved the Rocket, but he was our hero, too."

Lawrence Martin, author of several books on Canadian politics, on Mario Lemieux and on the Canada-USSR hockey series of 1972, carried the pan-Canadian appropriation of Maurice Richard farther than anyone else: "Outside of Quebec, Richard is not seen, nor was he ever seen, as a symbol of a solitude." To underscore the argument Martin, a political columnist for the former Southam newspaper chain, drew a parallel, startling for French speakers, between Richard and Pierre Elliott Trudeau:

> Pierre Trudeau always had a remarkable air of defiance about him. On the international stage he made short work of the image of Canadians as cattle. On the home front, few could challenge him. From the blue line in, he would carve you to pieces.

Richard and Trudeau (who would die in September 2000): to connect those two names, and to plead their case as models of Canadian patriotism, to marry a nationalist icon with the champion of federalism, one should either not be a French-speaking Quebecker, or be prepared to resist the common discourse on Maurice Richard, what could be termed the vulgate. (It is useful to be aware that Martin sees the Rocket almost everywhere he turns. In *Iron Man*, the second volume of his biography of former Canadian prime minister Jean Chrétien, he compares the fiery gaze of sovereignist leader Lucien Bouchard to that of Maurice Richard.)

That there exists a Québécois Maurice Richard and a Canadian Maurice Richard should come as no surprise. The Rocket of the Quebeckers and that of the Canadians are not the same, although there is little to distinguish them. Nor are they myths of the same order; in fact, while *myth* is the appropriate term in Quebec, it is not at all certain that it can be applied to Maurice Richard the Canadian.

The last Maurice Richard to be buried on May 31, 2000, could not have been predicted. For Alain Gerbier, of the Paris daily *Libération*, Quebec had lost, in Richard, its "saint of the skating rink." Local media, in a typically Francophobe reaction, mocked the "religious" conception of Richard's character, but they might have asked themselves if such an image had not already surrounded them. They would have soon realized that it was alive and well in Quebec. *Le Devoir*, in an editorial cartoon by Garnotte; *La Presse*, by Chapleau; not to mention the *Journal de Montréal*, insisted that a saint had died. That selfsame *Journal de Montréal* went as far as to speak of a "god." The people who signed the register at the Cours Windsor were thinking along the same lines: "The Rocket, chosen of God"; "After God is Maurice"; "Thank you, O God, for giving us Maurice." *The Gazette* (Montreal) struck a similar tone, when it quoted former referee Red Storey on May 28, 2000: "He wasn't the greatest skater in the world, he wasn't the greatest stickhandler in the world, but the guy upstairs sent him down to show everybody how determination could score goals." None better than He could give meaning to what must return to dust. (Five years later, under the pen of Alain de Repentigny, the hockey star had almost been transformed, in the eyes of his fans, into a holy relic: "Talking to Maurice was like touching a holy shroud." And in 2007, Réal Béland was to pray to "Our Father the Rocket Who Art in Heaven.")

A final resting place

Maurice Richard was buried in a casket manufactured by the Victoria-ville Group. The fact became public knowledge following publication of an "infomercial" published in *La Presse*. Headlined "Entrepreneur," the "news story" went on to describe how the Roynat Capital Corporation, "Canada's business banking leader," had sponsored a series of portraits "paying tribute to successful Canadian businesses." The May 6, 2005, item began with the following words:

> What do Maurice Richard, Robert Bourassa, Jeanne Sauvé and even the Unknown Soldier have in common? Each of them has been laid to final rest in a casket signed Victoriaville Group, Canada's leading wooden casket manufacturer, and the second largest in North America.

Alongside a former Quebec premier, a former governor general of Canada and the personification of military sacrifice, the unknown soldier of World War I whose remains had been repatriated to Ottawa a few days before Richard's death, the onetime hockey great, five years after his death, continued to be an excellent advertising vehicle for the 100,000 caskets and "cremation oriented receptacles" built annually by the Victoriaville Group. Many other firms likewise profited from Richard's death to promote themselves: Ultramar oil, Staples business supply chain, Molson Brewery, financial institutions (Desjardins Financial Services, the National Bank of Canada), McDonald's Restaurants, the Sports Experts sporting-goods store chain, radio stations CKAC and CJAD, Air Canada, Warner Brothers, *La Presse* and Loto-Québec ("Loto-Québec salutes a great winner"...). The Victoriaville Group had simply delayed a little longer than the others. True enough, it would have been indelicate to advertise caskets any earlier.

The Rocket's ashes were inhumed at Montreal's Notre-Dame-des-Neiges cemetery. Daily newspaper readers would have found out when his funerary monument was inaugurated on August 4, 2001, which would have been his eightieth birthday. Visitors to the cemetery have a hard time avoiding the massive composition, with its square base, its five truncated, unequal granite columns, the torch in the middle, the inscriptions ("RICHARD" appears twice, along with "NE JAMAIS ABANDONNER / NEVER GIVE UP," his motto), his hand cast in bronze, his signature and the insignia of his team, a portrait of himself and his wife, young and smiling, all in bronze. The statue, by Jules Lasalle, to whom we owe the statue of Richard in front of the arena of the same name, stands close to that of a former mayor of Montreal, beside whom he was often photographed: Jean Drapeau.

Let us compare, for a moment, his monument with that of baseball hero Roger Maris. In 1944–45, Maurice Richard had accomplished a feat that was to remain unmatched for many years: fifty goals in fifty games. Maris had beaten Babe Ruth's record for home runs in a single season—sixty-one—in 1961. He lies buried in the Holy Cross cemetery, in Fargo, North Dakota. His gravestone is simple: a black square resting upon one of its corners. His last name, Maris, is inscribed on the back of the stone; on the front, the name is repeated, and beneath it, the image of a baseball slugger, the numbers "61 / 61" and the words "Against all odds." It is the grave of a great baseball player, not that of a myth.

AGAINST MAURICE RICHARD

Is it possible, in 2009, to reject Maurice Richard's mythical stature? Has anyone ever attempted to do so? The first answer that pops into one's mind is the question: Why shouldn't they? The second is that though such a position is indeed feasible, it is not widely accepted, nor has it left its mark. Though the author of these lines has heard, as a guest on an open-line radio show, the case *against* Maurice Richard as being supposedly untalented and lazy, it should be seen as one of those exceptions that confirm the rule.

Michel-Wilbrod Bujold admires Maurice Richard the man, the victim of Clarence Campbell, but he finds Maurice Richard the player less convincing. While he accuses him neither of lack of talent nor of laziness, he blames him, in *Les hockeyeurs assassinés* [The Murdered Hockey Players] (1997), for not knowing how to use his stick as a true artist should have. Richard is not among the chosen few stickhandlers to be admitted to his "Hall of Obscure Fame"; Bujold judges Camille Henry to be his superior, or, keeping it in the family, his brother Henri.

Among the other (rare) exceptions, we can point to expressions of exasperation at the time of Richard's death, only to put them immediately aside. The commemorative frenzy that swept over Quebec society in May 2000 did not incriminate the figure of the Rocket. The target was "media puffery," which the weekly paper *Ici* twice lashed out at in its June 1, 2000, issue. One writer attacked the "cold meat" devoted to Richard, as the death notices prepared in anticipation of the death of public figures are known in the journalists' trade. The second one went even farther:

> Obscene, pitiable, smutty, rotten-fleshed, sick, abject, wretched, indecent or scabrous: those are only a few of the objectives that come to mind when it comes to describing the behaviour of certain media after Maurice Richard's death.

Michel Brunelle, in the fall of 2000, would prove equally cynical, but on a different level. "Rocket Knock-out," published in the literary journal *Moebius*, began with these words: "The Rocket is dead. Considering the immense mobilization touched off by the event, it is entirely legitimate to scrutinize the social phenomenon that it has embodied. Maurice Richard was a hero. *The idol of a people.*" Moving from a preliminary statement of fact, the author offers a critique of the Richard mythology, that "credulous credo," the *"Maurice Richard effect."* Brunelle grounds his critique in a political assertion: the veneration of "our supposed hero" has had no impact whatsoever on the demand for the creation of a Quebec state. Hockey had nothing more to offer the nation than "proxy victories"; it led, in fact, to no veritable liberation; the March 1955 riot had been nothing more than a "flash in the pan," a "placebo." His (historical) diagnosis is anything but dainty:

Seeing Maurice Richard win was enough to satisfy the ambitions of people [two generations of Quebeckers] who did not believe in themselves, to soothe artificially their feelings of submissiveness, to relieve them of attempting to free themselves, either individually or collectively.

To put it in the manner of Karl Marx, or of the 1970s: sport is "the opium of the people." Just as Richard, seen in such terms, would have been a passive object in the hands of the mythmakers, Brunelle in turn transforms him into a symbol: that of failure—of a collective and not an individual failure. Ultimately Maurice Richard, whom he recognizes as "an . . . exceptional man," means little to Brunelle. What counts for him are the relations between the Québécois and "the English."

In his overview of masculine models in Quebec, *Échecs et mâles* [Failures and Men] (2005), Mathieu-Robert Sauvé enumerates "fourteen types of men," among which we find "the hero." He goes on to identify specimens in several spheres of activity, including sports. "Authentic" Quebec sports heroes really do exist, and most of them are hockey players. Maurice Richard is among them, but he does not occupy a prominent place. Sauvé levels the same reproach at him as he does at the others: you are all heroes, but one-dimensional heroes only. For you, there is no such thing as life off the ice. Sauvé is particularly occupied by athletes' lack of involvement in politics, a point on which he and Michel Brunelle see eye to eye.

After the great excess of 2000, of which the *Ici* and *Moebius* articles were part and parcel, the year 2005 witnessed an effusion of panegyrics. The occasion was the release of *Maurice Richard,* the feature film directed by Charles Binamé with a script by Ken Scott. Praise was unanimous, for the actors and for the quality of the historical reproduction of Quebec society between the 1930s and 1955. The publicity campaign that preceded the opening was the costliest in the history of Quebec cinema, estimated at $2 million for a film that had cost $8 million. The media—the Internet, radio, television and the press— did their part. A contest was organized to recruit young athletes whose determination could be compared to the film's hero.

Amidst the concert of praise, a single, radically discordant voice was heard: that of Lysiane Gagnon, writing in *La Presse* on December 13, 2005. Wondering aloud about the Quebec embodied by Maurice Richard in the 1950s, and about his connection with twenty-first-century Quebec, the columnist baldly asserts: "Off the ice, Maurice Richard was a loser." She is less concerned with the film as such than with the light it sheds on the evolution of society. For Gagnon, the process of evolution had been such that Quebec movie-goers could not possibly recognize in the film the society in which they live today. Montreal has been transformed, French speakers have risen to dominant positions in the economy, and the French language has acquired a new status since the 1970s: in short, everything has changed. Quebeckers "no longer see themselves" in the image of a "loser" like that of the Rocket. Where Michel Brunelle saw the Maurice Richard cult as the source of political failure, Gagnon believes that, in 2005, it is impossible to identify politically with the hero of the film. (Gagnon's consistency should be noted: on June 1, 2000, she had written about the tactical manipulation of Maurice Richard, seen as a "winner" at the time, for partisan political purposes.)

Her dissonant interpretation would have meant little had it been an entirely isolated one. But, in an implicit and perfectly unexpected way, it confirmed the Binamé-Scott duo's reading of the Richard phenomenon. The film's advertising campaign, reinforced by the film critics, hammered away at one central argument, the one that dominated the funereal discourse of 2000: Maurice Richard was a model of determination. And yet, in the film, that same determination is not seen to match the claims being made for it.

There was no doubt whatsoever that, on the ice, Richard was the personification of determination. The film's creators had made the principal components of the Richardian legend their own: the five goals against Toronto, which won their author three game stars; the eight points on the evening after moving house in the snow; the goal scored with Earl Siebert on his back; the goal against "Sugar" Henry only a few moments after being seriously injured; the September 13, 1955, game in Boston during which Richard attacked an official; the Riot. In each of these sporting circumstances, Richard surpassed himself; nothing could have stood in his way.

But no sooner did he step off the ice than Richard lost that determination. The Binamé-Scott film addresses the Rocket's double life with considerable subtlety. When it came to politics, to questions of how to behave and to think, others answered for him: a union shop steward at the factory where he works as a machinist; his wife; a teammate (Émile Bouchard); the team's general manager (Frank Selke); his barber (Tony Bergeron). After a flare-up of rebellion, he just as quickly falls back into line: after Richard signs an article bitingly critical of Clarence Campbell, Frank Selke forces him to retract. Others may rebel in his name, but Richard remains a timorous soul. Such is the meaning of his message to the fans the day after the Riot, when he calls upon them to stop "making trouble." Maurice Richard was no Muhammad Ali.

Among those who show the film's Maurice Richard the way, one plays a key role: his coach Dick Irvin. In Charles Binamé and Ken Scott's hands, he emerges as a complex individual. Irvin incarnates the "Englishman," the local boss, the foreman. Unable to speak French to players who do not speak English (well), this English speaker gives them instructions in his own language, thereby representing a power that is insensible to the values of those over whom it is exercised. The same is true for the persona of the local boss: the film's Dick Irvin never hesitates to humiliate Richard (having one of his teammates attack him, not giving him a chance to play, berating him). At the same time, the film blunts the two-faced aspect of his character. On the one hand, after the Canadiens have won the Stanley Cup, Irvin, a sheaf of paper in hand, congratulates his players in broken French; the locker room erupts in cheers. On the other, in one of the final scenes, he confesses to Richard that he had pushed him as far as he could only to make him a better player. By then, the viewer is up to his neck in stereotypes: the ostensibly hard-hearted coach who attempts to bring out the best from an unwitting champion is one of the hoariest standbys of popular films.

In the end, the Maurice Richard depicted by the film is a man (often) and a hockey player (sometimes) incapable of personal initiative. To assert that for many years he had remained under other people's thumbs should not be taken to mean that he was a "loser." But it would be appropriate to wonder if he was truly the determined "winner" that the commonly accepted discourse so readily makes him out to be.

If we are to take the full measure of the myth, it may be useful to discover who has agreed to speak *against* him.

THE ROCKET AMONG THE ENGLISH

"The Rocket is not just a hockey player, he's a true piece of Canadiana."
—JEFFREY MORRIS, *Beckett Hockey Card Monthly*, September 1998

Among French-speaking Quebeckers, the prevailing discourse is (virtually) unanimous: Maurice Richard was the (athletic) knight of the French Canadians in their struggle against the (nasty) English, whether English Montrealers, English Canadians or Americans.

Let us test this hypothesis against two contemporary texts.

It is certainly this widely shared discourse that we find in the person of Philibert, the hero of Roch Carrier's *Is it the Sun, Philibert?*

(1970), and in the novel's narrator. Philibert, inebriated, finds himself at the Forum, in a state of high excitement at being there, and having Maurice Richard before him:

> And there it was! Number nine, the great Maurice Richard, the man with dynamite in his fists, the rocket-man who sped down the ice like a solitary bird in the vast blue sky.
> "*Baptême!* It isn't true! It's real but it isn't true! *Hostie!* I can see Maurice Richard. It can't be! I don't see him!"

When Richard played in the National Hockey League, it consisted of six teams, four American (Boston, Chicago, Detroit and New York) and two Canadian (Montreal and Toronto), even though the players, with the odd exception, were Canadian. On that night, the two Canadian teams were meeting, that of the French Canadians and that of the English Canadians. As Philibert looks on, the Rocket charges into the zone of the opposing team, the Maple Leafs.

> Maurice Richard crossed the blue line, then the red line, into the territory of the *maudits Anglais* from Toronto.
> "Kill 'em!"
> Philibert stood up.
> "Kill 'em, Maurice!"

At that moment, a Maple Leafs player trips up Richard: "The *maudit Anglais* had hooked Maurice Richard! They couldn't take it when a little French Canadian like Richard was better than them." The act sends Philibert into a fury; he leaps onto the ice to avenge his idol.

> The Leaf turned his head and Philibert's fist landed in his teeth. The player wobbled foolishly, unable to locate the ice under his skates. He teetered and then fell full-length on the ice, crushed by the laughter all around him.

It is Philibert's day of glory. "He was surrounded by so much warmth and friendship that he wouldn't need to be liked by anyone else as long as he lived." The crowd applauds, people pat him on the back, stroke his head. But that is not all, nor is it enough: "Because he was watching through tears, Maurice Richard was moving down below with unbearable awkwardness across the ice." Philibert has brought tears to Maurice Richard's eyes! (One might have the impression that Philibert is crying, due to the ambiguous syntax of the sentence, but it is more interesting to see a myth shed tears than a character from a long-forgotten novel.)

Few would criticize Montreal-born novelist and essayist Mordecai Richler for excessive sympathy for Quebec nationalism, against which he would lash out at every possible opportunity. But that did not stop him from being a fervent Maurice Richard fan. Richard is present in several of his novels, including *Barney's Version* (1997). In a profile of Gordie Howe for *Inside Sports* (1980), he wrote, of necessity, of the other number 9. In the Richlerian representation of Richard, what is perhaps the critical scene is played out in Eilat, in Israel, in March 1962. Richler describes it in an essay entitled "This Year in Jerusalem: The Anglo-Saxon Jews." At the bar of the Eilat Hotel, Richler is having a discussion with a drunken Israeli fisherman. The fisherman, named Bernard, does not like Canadians, something he takes pains to repeat. Richard can respond only in these terms: "Well, I'm a Canadian . . . Like Maurice Richard." What could be seen only as absurd humor—it strains credulity that Bernard could recognize the hockey player—rapidly turns to questions about identity. From Richard, Richler moves on to the definition of what constitutes a Canadian Jew ("I am a Canadian Jew"), and on to the defense of all Canadian Jews. Richler never manages to convince Bernard (who accuses him of trying to assimilate) nor the hotel bartender; the evening turns out to be "altogether unsatisfactory." The important thing is Richler's search for an identity, and its source. MR needed MR.

What then are we to conclude? Was Maurice Richard the exclusive champion of the French Canadians against the "nasty English"? A marker of identity for English Canadians? A myth for the former, or for the latter, or for both? Is "le Rocket" also "the Rocket"?

THE ROCKET

To assess the status of Maurice Richard in the eyes of English speakers, in both Quebec and Canada, we must take into account his undisputed success on both sides of the language barrier, and the invitations he received from one end of the country to the other. We must attempt to surmount the seemingly endless opposition between Gordie Howe and Maurice Richard, with each number 9 symbolizing a Canada distinct from its counterpart. Both before and after the 1955 riot, who was *the others'* Maurice Richard? Indicators of his importance, and of his success, abound.

Some of the products that used the Rocket's name were destined exclusively for the French-speaking market, while others were intended for the English-speaking public. In the National Hockey League, when the Nordiques abandoned Quebec City, they became the Colorado Avalanche; the Montreal Rocket, of the Quebec Major Junior Hockey League, did not change its name when it moved to Charlottetown, where it simply became the PEI Rocket. In a bygone era, skate manufacturers Daoust Lalonde, Equitable Life (USA) and Prudential Life (Canada), Vitalis hair conditioner and the inventors of General Electric's Show'n Tell, to name but a few, had a message to convey, and they decided to address the English-Canadian or American audience in their language, using the image of Maurice Richard. Their motivation was certainly not philanthropic; there was a dollar to be made.

Several books about Maurice Richard, or about his life and times, exist in both official languages. They include works by Ed Fitkin (1951),

Will he charge the net like Maurice Richard?

Charge, fake, turn and shoot — Maurice Richard made the hard shots look easy. He could shoot and score lying flat on the ice, or make the goal while pinned to the boards. In his exciting 18-year career, "Rocket" Richard scored 544 goals, nearly twice the total of any player before him.

Not every youngster can be a Maurice Richard. In fact, very few even participate in organized sporting events, much less become stars. But every young person — if only a spectator — can be as physically fit as the star athlete.

Our national leaders have stated that physical fitness, particularly the fitness of our young people, has never been more important than it is today.

To support the national fitness program, Equitable has prepared a special film: "Youth Physical Fitness—A Report to the Nation." If you would like to borrow a print of this film for showing to community groups, contact your nearest Equitable office or write to Equitable's home office.

The **EQUITABLE** Life Assurance Society of the United States

Home Office: 1285 Avenue of the Americas, New York, N.Y. 10019

For an attractive 7¾ by 11 inch reproduction of this drawing, send your name and address and the words, *Maurice Richard*, to: Equitable, G.P.O. Box 1828, New York, N.Y. 10001.

© Equitable 1965

Advertisement for the Equitable Life Assurance Society of the United States.

Andy O'Brien (1961), Maurice Richard and Stan Fischler (1971), Craig MacInnis (1998), Chrystian Goyens, Frank Orr and Jean-Luc Duguay (2000), Roch Carrier (2000), David Bouchard and Dean Griffiths (2002), Jack Siemiatycki and Avi Slodovnick (2002), and I. Sheldon Posen (2004). Most of them were first written in English and then translated. Two were written for young people and were published in 2002, which demonstrates that the impulse to hand down the Richard legacy from one generation to the next is still strong. Likewise, Roch Carrier's short story "Une abominable feuille d'érable sur la glace / The Hockey Sweater" (1979), Sheldon Cohen's short animation film based on it for the National Film Board and the young people's inspirational story *The Value of Tenacity: The Story of Maurice Richard* not only exist in French and English, but are used as pedagogical material in French courses for schoolchildren in English Canada: those who used it would be learning something more than a second language.

On the subject of the Rocket, English-speaking singers, composers and musicians have proven no less prolix than their French-speaking counterparts. Jeanne d'Arc Charlebois, Oscar Thiffault, Denise Fili-atrault, Pierre Létourneau, Éric Lapointe, Les mecs comiques, Marie-Chantal Toupin, Réal Béland and Alain-François all sang of the Rocket. The same year as Thiffault (1955), as we have already noted, Bob Hill and his Canadian Country Boys launched their "Saga of Maurice Richard." At the end of the 1950s, reports Andy O'Brien in his *Rocket Richard*, "The Rocket, the Pocket and Boom," a song with words by Bob Sabloff and music by Rusty Davis, enjoyed considerable success in Montreal, and in Toronto, as part of a musical show entitled *Up Tempo*. Nearly fifty years later, a British Columbia resident, Robert G. Anstey, was to do even better, with his *Songs for the Rocket* (2002), comprising not one song but twenty-seven. At the 2003 Juno Awards, country diva Shania Twain wore a costume inspired by the Rocket, with a dusting of sequins. There exists a "Reel de Rocket Richard," which was interpreted by Gabriel Labbé (1999) and by *Le rêve du diable* (2002); written circa 1956, it was composed in Ontario by Graham Townsend before being popularized in the Maritimes by fiddler Gerry Robichaud (1973).

The world of motion pictures and television has proved to be no different. Some productions were originally in English, then translated into French: *Here's Hockey! / Hockey* (1953), *Life after Hockey / La vie après le hockey* (1989), *Fire and Ice: The Rocket Richard Riot / L'Émeute Maurice Richard* (2000). In some cases, the French version came first: *Le sport et les hommes / Of Sport and Men* (1961), *Histoires d'hiver / Winter Stories* (1996), *Maurice Richard: Histoire d'un Canadien / The Maurice Richard Story* (1999). In certain cases, it is difficult to know which language came first: *Le chandail / The Sweater* (1980), *Le Rocket / The Rocket* (1998), *Maurice "Rocket" Richard* (1997). Of the twenty-some films and television programs viewed in preparation for this book, eight were produced by the National Film Board of Canada; of those eight, four exist in both languages. Charles Binamé's *Maurice Richard* (2005) becomes, in English, *The Rocket* (2006). The film is also peculiar in that while it was filmed in French, it has almost as many lines in English. Some audiovisual documents exist in one language only (*Hockey Lessons*, 2000), but most of them are for television broadcast, which may provide an explanation.

And what of writers and poets, you ask? Born in North Dakota of an English-Canadian father and a French-Canadian mother, Clark Blaise often turns to sports in his novels, particularly baseball, but also hockey. In "I'm Dreaming of Rocket Richard" (1974), the narrator recalls his childhood and how he used to go to the Forum in the 1950s dressed in a Boston Bruins hockey sweater, the better to cheer on Richard. Better (or worse) still, his father had had the Rocket tattooed on his back: "The tattoo pictured a front-faced Rocket, staring at an imaginary goalie and slapping a rising shot through a cloud of ice-chips." Like his mother, the lad feels nothing but shame for his

Advertisement for Daoust skates in the *Star Weekly*, Toronto, November 24, 1951.

father and his tattoo, mostly because his Florida cousins make fun of it. Perhaps it was "a kind of tribal marking"? Perhaps the boy bore the same mark as his father? Adore the Canadiens and the Rocket though he might, he does not (literally) wear them on his skin.

Scott Young knows Maurice Richard's career like the back of his hand. His novel *That Old Gang of Mine* (1982) features a Finnish hockey player, Juho Juontainen, a quiet, quick, strong, sometimes violent, short-fused and vindictive man with a knack for the offensive game. "He looked like old pictures Pete had seen of Rocket Richard." But Young is interested in more than appearances. At the beginning of chapter 20, he brings to life, without saying so, the events of March 13, 1955, in Boston, with Juontainen in the role of the Rocket, rewriting in the end Clarence Campbell's decision, which had led to the Riot. We are dealing with a scholar and a connoisseur.

Kevin and Sean Brooks's anthology *Thru the Smoky End Boards* (1996) and that of Michael P.J. Kennedy, *Going Top Shelf* (2005), include five poems containing Richard's name. In "Arena," Don Gutteridge speaks to the man who, via television, had "carried [his] boyhood," pointing to his greatness, and imagines that he is standing beside the diminished former star who leaves the rink "in Roman ruin" upon retirement. Jane Siberry, in her song "Hockey," thinks back fleetingly to the Riot. Roger Bell broke into tears on the day that he discovered that Richard was a man of flesh and blood: "In the Hockey Hall of Fame I Sat Down and Wept." Al Purdy's "Hockey Players" links the grandstands with the rink: the orgasm of the spectators becomes indistinguishable from that of the three players he most admires, including Richard. The most complex poem, in English and French, is "Homage to Ree-shard," again by Purdy. It is clear that the Canadiens' number 9 occupies a lofty place in the Canadian imagination, and that the evocation of him strikes to the depths of individual and collective memory. Let us have a closer look at this long (114 verses) poem.

From its very first words, Purdy summons up commonplaces. "Frog music in the night" evokes the countryside, where the poet lives and writes; it also echoes one of the most venerable Canadian racial insults, "frogs" being French speakers—an insult to which Maurice Richard never failed to react violently. The poem is also a locus of memory, which draws upon conversations between the poet and his friend Dave Williams at Roblin Lake, upon childhood souvenirs and lingering regrets. What we encounter is a fabulous collection of bric-a-brac: historical allusions (the founding of Montreal by Maisonneuve, the battle on the Plains of Abraham in 1759, Marie-Antoinette, Napoléon); reminders of Richard's exploits (goals scored carrying players on his back, his fights); sports (baseball, hockey) and mythological (Achilles, Alexander) comparisons; a brief reference to the Riot; reflections on the mythical dimension of hockey in Canada, from Saskatchewan to Quebec by way of Ontario; conventional images (eyes, speed); other less conventional ones (poverty surrounding the factories of Montreal's east end); surprising proper names (Jung, Freud); a false disclaimer ("Rocket, you'll never read this"). As in Blaise, dreams play a prominent role: "And then I dreamed Ree-shard." The penultimate verse of Purdy's homage—for it is indeed a homage—ends with a line fraught with significance: Richard "made Quebec Canadian." Could there be more conclusive proof that Richard is a national treasure "from shore to shore"?

A pan-Canadian icon

We might well limit ourselves to enumerating parallels, matching discourses and comparing descriptions. But we might also investigate what values English Canadians associate with the image of Maurice Richard.

Feelings of familiarity were no less intense than among French speakers. The magazine *Les Canadiens*, in 1999–2000, quoted a

Shania Twain (2003) and Céline Dion (1998) pay tribute to the Canadiens' number 9.

sentence by Red Fisher, of *The Gazette*, which made it perfectly clear: "Maurice Richard was family."

Pride was a factor. Ken Dryden was adamant in his panegyric, written for *Time* magazine:

> No other Canadian could have generated such a gathering. There was sadness and celebration, but deeper than that, there was pride. In that church and outside, the feeling was unmistakable: pride in being Montrealers and Montrealais, Quebeckers and Quebecois, Canadians and Canadiens; pride in being current players and old-time players; pride in being whatever it is that makes you proud. Pride in sharing the same space and time as Maurice Richard. Forty years after his retirement, he had made us proud again.
>
> Good for you, Maurice. *Merci.*

An "us" had fused together, and for that, Maurice Richard was to be thanked. That "us," furthermore, did not exist in one language to the exclusion of the other.

Nationalism, too. Hockey insider Pat Quinn used striking terms in an interview with a reporter from the *Calgary Herald* the day after Richard's funeral:

> He was a symbol of struggle to all Canadians, not just Quebeckers... For my generation, he symbolized the desire to get out from under the British flag, that we were no longer a colony and we had to stand on our own as a country. He made us proud to be Canadian.

This particular form of national pride, even though it was not that of the French Canadians / Québécois, nor as systematically asserted, was no less real. (It is unlikely that our subject, who had some difficulty in identifying with his political portrait in Quebec, could have identified with the above either.)

Familiarity, pride and nationalism were easy to recognize in 2000, in English as in French. The concert of praise had the effect of concentrating the public mind: it was an occasion, each person for him or herself, and collectively, to assign a meaning to what Richard had been, in Canada as well as in Quebec. Declarations on the Canadianness of the hockey star, however, were far removed from the French-language media discourse.

But we would be wrong to presume that the Canadian national claim to Maurice Richard dates back only to recent years. The products, texts, pieces of music and audiovisual documents we have been discussing all remind us that the process really began more than fifty years ago. Before the Riot and the contradictory views that boiled up around it, questions relating to Maurice Richard's place in Canadian society had begun to be raised. It is in this perspective that the two articles by Hugh MacLennan published in 1955, one a few weeks before the Riot, the other several days after, must be placed. The journalist-novelist examines in what way Richard is a hero for French speakers, what he represents for English Montrealers, how he had become almost "a tribal god" for the "Canadians" (i.e., French Canadians), what is "the real focal point" of Canada. That an author of his celebrity should take interest in Maurice Richard confers a certain respectability on this kind of speculative thinking. The same would be true of other renowned English-Canadian authors, among them Mordecai Richler and Al Purdy.

The two solitudes

There can be no doubt about the Rocket's specific function among English Canadians, nor that he had become a pan-Canadian icon. From Waterloo (Ontario) to Sardis (British Columbia) and from Turtleford (Saskatchewan) to Halifax (Nova Scotia), he lent cohesion to Canadian society, if only at the level of sports. That being the case, it remains unlikely that the English speakers' Maurice Richard would be exactly the same as the French speakers'. Let us then attempt to tell them apart.

"A mari usque ad mare" (From sea to sea), to employ the motto of Canada, Maurice Richard was a sports star, perhaps one of the first superstars. He was also a symbol: about this there is little disagreement.

That he was a hero is an oft-repeated truism. Whether we are reading Hugh MacLennan, Andy O'Brien, George Sullivan, Stan Fischler or Craig MacInnis, listening to Bob Hill or to the cast of the *Up Tempo* review, watching Kenneth Brown in Tom Radford's film or being browbeaten by Don Cherry in the media, the word keeps popping up. *Reluctant Hero* was the title of Chrystian Goyens and Frank Orr's book. The operation undoubtedly coincided with the cautious Canadian search for heroes, as Charlotte Gray, Lawrence Martin and Peter C. Newman had described it in 2000.

The term *legend* occurs just as often, sometimes in works by the same commentators, sometimes by others. In 1995 a Richard figurine belonging to the series Canadian Timeless Legends Starting Lineup (for children four years and up) appeared on the market. Four years later several individuals, appearing on the RDI tribute to Maurice Richard, were to employ the term, both French speakers (Bruny Surin, Robert Guy Scully, Marie-José Turcotte, Roy Dupuis) and English speakers (Jack Nicklaus, Elvis Stojko, Donald J. Trump). The Canadian Museum of Civilization in 2004 staged its commemorative exposition "Une légende, un héritage: 'Rocket Richard': The Legend—the Legacy," with its perfectly symmetrical and impeccably bilingual title.

But was he a *myth* for English Canadians? Probably not, despite the lyrical flights of people like filmmaker Brian McKenna, who admitted to Dave Stubbs when his *Fire and Ice* was televised: "I look back at how I saw Maurice Richard ... and I understood how kids growing up in ancient Greece must have felt about the gods." From the gods of ancient Greece to Maurice Richard was but a step, rarely taken. Why?

Let us return to the definition of myth given above. The mythical figure, as we understand it here, is a narrative that must be approached on several levels. Its subject must belong to suprahistorical time. It must have a dimension of the marvellous. It must be culturally transmitted. It has a collective dimension. It is malleable. Chance impinges on its transmutation from cultural icon to myth.

On most levels, English Canada's Maurice Richard corresponds to our hypothetical definition. He commands the limelight, not merely in the sports world, since the 1940s. His praises are sung in both languages. He has been taken up by popular culture as well as by literary culture. He became the vehicle of collective aspirations: the Canadian par excellence, up to and including his duality. In Tom Radford's film *Life after Hockey*, the principal character, Brown, who had grown up in a prairie village, explains that in 1961 little boys in Canada had to choose between the Canadiens and the Maple Leafs. He adopted Montreal, because people there spoke French; French was synonymous with "fascination," with "mystery," with a "magical aura." By selecting Maurice Richard over Frank Mahovlich, Brown refused to be like those he called the Protestants of Toronto, and constructed his Canadian identity around an idealized society where French was spoken. He understands the contribution of French speakers as an *internal* one. His Canada is also, indissociably, French Canada. Wherever in the country we look, chance seems to have played the same role in the transformation of Maurice Richard.

Is his public persona malleable enough to affirm that he is a myth in English Canada? That would seem to be less certain, even though Canada is also seeking myths that are more than merely regional, as Daniel Francis argues in his book *National Dreams: Myth, Memory and Canadian History* (1997). Over time, the Maurice Richard of

French speakers has been constantly reinvented. He has been, successively, a sports figure, a newspaper columnist, a cultural icon, a commercial representative, a dutiful son, devoted husband, attentive father, big-hearted grandfather, etc. He was said to be violent, but he knew how to calm himself. There was fire in his eyes, but those eyes were also capable of tears. For French speakers he could embody French-Canadian, then Québécois nationalism *and* Canadian federalism; in the Rest of Canada, the Rocket had no such luck. There was no way he could be, in the ROC, the conjunction in a single person of all the contradictions of his people.

Two cartoonists (Aislin, Garnotte); two visions.

LET US CONCLUDE with two images.

On May 28, 2000, Aislin, *The Gazette*'s editorial cartoonist, drew a flag flying at half-mast. The rectangular flag reminds us of the Montreal Canadiens sweater, and it bears the number 9. Four days later, in *Le Devoir*, Garnotte takes up the same theme, with a hockey stick substituting for the flagpole. And instead of the Canadiens colours, the flag being flown is that of Quebec. Not everyone was crying for the same reason on those emotion-charged days.

Epilogue

ODAY'S QUEBEC loves success, international success above all. Nothing gives it greater pleasure than the success of one of its divas in the United States, one of its circuses in Japan, one of its participants in an over-the-top sport (snowboarding, synchronized swimming, beach volleyball).

Today's Quebec prefers raw emotion to grandeur. Nothing, in its eyes, is more touching, more familiar, closer to home than the success of one of its divas, one of its circuses, or one of its participants in flashy sports.

Maurice Richard is the ideal myth for that particular Quebec.

He was a success in an era when his countrymen had been long in coming to the fore, and his success was Québécois, Canadian, North American and international. He broke numerous records in the course of his career. He was the one who triumphed: over other teams, over adversity, over violence and injustice. He was a national champion, and moreover, he had an innate sense of the dramatic. His successes were spectacular. He was a man of action.

And yet, nothing was more foreign to him than grandeur. He was a man driven by a simple idea (a man of one simple idea, perhaps): to score. His constant refrain was that he was "only a hockey player." He was a family man. Even in hard times, he remained one of his countrymen. When he scored, the effort was palpable. When he spoke, the words did not come easily. When people cheered, he did not know how to react. When suffering overwhelmed him, he showed it: the man with fire in his eyes was not afraid of tears. He was just like everybody else.

To speak of these things—his qualities and his failings—is in no way to diminish Maurice Richard. The cultural historian, if he is doing his job properly, must locate his analysis at another level. His is not to criticize the man, but to understand what a society, over a period of sixty years, has wished to make of that man, what Quebec and Canada hoped to invest in the figure of Maurice Richard.

Such a position might lead to a certain form of cynicism half avowed. By writing that he has read the same stories over and over again, the interpreter may convey the impression that he is totally removed from his subject; that he is merely sitting in judgment from on high, in his ivory tower. Such should not be the case, but it is a risk with which one must learn to live.

Worse things could happen.

Afterword

JEAN BÉLIVEAU

I WAS A young boy in the early 1940s when I would sit beside the family radio on Saturday nights and listen to the broadcast of the Montreal Canadiens games. For me, as for so many of us at that time, Maurice Richard was the hockey player we wanted to be. We let our imaginations magnify his magnificent feats when we listened to those games; then we would mimic his moves as best as we could on the outdoor rink beside the house.

But I never imagined that one day I would actually play on the same team with him.

For seven years, I sat beside Maurice in the dressing room, and for those seven years I was fortunate to be part of the power play with the Rocket, along with Dickie Moore, Burt Olmstead, Doug Harvey and Boom Boom Geoffrion.

Maurice was a quiet man who did not seek the attention of media or fans off the ice. Beside me in the dressing room he said very little, even after I had been a member of the team for some time. But he treated me well, like any other member of the team, and that was all a young player could ask for. It was on the ice that Maurice did his talking, where his leadership stood out. His offensive exploits were an inspiration to all of us. And of course it was those same exploits, those mesmerizing cobra-like eyes beaming toward the goaltender, that captivated young boys, fans and all of his teammates and opposing players alike.

I knew that Maurice was much more than a hockey player. He was a hero who defined a people emerging from an agrarian society in the postwar era and moving to the cities to seek their fortunes. For those people, he became a cultural icon.

And that is what Benoît Melançon's book is about, and why it is an important examination of a man who reached a status seldom dreamed of by athletes in any sport, and especially not by a man who never sought out the role himself.

It is this examination that helps us understand how, years after we played together, I could witness the outpouring of solemn respect and admiration, together with a profound sense of loss, for a man who had played his last hockey game forty years and a month before. At his funeral in May 2000, when one million Montrealers lined the streets of his hometown to bid a final farewell, I understood how powerful was the emotional connection between a people and Maurice "Rocket" Richard.

JEAN BÉLIVEAU
November 2008

Acknowledgements

Over the years, many individuals have contributed to the preparation of this book: Guillermina Almazan, Stéphane Amyot, Catherine Bernier, William Bernier, André Biron, Michel Biron, Moishe Black, René Bonenfant, Larry Bongie, Emmanuel Bouchard, Maude Brisson, Gianni Caccia, Craig Campbell, Nathalie Carle, Benoît Chartier, Jean-François Chassay, Sylvain Cormier, Donald Cuccioletta, Paola D'Agnolo, Gilbert David, Antoine Del Busso, Julie Dubuc, Michel Dumais, François Dumont, Gilles Dupuis, Edward Fraser, Gordon Fulton, Céline Gariépy, Michel Gay, Véronique Giguère, Francis Gingras, Guylaine Girard, Yan Hamel, Pierre Jampen, Bill Kinsley, Michel Lacroix, Geneviève Lafrance, Yvan Lamonde, Bruno Lamoureux, Étienne Lavallée, Carl Lavigne, Laurent Legault, Yves Lever, Michel Maillé, Marie Malo, Patricia Malo, Théo Malo Melançon, Denise Marcotte, Gilles Marcotte, Suzanne Martin, Gaston Massé, Catherine Mavrikakis, Gilles Melançon, Robert Melançon, Samuel Melançon, Jeannine Messier-LaRochelle, Michel Nareau, Carole Ouimet, Pierre Popovic, I. Sheldon Posen, Katherine Roberts, Daniel Roussel, Denis Saint-Jacques, Rob Sanders, Marguerite Sauriol, Emmanuelle Sauvage,

Acknowledgments

Madeleine Sauvé, Pierre Savard, Sylvain Schryburt, Jim Sentance, Ray Stephanson, Isabelle Thellen, Robert Thérien, Lyne Vaillancourt, Madeleine Vernier, Marie-Éva de Villers, Jon Weiss, Morwenna White and Jon Willis. My thanks to all of them, as well as to those whom I may have forgotten, and to whom I apologize before the fact.

All texts cited in this work are listed in the bibliography that follows. But additional information on sources used is necessary.

Introduction
For an introduction to cultural history, see works by Pascal Ory (2004) and Philippe Poirrier (2004). I have dealt at length with my choice of methodologies in an article published in the periodical *Globe* in 2007, "Écrire Maurice Richard: Culture savante, culture populaire, culture sportive" [Writing Maurice Richard: High Culture, Popular Culture, Sporting Culture]. La Commission de toponymie du Québec is the source of all information relating to place names.

Portrait of the Rocket as a Hockey Star
There are several biographies of Maurice Richard, the most extensive written by Jean-Marie Pellerin, published in 1976 and updated in 1998. Each of them was consulted for confirmation of the dates of the principal events of Richard's life and career. Furthermore, wherever possible, those dates were cross-checked against contemporary

newspaper accounts. Statistics have been drawn from Pierre Bruneau and Léandre Normand's *La glorieuse histoire des Canadiens* (2003). On Maurice Richard's short-lived stint behind the Quebec Nordiques bench, see *Just Another Job* (1972), a film by Pierre Letarte and the book by Claude Larochelle (1982). In 1998, David McNeil published an article on the overtime games of the 1950–51 season playoffs in which his father, Gerry McNeil, and Maurice Richard are discussed.

When the eyes speak...
Robert Guy Scully's remarks on the look in Roy Dupuis / Maurice Richard's eye can be heard on the television program *Soirée Maurice Richard* [Maurice Richard Night] (1999). Denise Robert made her comments on *Flash*, May 26, 2005. The cover of the December 19, 1998, issue of *Dernière heure*, not long after Maurice Richard's appearance at the Céline Dion show, carried the words: "Céline and Maurice cry."

What's in a name?
Jean-Marie Pellerin quotes Hy Turkin ("The Brunette Bullet"), Happy Day ("V5") and the Toronto *Telegram* ("Sputnik Richard").

Selling a myth
For a better grasp of the products that made use of Maurice Richard, two catalogues should be consulted: *The Maurice "Rocket" Richard Auction, May 7th,* 2002 and 626 *par 9: Une énumération chronologique des buts marqués par Maurice "Rocket" Richard en photos, statistiques et récits /* 626 *by 9: A Goal-by-Goal Timeline of Maurice "The Rocket" Richard's Scoring Career in Pictures, Stats and Stories* (2004). Jim Sentance (1999) has studied, from his perspective as an economist, the hockey card business. Cultural studies are sensitive to what is known as the "commodification" of cultural icons; for an example, see Nick

Trujillo's *The Meaning of Nolan Ryan* (1994) and particularly the chapters entitled "A Hero for All Ages" and "Nolan Ryan Inc."

The Rocket's body

The story of Maurice Richard and Jean-Paul Riopelle playing hockey against each other can be found in Alain de Repentigny's 2005 book. It is possible to visit the studio of sculptor François Corriveau at www. virtuel.net/users/mecoriv/index.html and that of Paule Marquis at http://www.paulemarquis.com. On Quebec political statuary and its "dull-witted realism," see Antoine Robitaille's article in *Argument*, 2004. Lucie Lavigne reproduces the advertising scenario for Grecian Formula 16 in *La Presse*, May 31, 2000.

Comparing the incomparable

Robert Hamblin analyzed William Faulkner's article in 1996.

Maurice Richard as told to children

The words "The skating rink is a great school of life" could be heard on a video broadcast as part of the exhibition "L'univers Maurice 'Rocket' Richard" held in the late 1990s at the Maurice Richard Arena.

Maurice Richard's writings

Richard's *La Presse* columns quoted are those of November 26, 1995, and March 27, 2000. His comments on the Geoffrion-Murphy affair and Richard's letter of January 14, 1954, appeared in *Samedi-Dimanche*, reproduced by Jean-Marie Pellerin.

December 29, 1954–March 18, 1955

The report of Clarence Campbell's investigation is quoted from *The Gazette* (Montreal) of March 17, 1955. Richard is quoted in *La Presse* of

March 17, 1995, as saying that he followed the Riot on the radio. Several learned texts have been written about the Riot: articles by Jean R. Duperreault (1981), Anouk Bélanger (1996), Suzanne Laberge and Alexandre Dumas (2003), a master's thesis by David Di Felice (1999) and a portion of a doctoral dissertation by Michel Marois (1993).

In song

On songs about Maurice Richard, I. Sheldon Posen's article is indispensable; it quotes the lyrics of Oscar Thiffault and Bob Hill's songs. I thank the author for agreeing to answer questions raised by the article, as well as Robert Thérien for his assistance in tracking down obscure musical tracks.

... in print and on the air

Maurice Richard states that he first took an interest in professional hockey thanks to the radio in the book upon which his name appears as co-author, along with Stan Fischler. The accounts of Claude Béland and Dominique Michel are quoted from *La Presse*, March 17, 2005.

... in story

As Jean-Claude Germain suggests in his play, Richard was often invited to schools to speak to the pupils. For example, Jacques Lamarche's 2000 souvenir photo album shows him visiting the Amos Seminary in 1957, and the woodworking class of a Montreal school in 1961. Robert Guy Scully reminisces about one of his school visits on *Soirée Maurice Richard* (1999). Mary Jane Miller (1980) and James J. Herlan (1983) have analyzed Rick Salutin's play. Jean Cléo Godin and Laurent Mailhot (1980), Cheryl Bodek (2000) and Carlo Lavoie (2002) have written on Jean-Claude Germain's play.

...in pictures

A complete filmography constitutes the third part of the bibliography, which follows. Roland Barthes' text for the Hubert Aquin film was published in 2004; both the text and the film were commented on by Gilles Dupuis the following year; articles by Joyce Nelson (1977) and Scott MacKenzie (1997), who provides an English translation of the text, can also be consulted; another English translation was published in 2007. The double treatment of Gilles Groulx's short film is described in *Dictionnaire de la censure au Québec* [Dictionary of Censorship in Quebec] by Pierre Hébert, Yves Lever and Kenneth Landry (2006). *The Rocket/Le Rocket*, marketed by the National Film Board in 1998, is a montage of extracts from other NFB-produced films and contains no new material. A short film by Mathieu Roy (2005) depicts the making of Charles Binamé's film and espouses its reading of the Riot.

Rocket politics

The traditional interpretation of the Quiet Revolution as a radical break in Quebec history is receiving increased criticism. See, for example, Claude Couture's article on Maurice Richard as a symbol of the workers' movement (2004), the special section of *Globe* magazine entitled "Relire la Révolution tranquille" [Rereading the Quiet Revolution] (1999) or, on a less erudite note, the articles published in the periodical *Cap-aux-Diamants*, "Au seuil de la Révolution tranquille: Les années 1950" [On the Threshold of the Quiet Revolution: The Fifties] (2006). Jocelyn Létourneau has demonstrated that the traditional interpretation has remained dominant, particularly in "L'imaginaire historique des jeunes Québécois" (1988). Maurice Duplessis' letter to Maurice Richard can be read in *The Maurice "Rocket" Richard Auction, May 7th*, 2002. For Duplessis' use of language, see "Un opportuniste sans scrupule" in Pierre Popovic's *La contradiction du poème* [The Poem's Contradiction] (1992). For an appreciation of what fiction can teach us about a man and his fate, see *La mort de Maurice Duplessis et autres récits* [Maurice Duplessis' Death and Other Stories] by Gilles Marcotte.

Legend, hero, myth
Scholarly works on myth are too numerous to be noted here. I limit myself to pointing out that my conception of it is close to that developed by Pascal Brissette (1998). For him, the myth is a "mercenary" narrative.

Mythical time
According to Paul Daoust (2005, 2006), the Maurice Richard myth has been "fermenting" since 1944 and came into existence in 1955, even though French Canadians were unaware of it at the time; I do not agree with that reading. The function of hockey in *Le coeur de la baleine bleue / The Heart of the Blue Whale* has been studied by Carlo Lavoie (2003).

Lament for the Rocket
Analysis of the discourse on the death of Maurice Richard has been developed after an assessment of several newspapers and periodicals: *Allô-Vedettes, Barracuda Magazine, Les Canadiens, Dernière heure, Le Devoir, The Gazette,* the *Hockey News, Ici, Le Journal de Montréal, Libération, Le Magazine 7 jours,* the *New York Times, Paris Match, La Presse, Time, Voir,* etc. Jacques Lamarche has compiled articles published upon Richard's death in 2000. Also consulted were two scholarly texts dedicated to the question, by Howard Ramos and Kevin

Gosine (2001) by and Gina Stoiciu (2006). Paul Daoust was able to consult nearly one hundred of the Cours Windsor funeral registers; he analyzes a dozen of them in his 2006 book, where he underlines their triple dimension: family-oriented, religious and political. Neal Karlen describes his visit to the cemetery where Roger Maris is buried in *Slouching Toward Fargo* (1999).

The Rocket among the English

See www.curriculum.org/occ/profiles/9/pdf/FIFIDP.pdf and www. bced.gov.bc.ca/irp/cfrench512/sample2.htm for examples of the pedagogical use of Roch Carrier's story. On Maurice Richard's place in English Canada, my conclusions are closer to those of I. Sheldon Posen (2005) than to Ramos and Gosine (2001). In addition to his extensive commentary on the songs about Maurice Richard, Posen also examines the poetry of Don Gutteridge, Jane Siberry in her song "Hockey" and Al Purdy ("Homage to Ree-shard"). On English Canada and its sports heroes, in addition to the book by Daniel Francis (1997), see also the work of Don Morrow (2004).

Les hivers de mon enfance
étaient des saisons longues, longues.
Nous vivions en trois lieux:
l'école, l'église et la patinoire; mais
la vraie vie était sur la patinoire.
Roch Carrier

The winters of my childhood were
long, long seasons. We lived in
three places – the school, the church
and the skating-rink – but our real life
was on the skating-rink.

The Canadian five-dollar bill evokes Maurice Richard.

Bibliography

The bibliography does not contain everything about Maurice Richard that has been written, sung or filmed, nor does it cover all the documents I have consulted. In it, however, the reader will find all the texts, songs and audiovisual documents I have cited, in addition to several digital resources. A periodically updated, expanded version can be found at www.lesyeuxdemauricerichard.com.

Prior to writing this book, I have published three articles on the Maurice Richard myth: "Canadien, comme Maurice Richard, ou Vie et mort d'une légende" (1995); "Le Rocket au cinéma: Les Yeux de Maurice Richard, prise 2" (1998); "Maurice Richard expliqué aux enfants" (2005). Those articles have been completely revised and updated for this work.

Books, book chapters and articles

Allô-vedettes, special edition, no. 2, 2000. Special section: "Maurice Richard: L'idole d'un people."

Anstey, Robert G. *Songs for the Rocket: A Collection of Notes and Comments with the Song Lyrics for Twenty-Seven Original Songs About Maurice "The Rocket" Richard*. Sardis, BC: West Coast Paradise Publishing, 2002.

Aquin, Hubert, and Andrée Yanacopoulo. "Éléments pour une phénoménologie du
    sport." In *Problèmes d'analyse symbolique*, edited by Pierre Pagé and Renée
    Legris. "Recherches en symbolique" collection, no. 3. Montreal: Presses de
    l'Université du Québec, 1972, pp. 115–46.

Arsène et Girerd. *Les enquêtes de Berri et Demontigny: On a volé la coupe Stanley*.
    Montreal: Éditions Mirabel, 1975.

"Au revoir, Maurice." *Calgary Herald*, June 1, 2000, p. A3.

Bacon, Dick. "Mr. Hockey." *Hockey Blueline* 4, no. 7 (May 1958), pp. 18–24.
    www.xs4all.nl/~mspelten/MauriceRichard/interview.htm.

Barbeau, Jean. *Ben-Ur*. "Répertoire québécois" collection, no. 11–12. Montreal:
    Leméac, 1971. Presented by Albert Millaire.

Barthes, Roland. *Le sport et les hommes: Texte du film "Le sport et les hommes"
    d'Hubert Aquin*. Montreal: Presses de l'Université de Montréal, 2004.
    Preface by Gilles Dupuis.

——. "Of Sport and Men." *Canadian Journal of Film Studies/Revue canadienne
    d'études cinématographiques* 6, no. 2 (Autumn 1997), pp. 75–83. Translated
    by Scott MacKenzie.

——. *What is Sport?* New Haven and London: Yale University Press, 2007.
    Preface by Gilles Dupuis. Translation by Richard Howard.

Beaulieu, Victor-Lévy. "Un gars ordinaire, qui vise le sommet." *Perspectives*,
    October 14, 1972, pp. 22, 24, 27.

Bégin, Jean-François. "Le Canadien ultime." *La Presse*, April 3, 2004, p. S1.
    Drawing by Francis Léveillé.

Bélanger, Anouk. "Le hockey au Québec, bien plus qu'un jeu: analyse sociologique
    de la place centrale du hockey dans le projet identitaire des Québécois." *Loisir
    et société/Society and Leisure* 19, no. 2 (Autumn 1996), pp. 539–57.

——. "Le hockey et le projet d'identification nationale au Québec." Chapter 4 in "Le
    hockey au Québec: un milieu homosocial au coeur du projet de subjectivation
    nationale." Master's thesis, Université de Montréal, August 1995, pp. 76–103.

Béliveau, Jean, with Chris Goyens and Allan Turowetz. *Jean Béliveau: My Life
    in Hockey*. Rev. ed. Vancouver: Greystone Books, 2005. Foreword by Wayne
    Gretzky. Introduction by Allan Turowetz.

Béliveau, Jean, Chrystian Goyens and Allan Turowetz. *Ma vie bleu-blanc-rouge.* 1994. Re. ed., Montreal: Hurtubise HMH, 2005. Preface by Dickie Moore. Foreword by Allan Turowetz. Translated and adapted by Christian Tremblay.

Belleau, André. *Le romancier fictif: Essai sur la représentation de l'écrivain dans le roman québécois.* "Genres et discours" collection. Sillery, QC: Presses de l'Université du Québec, 1980. "Note liminaire" by Marc Angenot.

Berthelet, Pierre. *Yvon Robert: Le lion du Canada français.* Montreal: Éditions Trustar, 1999. Preface by Maurice Richard.

Bérubé, Renald. "En attendant les buts gagnants." *Moebius*, no. 86 (Fall 2000), pp. 9–18.

——. "Les Québécois, le hockey et le Graal." In *Voix et images du pays VI.* Montreal: Presses de l'Université du Québec, 1973, pp. 191–202.

Black, Conrad. *Duplessis.* Toronto: McClelland and Stewart, 1977.

Blaise, Clark. "I'm Dreaming of Rocket Richard." In *Tribal Justice.* 1974. New Press Canadian Classics Collection. Reprint, Toronto: General Publishing, 1984, pp. 63–72.

Blanchard, Michel. "La plus grande victoire du Rocket." *La Presse*, September 12, 1998, pp. A1, G5.

Bodek, Cheryl. "The Dual Identity of Maurice Richard: The Creation of a Myth in Prose, Theatre and Television." Master's thesis, Bowling Green State University, 2000.

Bouchard, David. *Ça, c'est du hockey!* Montreal: Les 400 coups, 2004. Illustrations by Dean Griffiths. Translation by Michèle Marineau.

——. *That's Hockey.* Victoria: Orca Book Publishers, 2002. Illustrations by Dean Griffiths.

Brissette, Pascal. *Nelligan dans tous ses états: Un mythe national.* "Nouvelles études québécoises" collection. Montreal: Fides, 1998.

Brodeur, Denis. *Denis Brodeur: 30 ans de photos de hockey.* Montreal: Éditions de l'Homme, 1993. Texts by Daniel Daignault. Prefaces by Jean Béliveau, Guy Lafleur and Maurice Richard.

Brodeur, Denis, and Daniel Daignault. "Maurice Richard: Un homme fier, une carrière glorieuse," in *Denis Brodeur présente les grands du hockey: Vedettes*

d'hier, Grands joueurs d'aujourd'hui, Étoiles de demain. "Sport" collection.
Montreal: Éditions de l'Homme, 1994, pp. 66–67.

Brooks, Kevin, and Sean Brooks, eds. *Thru the Smoky End Boards: Canadian
Poetry about Sports and Games.* Vancouver: Polestar Book Publishers, 1996.

Brown, Kenneth. *Life After Hockey.* Toronto: Playwrights Union of Canada,
1985. Photocopied text.

Bruneau, Pierre, and Léandre Normand. *La glorieuse histoire des Canadiens.*
Montreal: Éditions de l'Homme, 2003. Preface by Jean Béliveau.

Brunelle, Michel. "Rocket Knock-out." *Moebius*, no. 86 (Autumn 2000), pp. 21–24.

Bujold, Michel-Wilbrod. *Les hockeyeurs assassinés: Essai sur l'histoire du
hockey 1870–2002.* Montreal: Guérin, 1997.

"Campbell Statement on Richard Censure." *Gazette* (Montreal), March 17, 1955, p. 1.

Cap-aux-Diamants, no. 84 (Winter 2006), pp. 7–43. Special section: "Au seuil de la
Révolution tranquille: Les années 1950."

Carrier, Roch. "The Hockey Sweater." In *The Hockey Sweater and Other Stories.*
Toronto: Anansi, 1979, pp. 75–81. Reprinted in *The Hockey Sweater.*
Montreal: Tundra Books, 1984. Translated by Sheila Fischman.
Illustrated by Sheldon Cohen.

——. *Il est par là, le soleil.* "Romanciers du jour" collection, no. R-65.
Montreal: Éditions du jour, 1970.

——. *Is It the Sun, Philibert?* Toronto: Anansi, 1972. Translated by
Sheila Fischman.

——. *Le Rocket.* Montreal: Stanké, 2000.

——. *Our Life with the Rocket: The Maurice Richard Story.* Toronto:
Penguin / Viking, 2001. Translated by Sheila Fischman.

——. "Une abominable feuille d'érable sur la glace." In *Les enfants du
bonhomme dans la lune.* Montreal: Stanké, 1979, pp. 75–81. Reprinted as
Le chandail de hockey. Montreal: Livres Toundra, 1984. Illustrated by
Sheldon Cohen.

Chantigny, Louis. *Mes grands joueurs de hockey.* "Éducation physique et loisirs"
collection, no. 8. Montreal: Leméac, 1974. Preface by Marcel Dubé.

——. "Une fin tragique pour le Rocket." *Le Petit Journal*,
October 18–25, 1959, p. 132.

Chassay, Jean-François. *Les taches solaires.* Montreal: Boréal, 2006.

Cloutier, Eugène. *Les inutiles*. Montreal: Cercle du livre de France, 1956.

Corboz, Gaël. *En territoire adverse*. "Graffiti" collection, no. 37. Saint-Lambert, QC: Soulières, 2006.

Couture, Claude. "Le 'Rocket' Richard: reflet d'une société coloniale ou post-coloniale?" *Canadian Sports Studies/Études des sports au Canada*, March 2004, pp. 38–41. Published by the Association of Canadian Studies.

Daignault, Daniel. *Maurice Richard: Le plus grand héros du Québec*. Montreal: Édimag, 1999.

——. *Maurice Richard: La fierté d'une nation*. Montreal: Édimag, 2005.

——. *Maurice Richard: Un géant du Québec*. "Garnotte: Biographie" collection, no. 9. Montreal: Loze-Dion, 1996.

Daoust, Paul. "17 mars 1955: 50 ans plus tard. L'émeute au Forum, première révélation du mythe Richard." *Le Devoir*, March 17, 2005, p. A7.

——. *Maurice Richard: Le mythe québécois aux 626 rondelles*. Paroisse Notre-Dame-des-Neiges, QC: Éditions Trois-Pistoles, 2006.

De Koninck, Marie-Charlotte. "Quand les médias ont transformé la culture." In *Jamais plus comme avant! Le Québec de 1945 à 1960*. "Voir et savoir" collection. Montreal and Quebec City: Fides and Musée de la civilisation, 1995, pp. 141–69.

De Repentigny, Alain. *Maurice Richard*. "Passions" collection. Montreal: Éditions La Presse, 2005. Foreword by André Provencher. Preface by Stéphane Laporte.

Dernière heure. Special edition: *Maurice Richard*. "Les grandes biographies" collection. Montreal: Trustar, 2000.

Desbiens, Jean-Paul. *"Je te cherche dès l'aube": Journal 2001–2002*. Montreal: Stanké, 2002.

Desjardins, Maurice. *Les surhommes du sport: Champions et légendes*. "Sport" collection. Montreal: Éditions de l'Homme, 1973.

Desrosiers, Éric. "Une malchance transformée en bénédiction." *Le Devoir*, September 25–26, 1999, pp. A1, A14. Reprinted in *Le Devoir*, May 30, 2000, pp. A1, A8.

Diderot, Denis. *Le neveu de Rameau suivi de Satire première, Entretien d'un père avec ses enfants, et de Entretien d'un philosophe avec la maréchale de ***. "Classiques de poche" collection, no. 16074. Paris: Le livre de Poche, 2002. Edition established, presented and annotated by Pierre Chartier.

Di Felice, David. "The Richard Riot: A Socio-Historical Examination of Sport, Culture, and the Construction of Symbolic Identities." Master's thesis, Queen's University, 1999.

Dion, Jean. "Plus grand que nature." *Le Devoir*, May 29, 2000, pp. A1–A10.

Donegan Johnson, Ann. *Un bon exemple de ténacité: Maurice Richard raconté aux enfants*. "L'une des belles histoires vraies" collection. [N.p.]: Grolier, 1983. Illustrated by Steve Pileggi.

——. *The Value of Tenacity: The Story of Maurice Richard*. "ValueTales" collection. La Jolla, CA: Value Communications, 1984. Illustrated by Steve Pileggi.

Dryden, Ken. "Farewell to The Rocket." *Time*, June 12, 2000, pp. 40–44. Reprinted as "Il est arrivé à nous rendre fiers." *La Presse*, June 7, 2000, p. s6. Translated by Gilles Blanchard.

——. "Sports: What Could Mr. Eaton Have Been Thinking?" *Globe and Mail*, October 13, 2001, p. D8.

Duperreault, Jean R. "L'affaire Richard: A Situational Analysis of the Montreal Hockey Riot of 1955." *Canadian Journal of History of Sport/Revue canadienne de l'histoire des sports* 12, no. 1 (May 1981), pp. 66–83.

Dupuis, Gilles. "Les sports 'nationaux': du mythe à l'épiphénomène." In *Des mots et des muscles! Représentations des pratiques sportives*, edited by Yan Hamel, Geneviève Lafrance and Benoît Melançon. Quebec City: Nota bene, 2005, pp. 85–101.

Encan de la collection Maurice "Rocket" Richard, 7 mai 2002/The Maurice "Rocket" Richard Auction, May 7th, 2002. Saint-Constant, QC: Collections Classic Collectibles, 2002.

Enquist, Per Olov. *Écrits sur le sport. I: La cathédrale olympique. II: Mexique 1986*. "Lettres scandinaves" collection. Arles: Actes sud, 1988. Translated by Marc de Gouverain and Lena Grumbach.

Étiemble. *Le mythe de Rimbaud*. Volume 2: *Structure du mythe*. "Bibliothèque des idées" collection. Paris: Gallimard, 1961 (first edition 1952).

Faulkner, William. "An Innocent at Rinkside." *Sports Illustrated*, January 24, 1955, pp. 14–15.

Filion, Gérard. "Qui sème le vent . . ." *Le Devoir*, March 19, 1955, p. 4.

Fitkin, Ed. *Highlights from the Career of Maurice Richard: Hockey's Rocket*. Toronto: A Castle Publication, [n.d.: 1951?].

——. *Le Rocket du hockey: Maurice Richard*. Toronto: Une publication Castle,
    [n.d.: 1952]. Translation by Camil DesRoches and Paul-Marcel Raymond.

Foglia, Pierre. "Je veux être une tortue." *La Presse*, September 9, 1999, p. A5.

——. "Le dernier des héros." *La Presse*, May 28, 2000, p. A5.

Foisy, Michel. *La carte de hockey magique*. Sainte-Thérèse, QC: Michel Foisy, 2000.
    Preface by Maurice Richard.

——. *La carte de 1 000 000 $*. "Les héros du sport" collection, no. 2. Sainte-Thérèse,
    QC: Michel Foisy, 2003.

Forest, Michel. *Maurice Richard*. "Célébrités canadiennes" collection. Montreal:
    Lidec, 1991.

Francis, Daniel. *National Dreams: Myth, Memory and Canadian History*
    Vancouver: Arsenal Pulp Press, 1997.

Frayne, Trent. *The Mad Men of Hockey*. Toronto: McClelland and Stewart, 1974.

Gagnon, Lysiane. "Le Québec du Rocket." *La Presse*, December 13, 2005, p. A25.

——. "L'homme des années 50." *La Presse*, June 1, 2000, p. B3.

Gélinas, Marc F. *Chien vivant*. "Roman" collection. Montreal: VLB éditeur, 2000.

Gélinas, Pierre. *Les vivants, les morts et les autres*. Montreal:
    Cercle du livre de France, 1959.

Gerbier, Alain. "Hockey: Maurice Richard, véritable légende, est mort à 78 ans.
    Le Québec pleure son saint de glace." *Libération*, May 29, 2000, p. 32.

Germain, Jean-Claude. "L'émeute Maurice Richard: La mesure de la colère de tout
    un people." *L'Aut' Journal*, no. 246, February 2006, p. 8.

——. *Un pays dont la devise est je m'oublie*. Montreal: VLB éditeur, 1976.

Gingras, Yves. "Une association profitable?" *La Presse*, October 26, 2004,
    Affaires section, pp. 1–2.

Globe 2, no. 1 (1999), pp. 1–138. Special section: "Relire la Révolution tranquille."

Gobeil, Pierre. "'Maurice a été le plus grand!' Henri a pleuré en apprenant la mort
    de son frère." *La Presse*, May 29, 2000, p. 2.

Godin, Jean Cléo, and Laurent Mailhot. *Théâtre québécois II: Nouveaux auteurs,
    autres spectacles*. Montreal: Hurtubise HMH, 1980.

Gosselin, Gérard "Gerry." *Monsieur Hockey*. Montreal: Éditions de l'Homme, 1960.
    Preface by Frank Selke.

Gould, Stephen Jay. "Good Sports & Bad." *New York Review of Books*,
    March 2, 1995, pp. 20–23.

Goyens, Chrystian, and Frank Orr, with Jean-Luc Duguay.
  Maurice Richard: Héros malgré lui. Toronto and Montreal:
  Team Power Publishing Inc., 2000. Prefaces by Henri Richard
  and Pierre Boivin.

Goyens, Chrys, and Frank Orr, with Jean-Luc Duguay. *Maurice Richard:
  Reluctant Hero.* Toronto and Montreal: Team Power Publishing Inc., 2000.
  Prefaces by Henri Richard and Pierre Boivin.

Gravel, François. *Le match des étoiles.* "Gulliver" collection, no. 66. Montreal:
  Québec/Amérique jeunesse, 1996. Preface by Maurice Richard.

Gray, Charlotte. "No Idol Industry Here." In *Great Questions of Canada,*
  edited by Rudyard Griffiths. Toronto: Stoddart, 2000, pp. 81–85.

Hamblin, Robert. "*Homo Agonistes,* or, William Faulkner as Sportswriter."
  Aethlon: The Journal of Sport Literature 13, no. 2 (Spring 1996), pp. 13–22.

Hébert, Pierre, Yves Lever and Kenneth Landry, eds. *Dictionnaire
  de la censure au Québec: Littérature et cinéma.* Montreal: Fides, 2006.

Herlan, James J. "The Montréal Canadiens: A Hockey Metaphor."
  Québec Studies 1, no. 1 (Spring 1983), pp. 96–108.

Hickey, Pat. "Rocket Dies at Age 78: Hockey World Pays Tribute to Great Star."
  Gazette (Montreal), May 28, 2000, pp. A1–A2.

Hockey Montréal: Histoire du hockey à Montréal 1, no. 2 (March 27, 1992).

The Hockey News, June 30, 2000. Special section: "Maurice Rocket
  Richard: Fire on Ice. 1921–2000."

Hood, Hugh. *Puissance au centre: Jean Béliveau.* Scarborough, ON:
  Prentice-Hall of Canada, 1970. Translated by Louis Rémillard.

——. *Strength Down Centre: The Jean Béliveau Story.* Scarborough, ON:
  Prentice-Hall of Canada, 1970.

Howe, Colleen, and Gordie Howe, with Charles Wilkins. "Maurice and Lucille
  Richard: In the Mood." In *After the Applause.* Toronto: McClelland
  and Stewart, 1989, pp. 164–84.

Jacob, Roland, and Jacques Laurin. *Ma grammaire.* "Réussite"
  collection. Boucherville, QC: Éditions françaises, 1994.

Kaminsky, Stuart. *High Midnight: A Toby Peters Mystery.* New York:
  Carroll and Graf Publishers, 2001 (first edition 1981).

——. *Pour qui sonne le clap.* "Série noire" collection, no. 1866. Paris: Gallimard, 1982. Translated by S. Hilling.

Karlen, Neal. *Slouching Toward Fargo: A Two-Year Saga of Sinners and St. Paul Saints at the Bottom of the Bush Leagues with Bill Murray, Darryl Strawberry, Dakota Sadie and Me.* New York: Spike, 1999. Reprint, Avon, 2000.

Katz, Sidney. "The Strange Forces behind the Richard Hockey Riot." *Maclean's,* September 17, 1955, pp. 11–15, 97–100, 102–06, 108–10.

Kennedy, Michael P.J., ed. *Going Top Shelf: An Anthology of Canadian Hockey Poetry.* Surrey, BC: Heritage House Publishing Company, 2005. Prefaces by Kelly Hrudey and Roch Carrier.

King, Ronald. "Le Noël de René, Céline, Rocket et . . . Magda!" *La Presse,* December 23, 2003, pp. S1–S2. Illustrated by Francis Léveillé.

Laberge, Suzanne, and Alexandre Dumas. "L'affaire Richard / Campbell: un catalyseur de l'affirmation des Canadiens français." *Bulletin d'histoire politique* 11, no. 2 (Winter 2003), pp. 30–44.

Lalonde-Rémillard, Juliette. "Lionel Groulx intime." *L'Action nationale* 57, no. 10 (June 1968), pp. 857–75.

Lamarche, Jacques. *Maurice Richard: Album souvenir.* Montreal: Guérin, 2000.

Lamonde, Yvan, and Pierre-François Hébert. *Le cinéma au Québec: Essai de statistique historique (1896 à nos jours).* Quebec City: Institut québécois de recherche sur la culture, 1981.

Laporte, Stéphane. "Mes oncles et Maurice Richard." *La Presse,* March 15, 1998, p. A5.

Larochelle, Claude. "7: Richard ne dure que dix jours," In *Les Nordiques.* Montreal: France-Amérique, 1982, pp. 175–93.

Laurendeau, André. "Blocs-notes: On a tué mon frère Richard." *Le Devoir,* March 21, 1955, p. 4.

Lavigne, Lucie. "Vrai . . . jusque dans la publicité!" *La Presse,* May 31, 2000, p. A8.

Lavoie, Carlo. "Discours sportif et roman québécois: figures d'un chasseur du territoire." Doctoral dissertation, University of Western Ontario, 2003.

——. "Maurice Richard: du joueur à la figure." *Recherches sémiotiques / Semiotic Inquiry* 22, nos. 1–2–3 (2002), pp. 211–27.

Leclerc, Félix. "Maurice Richard." *La Presse,* October 28, 1983, p. 25.

Leclerc, Mario. "Le Rocket ne voulait pas que Kirk Muller porte son no 9."
    Le Journal de Montréal, May 28, 2000, p. 87.

Le Magazine 7 jours, June 10, 2000, pp. 3 and 8–25. Special section:
    "Édition souvenir: Adieu Maurice, 1921–2000."

Les Canadiens (1999–2000 season). Special edition. "Maurice Richard 1921–2000."

Létourneau, Jocelyn. "L'imaginaire historique des jeunes Québécois." *Revue
    d'histoire de l'Amérique française* 41, no. 4 (Spring 1988), pp. 553–74.

Lever, Yves. *Histoire générale du cinéma au Québec*. Montreal: Boréal, 1988.

MacGregor, Roy. *The Night They Stole the Stanley Cup*. "The Screech Owls" series,
    no. 2 Toronto: McClelland & Stewart, 1995.

MacInnis, Craig, ed. *Maurice Richard: L'inoubliable Rocket*. Montreal:
    Éditions de l'Homme, 1999. Translated by Jacques Vaillancourt.

——. *Remembering the Rocket: A Celebration*. Toronto: Stoddart (A Peter
    Goddard Book), 1998.

MacKenzie, Scott. "The Missing Mythology: Barthes in Québec." *Canadian
    Journal of Film Studies/Revue canadienne d'études cinématographiques)*
    6, no. 2 (Autumn 1997), pp. 65–74.

MacLennan, Hugh. "Letter from Montreal: The Explosion and the
    Only Answer." *Saturday Night*, April 9, 1955, pp. 9–10.

——. "Letter from Montreal: The Rise of the New Challenger."
    Saturday Night, January 15, 1955, p. 9.

Major, Henriette. *Comme sur des roulettes!* "Papillon: C'est la vie…"
    collection, "Mamie Jo et Papi Chou" series, no. 68. Montreal: Éditions
    Pierre Tisseyre, 1999. Illustrated by Sampar.

Marcotte, Gilles. *La mort de Maurice Duplessis et autres récits*.
    Montreal: Boréal, 1999.

Marois, Carmen. *Maurice Richard (1921–2000)*. "Tous azimuts" collection,
    "1er cycle du primaire. Mini-série 2," no. 21. Boucherville, QC: Graficor,
    2000. Illustrated by Jacques Lamontagne.

Marois, Michel. "Le Rocket, les Habitants et leurs adorateurs; deux études de
    cas exemplaires." Part 3 in "Sport, politique et violence: une interprétation
    des dimensions politiques du sport, de la violence des foules aux événements
    sportifs et de la médiatisation de cette violence." Doctoral dissertation,
    Université de Montréal, 1993, pp. 223–98.

Martin, Lawrence. *Iron Man: The Defiant Reign of Jean Chrétien.*
Volume 2. Toronto: Viking Canada, 2003.

———. "Richard Fills Hero Void." *Gazette* (Montreal), June 1, 2000, p. B3.

"Maurice Richard. 'Le point sur ma maladie.' Texte intégral de sa conférence
de presse." *Dernière heure*, July 4, 1998, pp. 7–11.

"Maurice 'The Rocket' Richard: Hockey's Battling Terror." *Babe Ruth Sports
Comics* 1, no. 6 (February 1950).

Mayer, Charles. *Charles Mayer présente L'épopée des "Canadiens":
De Georges Vézina à Maurice Richard: 40 ans d'histoire, 1909–1949.*
Montreal: [n.p.], 1949. Preface by Léo Dandurand.

McNeil, David. "The '51 Stanley Cup: A Spectacle of Sudden-Death
Overtime." *Textual Studies in Canada: Canada's Journal of Cultural
Literacy/Études textuelles au Canada: Revue de l'éducation culturelle au
Canada*, no. 12 (1998), pp. 5–18.

Melançon, Benoît. "Canadien, comme Maurice Richard, ou Vie et mort d'une
légende." In *Miscellanées en l'honneur de Gilles Marcotte*, edited by Benoît
Melançon and Pierre Popovic. Montreal: Fides, 1995, pp. 179–94.

———. "Écrire Maurice Richard: Culture savante, culture populaire, culture sportive."
Globe: Revue internationale d'études québécoises 9, no. 2
(2006 [2007]), pp. 109–35.

———. "Le Rocket au cinéma: Les yeux de Maurice Richard, prise 2." *Littératures*
(Department of French Language and Literature, McGill University),
no. 17 (1998), pp. 99–125.

———. "Maurice Richard expliqué aux enfants." In *Des mots et des muscles!
Représentations des pratiques sportives*, edited by Yan Hamel,
Geneviève Lafrance and Benoît Melançon. Quebec City: Nota bene,
2005, pp. 13–30.

Meloche, Roger. "Le mot de la fin: Maurice Richard . . ." *La Patrie*,
April 8, 1957, p. 28.

Miller, Mary Jane. "Two Versions of Rick Salutin's *Les Canadiens*."
Theatre History in Canada/Histoire du théâtre au Canada 1, no. 1
(Spring 1980), pp. 57–69. www.lib.unb.ca/Texts/TRIC/bin/
getPrint.cgi?directory=vol1_1/&filename=Miller.html.

Morris, Jeffrey. "The Rocket and Me." *Beckett Hockey Card Monthly*,
    September 1998, p. 80.

Morrow, Don. "A Riotous Reflection: The Heroic, Richard, and Canadian Sport
    History." *Canadian Sports Studies/Études des sports au Canada*,
    March 2004, pp. 48–52. Published by the Association of Canadian Studies.

Nelson, Joyce. "Roland Barthes and the NFB Connection."
    Cinema Canada, no. 42 (November 1977), pp. 14–15.

Newcombe, Jack. "Montreal's Flying Frenchmen." *Sport* 18, no. 4
    (April 1955), pp. 48–57.

Newman, Peter C. "We'd Rather Be Clark Kent." In *Great Questions of Canada*,
    edited by Rudyard Griffiths. Toronto: Stoddart, 2000, pp. 86–90.

O'Brien, Andy. *Fire-Wagon Hockey: The Story of the Montreal Canadiens*.
    Toronto: Ryerson Press, 1967.

——. "Maurice Richard." In *Superstars: Hockey's Greatest Players*. Toronto:
    McGraw-Hill Ryerson Limited, 1973, pp. 30–44.

——. *Numéro 9*. Saint-Laurent, QC: Éditions Laurentia, 1962. Translated by
    Guy and Pierre Fournier.

——. *Rocket Richard*. Toronto: Ryerson Press, 1961.

O'Donnell, Chuck. "Remembering the Rocket's Glare — Hockey Player
    Maurice Richard. *Hockey Digest*, November 2000. www.findarticles.com/
    p/articles/mi_moFCM/is_1_29/ai_66240077.

Ohl, Paul. *Louis Cyr, une épopée légendaire*. Montreal:
    Libre expression, 2005.

Ory, Pascal. *L'histoire culturelle*. "Que sais-je?" collection, no. 3713.
    Paris: Presses universitaires de France, 2004.

Pagé, Pierre, in collaboration with Renée Legris and Louise Blouin.
    Répertoire des oeuvres de la littérature radiophonique québécoise, 1930–1970.
    "Archives québécoises de la radio et de la television" collection,
    no. 1. Montreal: Fides, 1975.

Paris Match, June 8, 2000, pp. 38–47. Special section: "Adieu 'Rocket.'"

——. June 15, 2000, pp. 49–59. Special section: "Maurice Richard: L'hommage
    national au géant du Québec."

Parker, Robert B. *Hush Money*. New York: G.P. Putnam's Sons, 1999.

Pellerin, Jean-Marie. *L'idole d'un peuple: Maurice Richard*. Montreal:
Éditions de l'Homme, 1976.

——. *Maurice Richard: L'idole d'un peuple*. Montreal: Éditions Trustar, 1998.
Revised edition of *L'idole d'un peuple: Maurice Richard* (1976).

Plante, J.R. "Crime et châtiment au Forum (Un mythe à l'oeuvre et à l'épreuve)."
Stratégie, no. 10 (Winter 1975), pp. 41–65.

Poirrier, Philippe. *Les enjeux de l'histoire culturelle*. "Points-histoire" collection,
"L'histoire en débats" series, no. H342. Paris: Seuil, 2004.

Popovic, Pierre. *Entretiens avec Gilles Marcotte: De la littérature avant toute
chose*. "De vive voix" collection. Montreal: Liber, 1996.

——. *La contradiction du poème: poésie et discours social au Québec de 1948 à 1953*.
"L'univers des discours" collection. Candiac, QC: Balzac, 1992.

Posen, I. Sheldon. *626 by 9: A Goal-by-Goal Timeline of Maurice "The Rocket"
Richard's Scoring Career in Pictures, Stats and Stories*. Gatineau, QC:
Canadian Museum of Civilization, 2004. Foreword by Roch Carrier.

——. *626 par 9: Une énumération chronologique des buts marqués par Maurice
"Rocket" Richard en photos, statistiques et récits*. Gatineau, QC: Musée canadien
des civilisations, 2004. Translated by Marie-Anne Délye-Payette. Revised by
Jean-Luc Duguay. Foreword by Roch Carrier.

——. "Sung Hero: Maurice 'The Rocket' Richard in Song." In *Bean Blossom
to Bannerman, Odyssey of a Folklorist: A Festschrift for Neil V. Rosenberg*,
edited by Martin Lovelace, Peter Narváez and Diane Tye. "Folklore
and Language Publications" series. St. John's: Memorial University of
Newfoundland, 2005, pp. 377–404.

Poulin, Jacques. *The Jimmy Trilogy: My Horse for a Kingdom; Jimmy;
The Heart of the Blue Whale*. Translated by Sheila Fischman. Toronto:
Anansi, 1979.

——. *Le coeur de la baleine bleue*. "Les romanciers du jour" collection,
no. 66. Montreal: Éditions du jour, 1970.

Pozier, Bernard. *Les poètes chanteront ce but*. "Radar" collection, no. 60.
Trois-Rivières, QC: Écrits des Forges, 1991.

Purdy, Al. "Homage to Ree-shard." In *Sundance at Dusk*. Toronto: McClelland
and Stewart, 1976, pp. 36–39.

Ramos, Howard, and Kevin Gosine. "'The Rocket': Newspaper Coverage of the Death of a Québec Cultural Icon, a Canadian Hockey Player." *Journal of Canadian Studies/Revue d'études canadiennes* 36, no. 4 (Winter 2001–2002), pp. 9–31.

"Real-Man Revisited: Rocket Richard, Hockey Player or Cultural Revolutionary?" *Barracuda Magazine*, no. 8 [2000], pp. 32–39. www.barracudamagazine. com/rocket.htm.

"Reportage publicitaire. Entrepreneur. Roynat Capital présente ce profil en hommage au succès des entreprises canadiennes." *La Presse*, May 6, 2005, Affaires section, p. 16.

Richard, Maurice. "Condamné à bien jouer." *La Presse*, March 27, 2000, p. s6.

——. "Dans l'album..." *La Presse*, June 21, 1987, p. s9.

——. "Dix ans à *La Presse.*" *La Presse*, November 26, 1995, p. s7.

——. "Je me sens très bien!" *La Presse*, March 14, 1998, p. A1.

——. "Je n'ai jamais brisé trois bâtons sur le dos de Laycoe." *La Presse*, March 20, 2000, p. s6.

——. *Jouez du meilleur hockey avec les Canadiens.* [N.p.]: [n.d. — early 1960s], 24 p.

——. "L'émeute du Forum: 40 ans plus tard. Souvenirs. 'Ce n'est rien à côté de ce qui va suivre'..." *La Presse*, March 17, 1995, pp. A1–A2.

——. "L'émeute du Forum: 40 ans plus tard. Souvenirs. J'ai souvent vu rouge." *La Presse*, March 15, 1995, p. s9.

——. "Les Panthers iront-ils jusqu'au bout?" *La Presse*, May 26, 1996, p. s7.

——. "Le tour du chapeau." *Samedi-Dimanche*, December 6, 1952, p. 32.

——. "Le tour du chapeau." *Samedi-Dimanche*, December 20, 1952, p. 32.

——. "On a consulté mon entourage." *La Presse*, June 21, 1998, p. s7.

——. *Playing Better Hockey with les Canadiens.* [N.p]: [n.d. — early 1960s], 24 p.

——. "The Rocket Speaks Out." *Maurice Richard's Hockey Illustrated*, February 1963, pp. 8–10.

——. "Un reportage sportif signé René Lévesque." *La Presse*, November 8, 1987, p. s9.

Richard, Maurice, and Stan Fischler. *The Flying Frenchmen: Hockey's Greatest Dynasty.* New York: Hawthorn Books, 1971.

——. *Les Canadiens sont là! La plus grande dynastie du hockey.* Scarborough, ON: Prentice-Hall of Canada, 1971. Translated by Louis Rémillard.

Richler, Mordecai. *Barney's Version: With Footnotes and an Afterword by Michael Panofsky.* Toronto: Alfred A. Knopf, 1997.

——. "Howe Incredible." *Inside Sports*, November 30, 1980, pp. 108–15.

——. *Le monde de Barney: Accompagné de notes et d'une postface de Michael Panofsky.* "Les grandes traductions" collection. Paris: Albin Michel, 1999. Translation by Bernard Cohen.

——. "This Year in Jerusalem: The Anglo-Saxon Jews." *Maclean's*, September 8, 1962, pp. 18–19, 34–44.

Robitaille, Antoine. "Tribune: L'homme empaillé, ou pourquoi notre statuaire politique est-elle platement réaliste?" *Argument* 6, no. 2 (Spring–Summer 2004), pp. 3–8.

Robitaille, Marc. *Des histoires d'hiver, avec des rues, des écoles et du hockey.* Montreal: VLB éditeur, 1987.

"Rocket Riopelle." *Newsweek*, May 27, 1963, pp. 97–98.

Rogin, Gilbert. "One Beer for The Rocket." *Sports Illustrated*, March 21, 1960, pp. 47–50.

Rompré, Paul, and Gaëtan Saint-Pierre, with Marcel Chouinard. "Essai de sémiologie du hockey: À propos de l'idéologie sportive." *Stratégie*, no. 2 (Spring–Summer 1972), pp. 19–54.

Roy, Gabrielle. *Alexandre Chenevert.* 1954. "10 / 10" collection, no. 11. Reprint, Montreal: Stanké, 1979.

——. *The Cashier.* Toronto: McClelland and Stewart, 1963. Translated by Harry Binsse. Introduction by W.C. Lougheed.

Roy, Pierre. *Rocket Junior.* "Sésame" collection, no. 26. Saint-Laurent, QC: Éditions Pierre Tisseyre, 2000. Illustrated by Alexandre Rouillard.

Rumilly, Robert. *Maurice Duplessis et son temps.* Vol. 1, 1890–1944; vol. 2, 1944–1959. "Bibliothèque canadienne-française: Histoire et documents" collection. Montreal: Fides, 1978.

Saintonge, Jacques. "Maurice Richard." In *Une demi-heure avec . . . Vingt sujets canadiens, de Monseigneur de Laval à Maurice Richard.* Montreal: Éditions du Service des publications de Radio-Canada, 1965, pp. 115–23.

Salutin, Rick, with the collaboration of Ken Dryden. *Les Canadiens.*
    Vancouver: Talonbooks, 1977. Preface by Ken Dryden.

Sarault, Jean-Paul. *Les grands du hockey au Québec.* Montreal: Quebecor, 1996.

Sauvé, Mathieu-Robert. *Échecs et mâles: Les modèles masculins au Québec, du*
    marquis de Montcalm à Jacques Parizeau. Montreal: Les Intouchables, 2005.

Selke, Frank J., with H. Gordon Green. *Behind the Cheering.* Toronto: McClelland
    and Stewart, 1962.

Sentance, Jim. "English-Canadian Attitudes to French-Canadian Hockey
    Players: Evidence from the Market for Vintage Hockey Cards (Should
    Gordie Howe really be worth two Rocket Richards?)." Paper presented at the
    Annual Conference of the Canadian Economics Association, University of
    Toronto, May 1999.

Siemiatycki, Jack, and Avi Slodovnick. *The Hockey Card.* Montreal:
    Lobster Press, 2002. Illustrated by Doris Barrette.

———. *La carte de hockey.* Montreal: Éditions Homard, 2002. Illustrated by
    Doris Barrette. Translated by Christiane Duchesne.

Stern, Bill. "The Man They Call the Rocket . . . Maurice Richard." In *World's*
    Greatest True Sports Stories: Bill Stern's Sports Book, Winter 1952.

Stoiciu, Gina. "Maurice Richard: Les funérailles d'une idole nationale."
    In *Comment comprendre l'actualité: Communication et mise en scène.*
    "Communication" collection. Sainte-Foy, QC: Presses de l'Université du
    Québec, 2006, pp. 223–238.

Stubbs, Dave. "The Rocket's Red Glare." *StarPhoenix* (Saskatoon) *TV Times*,
    March 10–16, 2000, p. 63.

Sullivan, George. "Maurice Richard, the Rocket." In *Hockey Heroes: The Game's*
    Great Players. Champaign, IL: Garrard Pub. Co., 1969, pp. 66–95.
    Illustrations by Dom Lupo.

Tétreault, Christian. *Quelques reprises.* Montreal: Les 400 coups, 2005.

Todd, Jack. "The Lion in Winter." *Gazette* (Montreal), March 9, 1996,
    pp. C1 and C6.

Tremblay, Réjean, and Ronald King. *Les Glorieux: Histoire du Canadien de*
    Montréal en images. Montreal: Éditions Transcontinental, 1996.
    Preface by Maurice Richard.

Tremblay, Victor-Laurent. "Masculinité et hockey dans le roman québécois."
    French Review 78, no. 6 (May 2005), pp. 1104–16.

Trujillo, Nick. *The Meaning of Nolan Ryan*. College Station, TX:
    Texas A&M University Press, 1994.

Tygiel, Jules, ed. *The Jackie Robinson Reader: Perspectives on an American Hero,
    with Contributions by Roger Kahn, Red Barber, Wendell Smith,
    Malcolm X, Arthur Mann, and more*. New York: Dutton, 1997.

Ulmer, Mike. "Rocket Ride to Superstardom." In *The Hockey News' Top 50
    NHL Players of All-Time*. Toronto: Hockey News, January 1998, pp. 38–40.

Walker, Alan. "Rocket Richard on the Brink of 50 — and Oblivion." *Canadian
    Magazine*, May 1, 1971, pp. 1–7. Special insert in *Edmonton Journal*,
    Gazette (Montreal), etc.

Will, George F. *Men at Work: The Craft of Baseball*. 1990. Reprint,
    New York: HarperPerennial, 1991.

Wind, Herbert Warren. "Fire on the Ice." *Sports Illustrated*, December 9, 1954,
    pp. 32–36, 70–75.

Young, Scott. *That Old Gang of Mine*. Toronto: Fitzhenry and Whiteside, 1982.

Sound recordings

"C'est pour quand la Coupe Stanley?" In *Alain-François*. CD. Afl Productions
    AFLCD9507, 2007, 2 minutes 27 seconds. Vocals: Alain-François.

"Essaye donc pas." In *À qui appartient l'beau temps?* 33 1/3 LP disc. Kébec Disc
    KD-932, 1977, 3 minutes 33 seconds. Vocals and lyrics: Paul Piché.

"Hockey." In *Bound by the Beauty*. 33 1/3 LP disc. Duke Street Records DSR 31058,
    1989, 3 minutes 58 seconds. Vocals, lyrics and music: Jane Siberry.

"Hockey bottine." In *Réal Béland Live in Pologne*. CD. Christal Musik CMCD9954,
    2007, 4 minutes. Vocals: Réal Béland.

"J'irai au sommet pour toi." In *Maurice Richard*. CD. Cinémaginaire et PMC ZCD-
    1060, 2005, 3 minutes 57 seconds. Vocals: Marie-Chantal Toupin. Lyrics:
    Claude Sénéchal. Music: Michel Cusson.

"Le hockey est malade." In *On chante toujours mieux dans not' char*. CD. 2001,
    3 minutes 17 seconds. Vocals: Les mecs comiques.

"Le rocket Richard." 78 rpm disc. Apex 17140-A, 1955, 2 minutes 40 seconds.
 Vocals: Oscar Thiffault, accompanied by his orchestra and a children's
 choir. Lyrics: Oscar Thiffault.

"Maurice Richard." 78 rpm disc. Maple Leaf 5018A, 1951, 2 minutes 32 seconds.
 Vocals: Jeanne d'Arc Charlebois, accompanied by Jean "Johnny" Laurendeau
 and his band. Lyrics: Yvon Dupuis. Music: Jean "Johnny" Laurendeau.

"Maurice Richard." In *Pierre Létourneau*. 33 1/3 LP disc. London LP.1012, 1971,
 2 minutes 20 seconds. Vocals and lyrics: Pierre Létourneau.
 Musical direction: Jean Bouchety and Jacques Denjean.

"Rocket." In *Les Boys II*. CD. YFB DY2-4512, 1998, 3 minutes 55 seconds. Music:
 Éric Lapointe and Stéphane Dufour. Instrumental version of "Rocket
 (On est tous des Maurice Richard)."

"Rocket (On est tous des Maurice Richard)." In *Les Boys II*. CD. YFB DY2-4512,
 1998, 3 minutes 59 seconds. Vocals: Éric Lapointe. Lyrics: Roger Tabra
 and Éric Lapointe. Music: Éric Lapointe and Stéphane Dufour.

"Rocket Richard Reel." 1956(?). Music: Graham Townsend.
 Labbé, Gabriel, Dorothée Hogan and Michel Donato. *L'harmonica, une
 passion*. CD. Interdisc TRCD 9514, 1999.
 Le rêve du diable. *Sans tambours ni trompettes*. CD. RCD0207, 2002.
 Robichaud, Gerry. *Down East Fiddling*. 33 1/3 LP Disc. VRLP 310-S
 Voyager Recordings, 1973.
 Townsend, Graham. *Fiddling Favourites*. 33 1/3 LP Disc.
 RBS 1116 Banff, 1963(?).
 ——. *The Best Damn Fiddling in the World*. Audio cassette.
 BDFM 5-7004 Rodeo, 1990(?).

"Rocket Rock and Roll." 45 rpm single disc. Alouette CF 45-758, 1957,
 2 minutes 37 seconds. Vocals: Denise Filiatrault. Lyrics: Jacques
 Lorrain. Music: Roger Joubert.

"Saga of Maurice Richard." 78 rpm disc. Sparton 136R, 1955, 2 minutes 53 seconds.
 Performers: Bob Hill and His Canadian Country Boys. Lyrics: Bob Hill.

Films and television programs

100 Québécois qui ont fait le XXe siècle: Les héros mythiques. Documentary, 2003, 51 minutes. Director: Jean Roy. Producer: Eurêka! Productions/Télé-Québec. The first of four segments deals with Maurice Richard.

Fire and Ice: The Rocket Richard Riot/L'émeute Maurice Richard. Documentary, 2000, 60 minutes. Director: Brian McKenna. Producer: Galafilm.

Here's Hockey!/Hockey. Documentary, 1953, 10 minutes. Director: Leslie McFarlane. Producer: Office national du film/National Film Board. Reproduced in the television program *Passe-partout: "Le sport est-il trop commercialisé?"* by Gérard Pelletier (1955).

Histoires d'hiver/Winter Stories. Fiction film, 1998, 105 minutes. Director: François Bouvier. Producer: Aska Film. Based on the book by Marc Robitaille (1987).

Hockey Lessons. Television program, 2000, 25 minutes. Director: John Hudecki. Producer: Paul Hunt and Five Corners Communications, with Vision TV. "Living Memories" series.

Hommage à Maurice Richard. Documentary, 2005, 21 minutes. Director: Mathieu Roy. Producer: Cinémaginaire. Byproduct of *Maurice Richard*, by Charles Binamé (2005).

Le chandail/The Sweater. Animated film, 1980, 10 minutes. Director: Sheldon Cohen. Producer: Office national du film du Canada/National Film Board of Canada. After Roch Carrier's short story (1979).

Le Rocket/The Rocket. Documentary, 1998, 42 minutes. Director: Jacques Payette. Producer: Office national du film du Canada/National Film Board.

Le sport et les hommes/Of Sport and Men. Documentary, 1961, 58 minutes. Director: Hubert Aquin. Text: Roland Barthes. Producer: Office national du film du Canada/National Film Board.

Life after Hockey/La vie après le hockey. Telefilm, 1989, 50 minutes. Director: Tom Radford. Producer: Great North Productions Inc. After the play by Kenneth Brown (1985).

Maurice Richard/The Rocket. Fiction film, 2005, 124 minutes. Director: Charles Binamé. Producer: Cinémaginaire.

Maurice Richard: Histoire d'un Canadien / The Maurice Rocket Richard Story. Docudrama, 1999, 4 hours, 2 parts: *1921; 1951*. Directors: Jean-Claude Lord and Pauline Payette. Producer: L'information essentielle.

Maurice "Rocket" Richard. Docudrama, 1997, 1 minute. Producer: Historica Minutes. www.histori.ca / minutes / minute.do?id=10492 (French version). www.histori.ca / minutes / minute.do?id=10217 (English version).

Maurice Rocket Richard. Documentary, 1998, 2 hours, 2 parts: *Racontez-nous Maurice...*; *Le hockey depuis Maurice Richard*. Directors: Karl Parent and Claude Sauvé. Producer: Société Radio-Canada.

Mon frère Richard. Documentary, 1999, 53 minutes. Directors: Luc Cyr and Carl Leblanc. Producer: Ad Hoc Films.

Mon numéro 9 en or. Animated film, 1972, 4 minutes 45 seconds. Director: Pierre L'Amare. Producer: Office national du film du Canada / National Film Board.

Passe-partout: "Le sport est-il trop commercialisé?" Television program, 1955, 30 minutes. Presenter: Gérard Pelletier. Producer: Office national du film / National Film Board. Contains *Here's Hockey / Hockey* by Leslie McFarlane (1953).

Peut-être Maurice Richard. Documentary, 1971, 66 minutes 38 seconds. Director: Gilles Gascon. Producer: Office national du film du Canada / National Film Board.

Soirée Maurice Richard. Television program, October 25, 1999, 102 minutes. Producer: Réseau de l'information.

Un jeu si simple. Documentary, 1964, 29 minutes 45 seconds. Director: Gilles Groulx. Producer: Office national du film du Canada / National Film Board.

Digital resources

Archives de la Ville de Montréal. "Hommage à Maurice Richard." http: / / ville.montreal. qc.ca / portal / page?_pageid=165,230392&_dad=portal&_schema=PORTAL.

The Canadian Encyclopedia. www.thecanadianencyclopedia.com / index.cfm?PgN
    m=TCE&Params=ATARTA0006811.

Centre d'études et de recherches internationales, Université de Montréal.
    "Maurice Richard, icône culturelle." Lecture by Benoît Melançon:
    www.cerium.ca / article4057.html.

Dictionary of Canadian Biography Online. www.biographi.ca / index-e.html

Hockey Hall of Fame, Toronto. www.legendsofhockey.
    net:8080 / LegendsOfHockey / jsp / LegendsMember.jsp?mem=P196108.

Le Canadien de Montréal, 1909–1995 / Montreal Canadiens, 1909–1995. CD-ROM.
    Montreal: MMI Multi Media Interactif and Malofilm Production, 1995. Design
    and script: Jean Maurice Duplessis, Jacques Beauchemin and Luc Hétu.
    Project head: Jean Maurice Duplessis. Narration: Claude Queneville.

National Library and Archives. "Regard sur le hockey / Backcheck: A
    Hockey Retrospective." www.collectionscanada.ca / hockey / .

Société Radio-Canada. "Le Rocket, héros d'un peuple."
    http: / / archives.radio-canada.ca / 300c.asp?id=0-60-62.

Index

List of Illustrations

PAGE 46: Advertisement for Vitalis hair conditioner, published in the *Saturday Evening Post*.

PAGE 47: Advertisement for Williams shaving cream for the Spanish-speaking public.

PAGE 50: A young boy wears the number 9 sweater on an ice-fishing trip. John Little: *Ice-fishing at Ste. Anne de la Pérade, Maclean's*, January 3, 1959.

PAGE 52: Maurice Richard advertises corn syrup (courtesy of Cargill Inc.).

PAGE 53: Maurice Richard advertises batteries (courtesy of Benoît Melançon).

PAGE 54: Still bridging the generations in 1966 (courtesy of Benoît Melançon).

PAGE 57: Maurice Richard, one of his sons, and Jean Béliveau endorse the Marabout series. "Tribute to Dimitri Kassan," *Le Devoir*, November 15, 2003, p. A5 (©Editions Anne Sigier, Sillery).

PAGE 61: Serge Lemoyne: *No. 1 de Bangkok*, 1981 (© Serge Lemoyne Estate/SODRAC 2006; photo: Daniel Roussel; collection of Benoît Melançon).

PAGE 64: Jean-Paul Riopelle: *Hommage à Duchamp (Hommage à Maurice Richard)*, 1990. Acrylic, oil, fluorescent paint, silver metallic paint, gold metallic paint with metal sequins on plywood (painted on both sides), 203.2 x 91.4 cm (gift of Mr. Maurice Richard; Montreal Museum of Contemporary Art, no. D 94 35 P 1; © Jean-Paul Riopelle Estate/ SODRAC 2006; photo: Richard Max Tremblay).

PAGE 68: Paul Marquis: *Maurice Richard* (detail), 2001, statue 5'7" × 5' (Pepsi Forum Entertainment Centre, Montreal).

PAGE 69: Maurice Richard stickhandling with one hand, as imagined in the 1960s and in 2000. (Top) Maurice Richard scoring his 500th goal against the Chicago Blackhawks, postcard, Ville Marie Wax Museum, 1198 Ste. Catherine St. West, Montreal. (Bottom) Michael Dusablon: *Statue of Maurice Richard*, 2000, Madame Tussaud's Wax Museum, London (photo: Merle Toole, Canadian Museum of Civilizations).

PAGE 71: Statue by Jean-Raymond Goyer and Sylvie Beauchêne, Les Ailes shopping centre, Montreal (photo: Daniel Roussel).

PAGE 72: Statue by Jules Lasalle and Annick Bourgeau, Maurice Richard Arena, Montreal, 1977, bronze and granite (photo: Daniel Roussel).

PAGE 84: Maurice Richard as Superman, by Henri Boivin.

PAGE 88: Luca Giordano: *The Martyrdom of Saint Sebastian*, 17th c., Musée Fesch, Ajaccio, Corsica (photo: Erich Lessing/Art Resources, New York).

PAGE 89: Portrait of Maurice Richard, *Sport: The Magazine for the Sports-Minded*, vol. 18, no. 4, April 1955, New York, Mcfadden Publications Inc., p. 48 (photo: Ozzie Sweet).

PAGE 94: One of the best-known photos of Maurice Richard, by David Bier (photo: ©Betteman/Corbis).

PAGE 97: The Rocket on the cover of *Maclean's*, Vol. 72, no. 7, March 28, 1959.

PAGE 98: Maurice Richard as a grandfather and reader, 1988. Chrystian Goyens and Frank Orr, with Jean-Luc Duguay, *Maurice Richard: Heros malgre lui*, Toronto and Montreal, Team Power Publishing Inc., 2000, 160, p. 131 (photo: Bob Fisher/ Club de hockey Canadien Inc.).

PAGE 100: Taken from *The Hockey Sweater* © 1984 Sheldon Cohen: illustrations published by Tundra Books

PAGE 103: Maurice Richard at his lathe, from *World's Greatest True Sports Stories: Bill Stern's Sports Book*, 1952.

PAGE 106: Maurice Richard, as seen by Arsène and Girerd, 1975 (©Jean-Pierre Girerd and Arsène). Three pages from *Babe Ruth Sports Comics*, 1950 (©Classic Media, New York; photo: Canadian Museum of Civilization).

PAGE 112: Jack Reppen: *Maurice Richard scoring a goal against Toronto*, March 23, 1944, #5 in the Prudential Collection "Great Moments in Canadian Sport," 1961 (©Jack Reppen Estate).

PAGE 118: *Playing Better Hockey with les Canadiens*, cover (courtesy of Benoît Melançon).

PAGE 121: Bert Grassick: a newspaper cartoon showing Maurice Richard and Clarence Campbell, Toronto *Telegram*, 1950.

PAGE 126: Cartoon depicting Maurice Richard and Clarence Campbell, Montreal *Gazette*, March 18, 1955, p. 26 (photo: Société canadienne du micro-film Inc., Montreal).

PAGE 181: Maurice Richard, Maurice Duplessis and Maurice Bellemare, Montreal *Gazette*, 1952.

PAGE 188: Maurice Richard with a child, Quebec, *Sports revue: Le magazine sportif des Canadiens-Français*, vol. 7, no. 12, December 1958 (photo: Alain).

PAGE 199: *Hérauts*, vol. 17, no. 3, October 1, 1959, cover, Montreal, Editions Fides.

PAGE 202: Russell Hoban: *Portrait of Maurice Richard*, New York, *Sports Illustrated: America's National Sports Weekly*, vol. 12, no. 12, March 21, 1960, cover.

PAGE 207: *Sportorama*, vol. 1, no. 8, January 1968, cover.

PAGE 223: An admirer weeps in front of the statue of Maurice Richard, Montreal (photo: Shaun Best/ Reuters/Corbis).

PAGE 242: Advertisement for the Equitable Life Assurance Society of the United States (©Equitable, 1965).

PAGE 245: Advertisement for Daoust skates in the Toronto *Star Weekly,* November 24, 1951.

PAGE 248: Shania Twain pays tribute to the Canadiens' number 9 at the Juno Awards, April 6, 2003 in Ottawa (photo: Tom Hanson/Canadian Press). Céline Dion sings at the Bell Centre in Montreal, December 1998, Special edition. Dossier "Maurice Richard 1921–2000," *Les Canadiens,* vol. 15, no. 7, 1999–2000 season, p. 72 (photo: Club de hockey Canadien Inc.).

PAGE 253: Cartoon by Garnotte, Montreal, *Le Devoir,* June 1, 2000. Cartoon by Aislin, Montreal *Gazette,* May 28, 2000.